Simone de Beauvoir Revisited

Twayne's World Authors Series

French Literature

David O'Connell, Editor

Georgia State University

TWAS 820

Simone de Beauvoir
Photograph by Jerry Bauer.

Simone de Beauvoir Revisited

Catharine Savage Brosman

Tulane University

Twayne Publishers
A Division of G. K. Hall & Co • Boston

Publisher's Note

Simone de Beauvoir Revisited by Catharine Savage Brosman introduces readers to the vocabulary and concepts specific to Beauvoir's aesthetic, political, and philosophical concerns. Drawing on recent criticism and biographical information made available since Beauvoir's death in 1986 and since the publication of Konrad Bieber's *Simone de Beauvoir* (Twayne Publishers, 1979), Brosman offers an objective consideration of Beauvoir's lasting contribution to literature and philosophy. We are pleased to present this new explication of Beauvoir's lifetime achievement.

Published by Twayne Publishers
A division of G. K. Hall & Co.
70 Lincoln Street
Boston, Massachusetts 02111

Copyediting supervised by Barbara Sutton.
Book production by Janet Z. Reynolds.
Book design by Barbara Anderson.
Typeset by Compset, Inc., Beverly, Massachusetts.

First published   .
10 9 8 7 6 5 4 3 2 1

The paper used in this publication meets the minimum requirements
of American National Standard for Information Sciences—Permanence
of Paper for Printed Library Materials, ANSI Z39.48-1984. ∞™

Printed and bound in the United States of America.

Library of Congress Cataloging-in-Publication Data

Brosman, Catharine Savage, 1934–
    Simone de Beauvoir revisited / Catharine Savage Brosman.
        p.   cm.—(Twayne's world authors series ; TWAS 820. French
    literature)
    Includes bibliographical references (p.   ) and index.
    ISBN 0-8057-8269-9
    1. Beauvoir, Simone de, 1908–   —Criticism and interpretation.
    2. Women and literature—France—History—20th century.   I. Title.
    II. Series: Twayne's world authors series ; TWAS 820.   III. Series:
    Twayne's world authors series. French literature.
    PQ2603.E362Z62   1991
    848'.91409—dc20   91-14646

For Kate

Contents

Preface

Two massive biographies have recently appeared on Simone de Beauvoir, and the past decade and a half have seen publication of a substantial bibliobiography and dozens of other critical and biographical volumes, in addition to vast numbers of essays, book chapters, and articles. Attesting to Beauvoir's continued fame, this abundance of material likewise reflects increased interest in women authors in general. To write on Beauvoir—at once novelist; philosophical, social, and political essayist; feminist; and activist—is to deal with a striking example of a creative and thoughtful woman. With her death in 1986, a remarkable intellectual, literary, and public career was ended, a career in which Beauvoir had witnessed and contributed to sweeping changes in social attitudes toward women in the Western world. While many—including me— would accept only with serious reservations the claim that spiritually Beauvoir is "the mother of us all,"[1] she is certainly one of the outstanding women intellectuals of the century, one whose mark is visible everywhere and whose influence is still making itself felt currently, even as other writers and activists denounce some of her positions in favor of more radical ones.

Despite the resources already in existence, a concise review and fresh evaluation of Beauvoir's accomplishments are appropriate, now that some time has elapsed since her death. From a practical viewpoint, the full-length critical biographies are too extensive for many readers' purposes and are marred by excess anecdotal material introduced in an attempt to re-create the period and the person. A number of studies are now clearly out of date, even some published in the past 15 years, since they do not treat Beauvoir's last works and cannot look at her career as a whole; nor do they take into account certain important biographical data. Other investigations are concerned with only one or two aspects of her career and literary production at the expense of others or are unbalanced; this is the case particularly with the numerous studies done from the feminist viewpoint.

In this volume I review and evaluate Beauvoir's literary, philosophical, and other works in the appropriate critical context by chronological and generic groupings, against the background of her life and career, which I survey in the first chapter. I treat her fictional technique in detail, in accordance with her conviction that technique is a vehicle of meaning, and pay special attention to her philosophical concepts and positions, as expressed directly in essays and indirectly in fiction and drama, since the philosophical rationalizing of experience was long one of her principal concerns and even provided the framework for her political activism and feminism. Some 50 years after Beauvoir first elaborated her positions, they retain the vigor and perceptiveness that helped make French existentialism a major midcentury intellectual movement. I also consider Beauvoir's production in the context of the French literary and intellectual tradition and midcentury writing in France. Her intellectual and personal relationships with Jean-Paul Sartre are taken into account throughout, as they must be. I consider current critical concepts, but no one school of thought is favored.

Unless noted otherwise, all translations of Beauvoir's works cited in this volume are my own.

I wish to acknowledge my debt to previous scholars who have provided documentation on Beauvoir, to Interlibrary Loan at Tulane University, and to my assistant, Sharon Bryant. As always, I am most grateful to my husband, daughter, and many friends, all of whom generously share this and my other intellectual concerns.

Chronology

1937   Contracts pneumonia. Collapse of the trio with Olga and Sartre. Begins liaison with Jacques-Laurent Bost. Travels to Greece.

1939   Teaches at the lycée Camille Sée in Paris.

1940   Leaves Paris 10 June and returns on the 28th. Returns to the lycée Victor Duruy.

1941   Georges de Beauvoir dies. Goes on cycling tour in the Free Zone.

1943   Suspended from teaching; works for the national radio. *L'Invitée.*

1944   Flees Paris in July but returns 11 August to witness the Liberation. *Pyrrhus et Cinéas.*

1945   Travels to Spain and Portugal. *Le Sang des autres;* premiere of *Les Bouches inutiles.* First issue of *Les Temps modernes.*

1946   Lectures in North Africa, Switzerland, Italy, Holland. *Tous les hommes sont mortels.*

1947   In January makes first trip to the United States, where she meets Nelson Algren. Returns to Europe in May and travels to London and Scandinavia during the summer. Visits Algren in September. *Pour une morale de l'ambiguïté.*

1948   Travels with Algren in the United States, Mexico, Guatemala; *L'Existentialisme et la sagesse des nations. L'Amérique au jour le jour.*

1949   Algren visits in Paris; Beauvoir goes with him to Italy and North Africa. *Le Deuxième Sexe.*

1950   Tours Africa with Sartre.

1951   Breaks with Algren while in the United States.

1952   Biopsy for breast cancer. Begins relationship with Claude Lanzmann.

1954   *Les Mandarins* (Prix Goncourt).

1955   Attends peace conference in Helsinki; travels to China and the Soviet Union (first trip). *Privilèges.*

1957   *La Longue Marche.*

1958   *Mémoires d'une jeune fille rangée;* relationship with Lanzmann ends.

1960   Travels to Cuba. Algren visits Paris; he and Beauvoir travel together. Travels with Sartre to Brazil; they return via Cuba. Signs "Manifesto of 121." Meets Sylvie Le Bon. *La Force de l'âge.*

1962   Travels to the Soviet Union.

1963   Françoise de Beauvoir dies. *La Force des choses.* Travels to the Soviet Union (twice) and Czechoslovakia.

1964   Travels to the Soviet Union. *Une Mort très douce.*

1965   Travels to the Soviet Union.

1966   Travels to the Soviet Union and Japan. *Les Belles Images.*

1967   Travels to Egypt and Israel. Participates in Russell Tribunal in Stockholm and Copenhagen.

1968   *La Femme rompue.* Visits Yugoslavia.

1970   *La Vieillesse.* Edits *La Cause du peuple* and *L'Idiot international.*

1971   Signs feminist manifesto in favor of abortion.

1972   *Tout compte fait.*

1973   Begins feminist column in *Les Temps modernes.*

1974   Becomes president of League of Women's Rights.

1975   Awarded the Jerusalem Prize.

1979   *Quand prime le spirituel.*

1980   Sartre dies 15 April.

1981   *La Cérémonie des adieux.*

1983   Edits *Lettres au Castor et à quelques autres.* Visits the United States.

1986   Dies 14 April.

Chapter One
Background and Career

Simone de Beauvoir is known worldwide as a major figure in contemporary French literature, a political activist, and a pioneer in feminism. Although some of her novels sold well and garnered favorable critical comment, readers have in general appreciated in her principally the essayist and the autobiographer, if one is to judge by the emphasis of many critical treatments and the sales figures of her books. Her study of women, *Le Deuxième Sexe* (1949; *The Second Sex*), has sold hundreds of thousands of copies and appeared in dozens of languages, and while recent feminists have disputed some of its findings and taken issue with certain positions, it remains a pioneering document, and a central text in women's studies; one finds it mentioned in nearly every contemporary book and countless articles that deal with the situation of women.[1] As the editorialist in *Signs* wrote in 1979, "Simone de Beauvoir essentially founded the new scholarship about women."[2] Beauvoir's four volumes of memoirs have similarly appealed to readers by the hundreds of thousands. Printed and televised interviews with her in several countries and two films in which she was featured, including *Simone de Beauvoir* (1979), have aroused enormous public interest in the writer herself. Her active support of many social and political causes, from the early 1960s on, made her a public figure in Western and Eastern Europe, the Americas, Africa, and even Asia.

Thus, like a number of other French writers of her century, including André Gide, Albert Camus, André Malraux, and her lifelong companion and collaborator, Jean-Paul Sartre, from whom she was virtually inseparable intellectually, Beauvoir occupied a position like that of the great eighteenth-century *philosophes* such as Voltaire and Diderot, who had intellectual contacts throughout Europe and remain as well known for the stands they took as for individual works. In some ways, principally because of vastly larger audiences and the publicity afforded modern writers, Beauvoir's stature is even comparable to theirs, although the literary merit of her works and her intellectual accomplishments are not so impressive. "Basically she was not an inventive or highly imaginative writer," Renée Winegarten has observed.[3]

This reservation notwithstanding, as the twentieth century draws to a close, it seems clear that, for the foreseeable future, Beauvoir will be considered one of the century's outstanding intellectual figures and perhaps the most important contemporary woman author in France, surpassing Colette, Nathalie Sarraute, Marguerite Yourcenar, Marguerite Duras, and younger writers now active such as Marie Cardinal and Hélène Cixous. Unlike Colette, Beauvoir did not have the state funeral that the French grant to their greatest or most beloved public figures, but some 5,000 people gathered around Montparnasse Cemetery for her burial. Her status is clearly the result of her career as a whole, including her activism and her close relationship with Sartre. It is also due in no mean part to the fact that she was a successful *woman* writer, one of a small number. As she asserted repeatedly, her career, which was coextensive with almost all her adult life, was born both of conscious decision—an act of the will—and from her circumstances, or "situation," in existentialist terms.

She herself recounted her life and explored this situation in her memoirs and in interviews and some of her fiction. She was, some would say, fascinated with herself and overly complacent; at times she is garrulous, and not every reader finds worth perusing all the details of her childhood, her adult intellectual pursuits, friendships, love affairs, and travels. To justify such extensive writing about the self and its experiences, one can observe that, for her, art was not a compartment of her life separated from the rest, still less an idol to which, in a Proustian fashion, her life would be subordinated and sacrificed. Indeed, perhaps it is not quite proper to speak of Beauvoir's *art,* if by that one means a literary enterprise undertaken for the sake of an aesthetic ideal. Although she was concerned with style, often reworking her prose to refine word choice and metaphoric expression,[4] and similarly took pains with the structure of her works, she is not primarily a stylist, concerned with a beautiful literary object. Writing for her was, rather, an aspect of her intellectual life, itself an aspect of her whole life. From girlhood to old age, Beauvoir was concerned with the experience of living, both immediately and as subsequently reflected, and she wanted that experience to be as intense as possible. For her, literature was a way of exploring experience. It was also a means of communicating that experience to others, as an enrichment for their lives and for hers, since what she felt and thought was thereby multiplied in the minds of her readers;

she did not subscribe to the view (codified as deconstructionism) that communication with others is impossible, because the self is solipsistic, or the text refers only to itself and constantly deconstructs itself, or because language, having no reference beyond subjectivity, is inadequate. (This view was one of her objections to the New Novel of the 1950s and 1960s and to its critical foundation.)[5] For her the self was an integral part of writing, just as writing was essential to the self.

This attitude is both romantic and existentialist. It was the romantics who bequeathed to the Western world the conviction that the self is the supreme subject of literature and taught their descendants how to make their egos interesting to others. This development took place against the background of the French Revolution, the ideological premise of which was the equality of human beings before the law and with respect to their metaphysical situation. The romantics were not, of course, the only ones who made themselves the subject of their books; Montaigne originated the personal essay fixed on the vagaries of the self. But the romantics gave such literature wide currency, and Chateaubriand, at whose grave Sartre showed his disrespect by a vulgar act, is not so distant from Beauvoir and Sartre as might be imagined.

Similarly, Beauvoir's work exhibits the very essence of the existentialist understanding of literature. Rooted in the concrete, the individual situation, it reveals a "freedom" (that is, a human being, defined as free) reflecting on itself and creating itself by choices, both biographical choices as *recounted* in writing and choices of value made in the very *act* of writing. In *Qu'est-ce que la littérature?* (*What Is Literature?*) Sartre distinguishes between two types of writing: poetry, the aims of which are aesthetic or ornamental, and all others, which are fundamentally functional, though not necessarily didactic, because they are directed by one freedom (writer) to others (readers) and express the values embodied and thus created by that freedom in the name of all others who share the human condition. Whether fiction, play, essay, or memoirs, Beauvoir's writing is clearly of the second type, although to say that her books express values and viewpoints on the human condition is not to say that they are thesis novels or other types of didactic works that attempt to impose one set of answers to a problem. Her viewpoints come from *le vécu* ("the lived"—that is, personal experience) and thus justify the direct expression of the self in her writing.

One could similarly argue, as in effect she herself has done, that Beauvoir's extensive self-expression is particularly justified because she is a woman. That is, the similarities in women's situation in many past and present societies make exemplary Beauvoir's exploration of the circumstances of being born and growing up in the feminine condition. While those who do not view woman's condition as being in any way problematic—either historically or currently—would see no value in Beauvoir's existentialist examination of her life as a woman, the tremendous worldwide sales of her books, especially those which touch most closely on her career and on the feminine condition, together with the vast numbers of letters she received from women readers, show that, for many, Beauvoir was successful in making of this self-examination a welcome revelation and object lesson for others.

Family and Childhood

Beauvoir's parents, Georges Bertrand de Beauvoir and Françoise Brasseur, both came from the upper bourgeoisie; they were genteel enough almost to pass for aristocracy.[6] Georges de Beauvoir's grandfather was a tax inspector who made a considerable fortune; his father was a successful and prosperous department head in the government, while his uncle lived simply on his own independent income. Georges grew up in ease and enjoyed the privileges and pastimes that wealth afforded. He studied law but chose not to practice, instead working as secretary to an attorney and pursuing pleasures—the racetrack and especially amateur theatricals, a substitute for the acting career his family would not let him follow. Beauvoir's maternal grandfather, Gustave Brasseur, originally from Belgium, became a prosperous banker in Alsace. In their 1985 biography of Beauvoir, Claude Francis and Fernande Gontier revealed the circumstances in which, after Brasseur's bank failed in 1909, he was forced into bankruptcy and convicted of fraud (Francis and Gontier 1987, 6, 8, 13–14).[7] Even before 1909, however, Gustave Brasseur experienced financial difficulties. He later launched other business ventures, including a shoe manufacture shortly after World War I, but was repeatedly unsuccessful and eventually pulled his son-in-law down with him into financial ruin. The dowryless marriage of Françoise Brasseur to Georges de Beauvoir was a respectable match but represented a compromise, since the wealthy cousin Champigneulles, whom Françoise had loved and whom the family had expected her to marry, abandoned his plans when Gustave's financial difficulties arose.

After their wedding in 1907, the couple settled in the Montparnasse section of Paris, in an apartment at the corner of the boulevard Montparnasse and the boulevard Raspail, where, in 1909, the Café

Rotonde opened on the ground floor. Simone Lucie Ernestine Marie Bertrand, their elder daughter, was born in Paris on 9 January 1908; her sister, Hélène, known throughout her life as Poupette, was born two years later. As Beauvoir noted, she spent nearly all her life in this neighborhood; the main exceptions occurred when she taught in Marseilles and Rouen and when, chiefly because of the war, she lived elsewhere in Paris, once in the Saint-Germain des Prés section. She identified with the Montparnasse neighborhood and attributed to her nearly lifelong residency there some of the continuity in her writing and her life.[8] When she was 11 years old, the family, in impecunious circumstances, moved to a less expensive and less comfortable apartment not far away, on the rue de Rennes, a lodging Beauvoir remembered with displeasure the rest of her life.

While never accepting orthodox Freudian doctrine and remaining for years rather skeptical concerning the conclusions reached by the Viennese doctor, Beauvoir recognized increasingly throughout her career the crucial role of early childhood in forming the mature person, both the affective and intellectual elements. She was persuaded that her mother's childhood, during which she was deprived of affection, had contributed to the woman's narrowness of mind and heart. Beauvoir's own childhood seems to have been affected especially by several circumstances. One was the family's straitened financial situation, which was responsible for the move and grew worse with the years. Georges de Beauvoir had spent, rather early in life, his personal fortune. In 1914 he was called up for service, despite heart trouble; after an attack that left him unfit for service, he was transferred to the War Ministry, but on a small salary. Later investments turned out badly. His impecunity was responsible for keeping the girls in plain, even ugly clothes, about which Simone grew self-conscious; for reducing their pleasures to few; and for provoking acrimonious domestic disputes. This financial situation led to everyone's recognition that Simone and Hélène would have to pursue careers, since they would have no other means of support and no desirable marriage could be foreseen for well-bred but dowryless girls. Beauvoir later realized that this circumstance had favored her by directing her without interruption into a university career.

Another crucial factor in Beauvoir's childhood was the respective characters of her parents. Georges de Beauvoir was urbane, indifferent to religion, and fond of women, with whom he had some extramarital contacts. It was he who encouraged the intellectual development of his young daughters. Françoise de Beauvoir participated in a few amateur plays with her husband, who was nearly 10 years older, but she was neither interested in society nor intellectually sophisticated. Moreover, she was very devout. Her education at the Couvent des Oiseaux (a school for daughters of the best members of the bourgeoisie) had nurtured her inclinations toward piety. While Simone's father expressed disdain for Christian practice and doctrine, her mother instilled and cultivated in the girls a strong sense of religious obligation, which Simone—possessing an intransigent, extremist character, always giving herself wholeheartedly to any project she chose and making great demands on herself—assumed with fervor. Françoise de Beauvoir also insisted on adhering rigorously to the code of proper social behavior. For some years, the young Simone felt very close to this "darling little mother,"[9] even closer than to her father, whose critical mind more nearly resembled hers, but eventually their differences in character, and particularly Françoise's total inability to accept any viewpoints other than those of her husband or the church, created conflict and strained relationships between mother and daughter.

A third crucial fact of Beauvoir's childhood was the existence of Hélène. While the latter admitted she had been dominated by her elder sister and long felt inferior to her, since her parents seemed to treat her so, she recognized that the relationship had been a friendly and even profitable one (Dayan, 34–35). This goodwill stemmed in part from the fact that Simone, showing early signs of a vocation to educate (which, at the outset of her adult life, was realized in the classroom but underlies much of her writing career also), undertook, quite successfully, to teach her young sister to read, add, and subtract, and in general served as her guide. The two remained friendly during most of their adolescence and were close as adults, although they were usually separated after Hélène, who became a respected painter, married Lionel de Roulet, assigned to the French cultural services in Lisbon, Milan, Vienna, and elsewhere and later to the European Community in Strasbourg. Both during their childhood and later their mother was uneasy about the girls' closeness because she felt excluded; Beauvoir told how as adults she and Hélène usually hid from her their meetings (MTD, 62).

A final crucial factor in Beauvoir's childhood was her parents' decision to send her, at age five and a half, to a Catholic school for girls, the Cours Désir. This school, serving a small number of students from good families, provided less-than-adequate training for a bright girl but furnished strong reinforcement of Christian belief and morals. What was most important about the Cours Désir was that there Beauvoir met Elisabeth Le Coin (Zaza Mabille in the memoirs), with whom she established a deep friendship that lasted until Zaza's death in 1929.[10] Her friend's tragic story appears in several works by Beauvoir. This friendship constituted her first commitment beyond the family, and for a time it even created a barrier between her and Hélène. Simone's devotion to Zaza was so strong that when Georges de Beauvoir offered to send Simone to a girls' lycée—a move that would have saved him tuition while providing her with much more solid training—she refused because it would mean separation from Zaza. Perhaps because the latter was very close to her mother and had numerous siblings, the friendship apparently meant less to her than to Beauvoir, but it did provide Zaza with a much-needed confidante during the girls' adolescence.

Adolescence and University Years

Midadolescence was no easy time for Beauvoir. Her long-standing intimacy with her father, a closeness that had nurtured her mind and may have been responsible for some of the development of her critical intelligence, decreased, probably as a result of his own bad humor (prompted by financial worries) and also, apparently, because his pretty little daughter had arrived at the awkward age and lost most of her charm. Simone felt as unattractive as she may have appeared, and social engagements—the kind required by even a modest family standing among the Parisian bourgeoisie—made her miserable. Moreover, at age 14 she began to doubt certain articles of Christian doctrine and soon realized that she no longer believed in God. For some years she hid her disbelief from her mother, admitting it only when questioned directly later. She also hid it from Zaza, whose natural inclination toward belief flourished in the pious atmosphere of both her home and the Cours Désir. With the loss of faith came a realization of the finality of death, together with a deep metaphysical revolt that Beauvoir recalled keenly all her life and that was first expressed by tears and screams, in a paroxysm of anguish. Her rejection of all religious belief and her revolt against the fact of death are obvious points she has in common with Sartre, Camus, Malraux, and others of the preexistentialist and existentialist generations. These reactions had an effect on all her subsequent life and her writing.

At age 15, at approximately the same time she lost her faith—and probably not coincidentally—Beauvoir became aware enough of herself and her capabilities to decide that she wanted to be a writer.[11] Although it took 20 years for this vocation to be first realized, the adolescent decision was genuine, based on a sense of self in relation to the world, not just an imitative impulse. Its significance will be explored further in later chapters, but for now it can be noted that Beauvoir was directly motivated by both her love of reading and her desire for celebrity, joined in the thought that someday readers would be moved by what she had written (Dayan, 16).

Throughout her schooling, Beauvoir was an excellent student, not merely the "dutiful daughter" of the translated title of *Mémoires d'une jeune fille rangée* (1958) but one for whom studies were fulfilling. She had both aptitude—a superior memory, verbal gifts, and ability in mathematics and abstract reasoning—and the willingness to work hard. For a while she intended to choose mathematics over literature and philosophy, because mathematics was Zaza's preference. A special teacher had to be engaged for the two girls in that subject. Beauvoir also undertook the study of Italian. Her first baccalaureate (literature and Latin) was awarded with honors in the summer of 1924. In 1925, having passed her baccalaureate in philosophy and mathematics, she enrolled in the Ecole normale libre (Institut Sainte-Marie) in Neuilly, a private school, for work toward a *licence-ès-lettres,* and in the Institut catholique, for mathematics. By this time, she had decided she would earn her living as a teacher. Her father, who had always been proud of her abilities, pushed her to study several subjects at once and accumulate diplomas, all the while ranting against modern literature and believing, or claiming to believe, that women's chief occupations should be domestic.

At the two institutes Beauvoir finally met professors who, unlike the severe and pious teachers at the Cours Désir, truly inspired her. One was Mlle Mercier (Mlle Lambert in the memoirs), a philosophy professor. Another was Robert Garric, a Catholic of liberal political leanings who in 1919 had founded the Equipes Sociales, a program for educational exchanges among young bourgeois and workers.[12] Beauvoir, who participated for a time in his project by teaching literature to workers, was very much struck by, and perhaps vaguely amorous of, him. In *Quand prime le spirituel* (1979; *When Things of the Spirit Come First*) one of the heroines is for a time fascinated by a liberal Catholic who organizes Christian cultural centers for young laborers.

As Beauvoir studied Latin, Greek, and philosophy and read voraciously, her mental horizons developed. At the same time she grew increasingly restless and unhappy at home. Having rejected her mother's religion, she also began to reject much of the code of behavior to which the respectable bourgeoisie subscribed, especially social requirements and ideas about marriage. She did not reject, however, basic middle-class morality, which she had interiorized before rebelling against it and its religious foundation. In sexual matters she remained almost puritanical until nearly the close of the 1920s and never entirely abandoned her sense of sexual proprieties. While her subsequent writings reveal a deep-seated resentment against the dominant institutions and values of her childhood—family, church, capitalism, middle-class code of conduct, and a nationalism to which most of the middle and upper classes subscribed, represented at its extreme by Charles Maurras and his Action française movement—she tended to express her revolt less violently, less radically, than many contemporaries, such as Louis-Ferdinand Céline, Jean Genet, and Sartre. In her personal life, her chief departures from ordinary morality were her decision not to marry and her several liaisons—not really a radical position. Her later espousal of Marxist economic principles went, of course, against the principles of her family and milieu, but, compared with the revolt of a Rimbaud, was very mild. Perhaps only at the time around 1960, when she supported the Algerian rebels, thus violating the law as well as defying French patriotic tradition, was her stance unusually bold. The relatively mild expressions of her rebellion may be read as a function of her femininity or of the powerful impact of her childhood training, or both. Never, though, did she outlive this adolescent rebellion, and while some may deem it heroic and farsighted, her enduring blanket condemnation of almost all established institutions, traditions, and classes in the West except the proletariat, intellectuals, and radicals suggests a somewhat arrested moral development, as well as a bias and intolerance that, as an intellectual, she should have been the first to condemn.

By her late teens, Beauvoir realized not only that the Le Coin family did not like her but, worse, that the parents were raising one obstacle after another to Zaza's happiness. When the latter fell in love with Maurice Merleau-Ponty, a university friend whom Beauvoir had introduced to her, Zaza's parents forbade their daughter to marry him; however, having realized how deeply attached to him she was, they decided to investigate his background. When his illegitimacy was discovered, M. Le Coin informed him of it (he had been completely unaware) and then informed Zaza, who gave up the idea of marrying

Maurice when her father threatened to make the scandal public (Bair, 152). Under the strain of this interdiction—the second time her parents had interfered with her sentimental choices—Zaza's physical strength began to collapse. The conflict rising from the strain of loving both her parents and the young man of whom they disapproved was too great; in 1929, after a brief illness, Zaza died.

All the rest of her life Beauvoir remained convinced that, in essence, Zaza's parents had killed her, and in Beauvoir's work Zaza represents the quintessential victim of bourgeois prejudices. By virtue of her innocence, she also represents the young victim who must be sacrificed, in the tradition of Iphigenia, so that others may succeed in their enterprises. Beauvoir stated that for a long while she felt that Zaza's death had paid for her own liberty (*MJF,* 359). What Meursault says in Camus's *L'Etranger* (*The Stranger*)—that everyone is always a little guilty—seems to apply to Beauvoir at both ends of her career, since, at the time of her mother's death, the question of the morality of survival is again expressed, if only implicitly. Zaza's death can also be read psychologically as representing for Beauvoir the death of a certain self and thus the passage of an initiation rite. [13]

In the mid-1920s, feeling she had little in common with an increasingly embittered, hostile father and a mother who was resentful and acrimonious, although basically affectionate, and who did not understand her elder daughter, Beauvoir threw herself wholly into her studies. Her only distractions were due to her second cousin Jacques Champigneulles (Jacques Laiguillon in the memoirs), only slightly older than she but considerably more sophisticated. Heir to a stained-glass factory, he was acquainted with members of artistic circles, including surrealists, and he introduced his cousin to avant-garde cinema and painting. On occasions he was allowed to take her out in the evenings, and she was thus able to participate in a side of Parisian life unacceptable to her family. They went to cafés, which proper women never entered, and nightclubs, and she learned to drink martinis and other cocktails. Emboldened by this experience, she later went out by herself or with girls her age (while her parents believed she was at Garric's cultural center), and she deliberately adopted provocative behavior, drinking too much, flirting with unsavory men in bars, accepting a ride with a stranger, allowing punks to pay her way at cheap pleasure arcades. This imprudent conduct led to nothing worse than a scare or so; perhaps she did not realize for years how fortunate she had been.

The relationship with Jacques was not simply friendship. On her part certainly, and probably on his, there was considerable attraction. Both she and her mother began to suppose that the two might marry; however, Beauvoir's maternal grandfather, who had been outraged when Jacques's father had turned down the match with Françoise Brasseur, had sworn that no member of his family would marry a Champigneulles. After the young man did his military service in Algeria, the subject was dropped. It may be that his mother had considered and then abandoned the idea of the match. After an unhappy marriage, and an unsuccessful career as manager of the family business, Jacques died at age 46 of the effects of alcoholism. Well before, Beauvoir realized she would not have been the sort of wife Jacques desired, and by age 21, what was left of her love for him had disintegrated. Like Zaza's death, Jacques's failure seemed to her the ransom for her own success.

After her classes at the two private institutes, Beauvoir transferred to the Sorbonne. In March 1926 she passed the first of the examinations for her certificate in literature; the following June, exams in Latin and mathematics. With the encouragement of Mlle Mercier, she decided to pursue her reading in philosophy and obtain the *agrégation* (the highest teaching certificate) in that discipline. By June 1927 she had passed (ranked number 2) her *certificat* in philosophy. During the academic year 1927–28, she taught philosophy at the Institut Sainte-Marie, while taking courses. By March 1928 she had passed all the examinations for her *licence* and begun writing a thesis or long paper—on Leibniz—and preparing for the *agrégation* exams. [14] In the spring of 1929 she was an apprentice teacher at the lycée Janson-de-Sailly for boys, along with Merleau-Ponty and Claude Lévi-Strauss, whose revolutionary studies in anthropology would later interest her.

If studies at the Institut Sainte-Marie had been broadening, the years at the Sorbonne represented an even greater step, furnishing rigorous training (with the respected neo-Kantian philosopher Léon Brunschvicg, among others) and a wider range of acquaintances, including some at the Ecole normale supérieure. Among them were Simone Weil, who was to become famous for her searching moral writings; Henri Lefebvre, who would be an outstanding Marxist historian; Merleau-Ponty (Pradelle in the memoirs), a major figure in French phenomenology and long a close friend; and René Maheu (Herbart in the memoirs), who later occupied an important position with UNESCO. Although married, Maheu spent a great deal of time with Beauvoir, in both intellectual discussions and the pursuit of Latin Quarter pleasures. It was Maheu who gave her the nickname "Castor" ("Beaver"), based on the resemblance between her surname and the English word, and on her industriousness. The name remained with her all her life. Two of Maheu's close friends at the Ecole normale supérieure were Paul Nizan, the brilliant novelist and social critic, and Sartre, who, although older, still had to pass his *agrégation* exams, having failed the previous year because he had composed an idiosyncratic exam paper instead of sticking to standard views. Thanks to Maheu, Beauvoir and Sartre became aware of each other and, after a false start or two, finally met in the summer. From the outset, they found each other immensely likable and invigorating intellectual company. In June 1929 she passed the written examination for the *agrégation* and began studying for the oral exam. When the results were announced, Sartre was first, Beauvoir second; some judges thought the order should be reversed (Francis and Gontier 1987, 92). She stated herself, however, that intellectually she was far less sophisticated than he at the time, and she generally considered him intellectually superior to her (Dayan, 20).

The Young Woman

With the *agrégation* behind her, Beauvoir's life changed radically. Moving away from the rue de Rennes, she rented a room on the rue Denfert from her grandmother, who was obliged to let rooms to supplement her income after Gustave Brasseur's death. Until Beauvoir won the Prix Goncourt in 1954 and bought with the prize money and royalties a studio apartment on the rue Schoelcher across from Montparnasse Cemetery, she would live in a series of rented rooms, usually in shabby hotels, and, later, in a modest apartment; she did not share a residence with Sartre at any time. The move to her grandmother's, where she was treated like other roomers, meant the end of her life at home, although she did continue to see her parents.

That same summer marked Beauvoir's initiation to physical love. Although intellectually liberated and politically liberal, she had remained quite prudish, insisting that physical love should be accompanied by admiration and companionship; she had not yet rejected marriage but had told her father that it must be based on absolute equality. Sartre was for her the true companion whom she could love both physically and intellectually. When he came to visit her in the neighborhood of Meyrignac, her uncle's family property, where she spent her 1929 vacation, Beauvoir was obliged to arrange clandestine meetings, since he could not be received by the family; when the family discovered his presence, he was asked to leave—an illustration of the bourgeois mentality Beauvoir had learned to detest—but he did not, and the meetings continued.

Intimate relationships with men were to remain, for several decades, an important part of Beauvoir's life. At the end of her career, she remarked that, were she to begin her work again, she would give more importance to the treatment of sexuality because it had been extremely meaningful for her. As it is, there are love affairs in all her novels, and in *Les Mandarins* (1954) one erotic experience is developed at length; similarly, she deals in her memoirs with her liaisons with Sartre, Nelson Algren, and Claude Lanzmann, while omitting relationshps with Jacques-Laurent Bost, Arthur Koestler, and others. Yet Beauvoir's work does not resemble that of Colette—a rival, along with Duras, for the position of greatest woman writer in France in this century. From the beginning, Colette's work centered on the exploration of a marginal eroticism—lesbians, *cocottes* (kept women), gigolos. It analyzed with grace and brilliance the amorous psychology of the heroes and heroines and their milieu, but its concern was usually with sexuality as such, not with its place in the characters' lives as a whole. Beauvoir, on the other hand, makes of sexuality an aspect of her characters' total experience.

Beauvoir was determined to live in Paris so that she would not be separated from Sartre. She gave private lessons and taught at the lycée Victor Duruy. Sartre, meanwhile, was having to fulfill his military obligation in the meteorological service and was assigned to various posts, usually reachable from the capital. Beauvoir explains in her memoirs how they agreed on the terms for their personal life. He proposed that they sign a *bail,* or lease, of two years, presumably based on fidelity, after which their "essential" love would be supplemented, but never replaced, by "contingent" loves (as he called them, using terms from their philosophical vocabulary). It was agreed that neither would let other love affairs threaten their devotion and commitment to each other. Sartre certainly had contacts with other women not long— perhaps only months—after he and Beauvoir became lovers, and he carried on a love affair in Berlin in 1933–34; Beauvoir, however, kept her part of the bargain through the early 1930s.

Sartre, who was aware of his nonmonogamous nature, had already had one torrid love affair, with Simone-Camille Sans (Camille in the memoirs), from Toulouse, who later became an actress under the name Simone Jollivet and the mistress of Charles Dullin, director of the

Théâtre de l'Atelier. Letters and other documents show that Sartre was very much attracted to women and, as he said, found them more pleasant and interesting companions than men.[15] It is also clear that he had an inordinate need to establish sexual relationships with women; while proclaiming, doubtless sincerely, to believe in equality of the sexes, he behaved very much like a Don Juan, except that his former lovers often remained in his circle as his friends. It was perhaps to offset his plain looks (which he called his ugliness) and his short stature that he sought the sort of preference that is expressed by sexual abandon; he seemed to believe also that sexual relations allowed for the establishment of a more thoroughgoing and honest friendship with a woman than would be possible otherwise.

Briefly, Sartre and Beauvoir did discuss marriage. After his military service was over in 1931, he applied for a lectureship to Japan, and Beauvoir for a teaching position in the French system. When the Japanese post was given to someone else, he was assigned to a lycée position in Le Havre; Beauvoir was assigned to Marseilles. She was so distraught over the separation that he suggested they marry so that, according to government practice, they would be sent to the same city. She declined, realizing, she claims, that, by convictions and habits, they did not really belong to the ranks of the married and that Sartre's offer, while doubtless sincere, went against the grain. He was rigorously anti-institution and especially antifamily; they both could have said, with Gide, "Families, I hate you." The irony is that subsequently, when both of them had a number of young disciples, some of the latter assumed the roles of children, for whom Beauvoir and Sartre felt morally and financially responsible; they were often called "*la famille.*" Sartre had amorous relationships with numerous students, including, in the 1960s, Arlette El Kaïm, whom he officially adopted; he thus in effect acted out the incest theme visible in his work.[16] On the particular matter of children, Beauvoir stated more than once that she had no desire for children of her own; she told Nelson Algren that she would choose abortion if she became pregnant (Bair, 373). Children play almost no role in her work, unless one counts those *lycéennes* and other adolescents who appear in her fiction as incarnations of psychological and metaphysical problems and as foils to the world of adults. There is both indirect and direct evidence that, sometime during the 1930s, Beauvoir had an abortion. In Sartre's *L'Age de raison* (1945; *The Age of Reason*) much of the plot turns on the efforts of the hero, Mathieu, to procure funds for an abortion for his mistress, Marcelle. The descriptions of Marcelle's uneasiness at being pregnant and of Mathieu's reactions convey the very feel of the physiological. Similarly, in Beauvoir's *Le Sang des autres* (1945; *The Blood of Others*) the pregnant heroine wants to abort her fetus; in contrast to what happens in Sartre's novel, in this one the grim operation really does take place. These fictional episodes would, of course, be worthless as evidence were it not for Beauvoir's own statement, made under oath at the time of the abortion controversy in France, that she had had an abortion (Francis and Gontier 1987, 337). There is at present no verification; nor is it known whether, if Beauvoir did indeed have an abortion, she regretted it at any time. But in any case, she participated vigorously in the campaign to make abortion legal in France.

On the occasions when Beauvoir spoke publicly of her relationship with Sartre, she maintained that it was entirely successful. Neither a marriage nor the classic "free union" of the sort practiced by a few French freethinkers (a relationship usually based on fidelity but without sanction by state or church), by definition it did not incorporate the adultery associated with the first (in which her own father apparently indulged) in many segments of French society, nor was it characterized by the quasi-puritanical rigor and limitations of the second. Certainly their common intellectual life and common undertakings provide evidence of the strength of the bonds between Beauvoir and Sartre. But after the first years, the relationship was in essence an intellectual and moral friendship, and the American subtitle of Francis and Gontier's biography, "A Love Story," is misleading.[17] Beauvoir confessed that she too was pleased not to have been monogamous (Dayan, 73). Still, the fact that she suffered frequently from Sartre's pursuit of other women, particularly younger ones, shows that their relationship was not unlike that of many married couples. When, much later, Sartre asked Arlette El Kaïm to marry him, before he chose instead to adopt her, Beauvoir is reported to have protested irately.[18] Nevertheless, the powerful intellectual bond between them, a bond that had strong affective elements and that love affairs with others did not destroy, makes their example unusual.

In the two years before Beauvoir left to assume her first teaching position at the lycée Montgrand in Marseilles, she lived the life of a young intellectual in Paris, thereby setting the pattern for the remainder of her career. While enjoying the companionship of Sartre and his circle, she attended concerts and art shows, insofar as her modest budget allowed. It must not be thought that hers was in any way a public life. She was only an apprentice writer, unknown; even Sartre had published nothing except pieces in obscure reviews. Of their close friends, only Paul Nizan had made a name for himself by 1931, with his remarkable *Aden Arabie*. The move to Marseilles in 1931, after a trip to Spain with Sartre in the summer—Beauvoir's first trip abroad—marked an abrupt change. She was separated from Sartre, her neighborhood, and her friends, and, as a civil servant, she was dependent on a government whose policies she disliked. From the outset, Beauvoir exercised as much independence as possible: she dressed, characteristically, in a more stylish fashion than her colleagues, she took liberties with the curriculum or at least in her presentation of the subject, and, instead of maintaining a suitably formal relationship with her students, she cultivated the friendship of those she found interesting and did not bother to hide her lack of concern for the others. Throughout her teaching career, which lasted until 1943, this conduct would become more marked. She associated with few of her fellow teachers; one friendship ended when the woman revealed herself as a lesbian. Perhaps the most important discovery Beauvoir made while in Marseilles was that of the surrounding countryside. She took frequent long hikes by herself and came to know the region intimately. Until she was no longer able to do so, decades later, Beauvoir remained an avid and energetic hiker and camper, and she was rarely happier than when she could enjoy a beautiful landscape, either alone or with friends.

In 1932 she was assigned to the lycée Jeanne d'Arc in Rouen, and Sartre, having finished his military service, was appointed to Le Havre, one hour away by train. They spent considerable time together during their four years in Normandy, and one must suppose that Beauvoir's teaching was sometimes neglected. When Sartre spent the academic year 1933–34 in Berlin, Beauvoir feigned illness in order to go visit him. It was in Rouen that she had as a pupil Olga Kosakiewicz, whom she introduced to Sartre and who came to play a major role in their lives. The model for Xavière of *L'Invitée* (1943; *She Came to Stay*), Olga was the daughter of Russian refugees. Although her capricious and demanding behavior made friendship difficult, Beauvoir acted as her mentor, persuaded Olga's parents to let her pursue independent studies in philosophy, and finally assumed some financial responsiblity for her when she came to live in Paris in 1936.

With Olga, Beauvoir and Sartre formed the "trio" described in the memoirs and reflected in *L'Invitée*. They considered this arrangement an experiment in relationships, an attempt to establish three-way bonds on the grounds of total openness and authenticity. In fact, the three-way relationship proved to be secondary to the pairs made with each other. To some degree, Beauvoir felt threatened by the relationship between Olga and Sartre, but she continued to support the idea of the trio and contributed to maintaining it. In 1937 Sartre became involved with Olga's younger sister, Wanda. When in that same year Beauvoir took as her lover a former pupil of Sartre's, Jacques-Laurent Bost (*"le petit Bost"* in the memoirs), she may have been making a gesture of independence as well as satisfying her own needs, which Sartre, despite his close ties with her, no longer met. Both sisters studied acting under Charles Dullin, took stage names, and later performed in plays by Sartre. Bost and Olga married in 1941.

Starting with her trip to Spain in 1931, followed by another in 1932 and by trips to London and Italy the next year, Beauvoir showed herself to be an avid traveler. In her visits to Europe and, later, to other continents, she revealed the same enthusiasm visible in her hiking and camping. Discomfort in lodgings and means of travel, as well as inedible food, was of almost no moment to her, nor was she deterred by unforeseen schedule changes and other annoyances inevitable in prolonged travel. She was willing, indeed determined, to see almost everything a city or region offered, and to see it thoroughly; the impatience that Lewis, in *Les Mandarins,* shows when Anne insists on climbing still another Yucatán pyramid reflects the reactions of Algren to Beauvoir's insatiable appetite for Mexican ruins. Unlike Sartre, who cared little for the outdoors and would sometimes read while his companions scampered over hills and fields, Beauvoir was as happy in the countryside as in cities. And she had no prejudice against either the closest or the farthest sites: she enjoyed exploring little corners of France as much as the Egyptian pyramids. Her eyes, ears, and palate were keen, and her accounts are marked by strong flavors that suggest how thoroughly she gave herself up to the sensation of the moment; to the objection that one never leaves oneself when traveling, she answered that she left herself and disappeared.[19]

Including additional travels in the 1930s—to Germany, Austria, Czechoslovakia, Switzerland, Belgium, Greece, Morocco, and elsewhere—Beauvoir would eventually take almost 200 trips abroad, some of them very lengthy; many are reported in her books, sometimes telescoped together. The volumes devoted exclusively to travel, *L'Amérique au jour le jour* (1948; *America Day by Day*) and *La Longue Marche* (1957; *The Long March*), are intended to be objective; the former com-

plements Sartre's essays on the United States. The memoirs' accounts of
her travels are sometimes more striking, however, as Beauvoir became
more skilled at transcribing both what she saw and the manner in
which she saw it. While she is not one of the great travel writers of the
century and thus cannot be ranked with such diverse French figures as
Gide, Paul Claudel, Paul Morand, and Henri Michaux, whose art was
more deeply changed by or more clearly oriented toward what they saw,
Beauvoir's success as a reporter and the importance of travel in her work
should be acknowledged.

In 1936 Beauvoir was assigned to the lycée Molière in Passy, a
suburb of Paris. Sartre was transferred to Laon, not far by train; the
following year he too began teaching in Paris, at the lycée Pasteur.
Beauvoir settled in Montparnasse and made the Dôme café, where she
had spent time in the 1920s, her social headquarters. In the winter she
went skiing, working assiduously on developing her skills in the sport
she had discovered in 1934–35. In the spring of 1937 she fell ill with
pulmonary congestion—one of the few times until her old age when
she would suffer from any physical disturbance.

Beauvoir had been writing for most of the decade. Sartre found her
early writing atrocious, partly because she had no style, partly because
she failed at creating characters different from herself (Dayan, 22).
Since she seemed to lack the ability to imagine and project into her
writing characters who differed from her, he suggested that she give up
the attempt to do so and instead draw her plots and characters from her
own experience and self. She took his advice and thus made what seems
to have been a major step in the development of her ability to write
fiction, although her maturity was also a factor. Throughout her career,
her work would remain very close to her own experience, and her
characters were frequently projections of herself. *Les Mandarins,* which
she maintained was not an autobiographical novel, is in fact no exception. Her short stories later published as *Quand prime le spirituel* were
turned down by publishers, justifiably, but it is now plain that she was
not without ability. By 1937 she was at work on a novel that was to
become, six years later, *L'Invitée.*

The War Years

A person of Beauvoir's intelligence and sensitivity could not remain
blind, during the 1930s, to the worsening political and social situation
in Europe. Yet, despite her friendship with the Trotskyite Colette

Audry (a fellow teacher in Rouen), Nizan (an active Communist), and other left-wing acquaintances, Beauvoir participated in no political movement and did not even vote. Part of this behavior she later attributed to what she called her blind optimism or her schizophrenia—that is, her unwillingness to believe in the possibility of catastrophe for herself (*FA,* 345). To the degree that she did take cognizance of real threats, she, like many others of liberal leanings, was more concerned with repressive elements at home than with growing fascism in other European countries. In 1936 she welcomed the Popular Front, a left-wing coalition government headed by Léon Blum. When war broke out that summer in Spain, she felt the same distress as many of her compatriots and deplored the subsequent defeat of the Republicans. The Munich Pact of 1938 seemed to her a victory for peace, although Sartre argued that Europe should not continue yielding to Hitler's demands. Only when war was declared in September of the following year did she acknowledge to herself that disaster had indeed befallen France, and that, despite her desire for autonomy, her life would henceforth be marked by history. Her young womanhood may be said to have come to an end at the conclusion of the between-the-wars period.

Information on Beauvoir's day-to-day life in wartime is abundant, because she included in *La Force de l'âge* (1945; *The Prime of Life*) substantial selections from a diary she kept then, and because Sartre's letters to her from his mobilization in September until his capture the following June (and, irregularly, thereafter) mirror her activities, since he discussed them with her. Her first concern was for his safety. She was soon reassured by him and by circumstances: for the eight months of the *drôle de guerre* (phony war) there was no fighting. She visited him in Brumath in the fall—contrary to regulations, since she was not his wife—and he came to Paris on leave in February, when he found himself obliged to divide his time among her, Wanda, and his mother. When Paris fell in June, Beauvoir left the city with almost everyone else and went to La Pouèze, the estate of Sartre's friend Mme Morel (Mme Lemaire in the memoirs). This exodus and Beauvoir's return (28 June) are described in *Le Sang des autres,* as well as in her autobiography. When Sartre was taken prisoner (28 June), she was frantic. In gloomy occupied Paris, she nevertheless began teaching again, at the lycée Victor Duruy.

Sartre was repatriated in March 1941. Beauvoir recognized on his return how the war and imprisonment had changed him, and she soon felt herself changing in response to him and the circumstances. He had adopted a strict moralism in political matters, based on a sense of solidarity and responsibility. He soon gathered like-minded friends to form a minor resistance movement, Socialisme et liberté, in which Beauvoir participated also. Though short-lived, it reflected their new political orientation. Later during the Occupation, Sartre became involved with the Comité national des écrivains, a resistance organization; Beauvoir, however, did not participate actively, because she believed her presence would add nothing. For years to come she would similarly remain in the wings, rarely writing on politics and doing no organizational work; only at the time of the Algerian rebellion did she start becoming more involved in the causes she and Sartre supported.

As the Occupation wore on, Beauvoir's chief concerns were often practical ones. Food shortages were severe in Paris; she was lodged in cold, miserable hotels; transportation was difficult. A demanding and parasitic disciple, Nathalie Sorokine (Lise in the memoirs and the model for Nadine in Les Mandarins), plundered a bicycle for her; without heat in her room, she spent many hours at the Café de Flore and even wrote there; she sometimes used the black market and on other occasions ate food sent by Mme Morel, even if such rations were half-spoiled. She continued teaching until 1943, when Nathalie's mother lodged an official complaint against her for having exercised undue influence on the girl. (The mother accused Beauvoir of encouraging Nathalie to leave her promising older lover for a student, Bourla.) Dismissed, Beauvoir found work with the national radio network. Despite the difficulties of daily life, Beauvoir and Sartre managed to take several bicycle trips, including one in the unoccupied zone in 1941. She also established several long-lasting friendships; among her acquaintances were Camus, Genet, the sculptor and painter Alberto Giacometti, and the surrealist and ethnologist Michel Leiris. In the summer of 1944, Beauvoir was urged by friends to go into hiding briefly, but she and Sartre returned to Paris in time to witness the Liberation in August.

The years 1943–45 saw Beauvoir's entry onto the literary scene. L'Invitée was published in 1943, Pyrrhus et Cinéas in 1944, Le Sang des autres in 1945, and, despite a poor press, her one play, Les Bouches inutiles (Who Shall Die?), ran for 50 performances that same year. These titles do not indicate the full scale of her writing then; she was also busy with philosophical essays, and with another novel, Tous les hommes sont mortels (All Men Are Mortal), which appeared in 1946, and she and Sartre planned as early as 1944 the new review that appeared in October

1945, *Les Temps modernes,* on whose editorial board she served henceforth and which remains one of the most prestigious French journals. By middecade she, with Sartre, was widely considered one of the significant new literary figures, and to her, as to him, was affixed, despite their protests, the label *existentialist,* introduced by the Christian writer Gabriel Marcel.

A Triumphant Career

The second half of the 1940s was marked by several important developments for Beauvoir. Her essay *Pour une morale de l'ambiguïté (The Ethics of Ambiguity)* was published in 1947, followed by other volumes, including the work that added most to her fame, *Le Deuxième Sexe* (1949). She contributed to periodicals abroad in addition to *Les Temps modernes* and was invited to lecture in Switzerland and Italy. She then arranged to visit the United States in 1947 and speak at numerous universities.[20] This tour proved to be of more moment than she had expected, for in Chicago she met and quickly fell in love with Nelson Algren (1909–81), whose novel *The Man With the Golden Arm* (1949) won the National Book Award. She made four other trips to the United States for lengthy visits with him, and he traveled to Paris to see her. While affirming her love for him, she turned down his proposal of marriage, saying that her life was established in France; she insisted later that, even had she not been tied to Sartre, she could not have agreed to live in the United States.[21]

This transatlantic liaison developed against the background of Sartre's love affair with Dolorès Vanetti (M. in the memoirs), a French actress who had gone to America at the outset of World War II and whom Sartre had met during his stop in New York in 1945. She was, if one is to judge from Beauvoir's reports, passionately in love with Sartre, and the sentiment was returned; each traveled several times to see the other, and Dolorès's increasing demands for Sartre's time intruded on time that he and Beauvoir had agreed to spend together. Beauvoir found Dolorès to be a more powerful rival for Sartre's affection than any previous mistress had been, and she came to wonder whether the commitment made by Sartre and herself would survive. Sartre showed no signs of jealousy toward Algren and encouraged Beauvoir to return to Chicago for visits. The Algren-Beauvoir romance ended, with considerable bitterness on his part, in 1951. A later reunion in Europe in 1960, when Algren may have hoped finally to persuade Beauvoir to live with him, lasted five months and was even-toned, but was without sequel. When Beauvoir returned to France in the fall of 1951 after her last stay with Algren, she felt forlorn. The following spring, her spirits worsened when a breast tumor was diagnosed; it was, however, benign.

In most ways, the patterns of the rest of her career were set in the 1940s. Almost-daily writing (except when she was traveling, and sometimes even then); lectures, interviews, and other public appearances; a set of close friends that included members of *la famille* and some of the most eminent writers and artists of the day; frequent travels; a deep and generous commitment to *Les Temps modernes,* for which she read hundreds of manuscripts; and an ongoing intellectual companionship with Sartre were permanent features of her life. From 1956 on, she and Sartre spent long portions of nearly every summer in Rome, where they alternately worked, relaxed, and visited with friends. In Paris they usually worked separately in the mornings, then together in the afternoons, saving time for films, plays, art shows, and drinks and meals with friends. Only when their notoriety became too great did they cease going out so much. Together more than separately, they were considered the spokesmen for French existentialism, sometimes praised, sometimes mocked (Beauvoir was called, for instance, "la Grande Sartreuse," a pun on La Grande Chartreuse, a monastery).

Beauvoir's political positions in the 1940s and 1950s cannot be separated from Sartre's. She did not lay claim to originality in political thought, and, save on certain issues, notably the condition of women, did not often directly treat in her work major political questions. *Les Mandarins,* which has as a principal theme the political choices facing France after the war, is an exception. Sartre, who accepted Marxist economic tenets and came to adopt dialectical reasoning, or rather to adapt it to his purposes, was concerned under the Occupation and afterward with forming a strong, nonaligned (that is, non-Communist) Left. Beauvoir did not participate directly in his short-lived Rassemblement démocratique révolutionnaire but did share his disappointment at its failure. In the early 1950s he tried to make a rapprochement with the French Communist party, a position he saw as the only viable one to take in a Europe divided by the cold war. Beauvoir shared his intense dislike of the policies of the United States, both domestic (in racial matters especially) and foreign, and disapproved especially of American involvement in the Korean War, just as she had attacked the French presence in Indochina as early as 1947; her friendship with Merleau-Ponty was strained by the Korean question, and this conflict, as much as the quarrel between Sartre and Camus in *Les Temps modernes* in 1952, also caused Beauvoir's estrangement from Camus. She sympathized with Marxist positions and with the Soviet Union in general, while ultimately having to recognize Stalinist excesses, when so much information about them became available that they could no longer be denied. When the Russians brutally suppressed the Hungarian uprising of 1956, Beauvoir and Sartre cooled their enthusiasm for the Soviet Union but remained hostile to the United States.

By 1950 Beauvoir began to feel that her life patterns were so established that nothing new of import would happen to her. She had experienced success as a writer; her love affair with Algren soon ended but she had lasting ties with Sartre and other friends; she had traveled widely. Somewhat gloomily, she saw the future as a prolongation of the past, with decline and death as the only modification. But in 1952, when Claude Lanzmann, a writer who was 17 years younger than she and who was on the staff of *Les Temps modernes,* invited her to the movies, Beauvoir, immediately after his call, realized intuitively that something new *had* happened. Asked later what impression he had of her then, Lanzmann replied that she had a smooth face and he wished to see what was behind it (Dayan, 13). The two became very close and, after a trip to Holland in December, decided to live together. Their cohabitation lasted some six years; thereafter, they remained close friends. Self-assertedly Jewish, Lanzmann was a militant admirer of the new state of Israel. He was a supportive partner, rejoicing with Beauvoir especially when *Les Mandarins* received the Prix Goncourt in 1954. They traveled together frequently, sometimes in a trio or quartet with Sartre and Michelle Vian.

For Beauvoir, as for Sartre and numerous other intellectuals and ordinary citizens, the Algerian rebellion against French rule, which began in 1954, and the consequent repression and war constituted a grave national crisis. Her long-standing opposition to French colonial presence in the Far East, a presence that finally ended in defeat in 1954, was paralleled by sympathy for the Muslim Algerians who wished to shake off what they regarded as the yoke of French imperialism. Far from condemning their recourse to terrorism, Beauvoir supported it and expressed solidarity with those in France who were engaged in providing clandestine aid to the rebels. She intervened in several cases, acted as a witness for the defense, demonstrated against the Gaullist government, and helped publish in *Les Temps modernes* testimonials of those who had been tortured in Algeria; she was president of a committee to procure justice for Djamila Boupacha, one of the victims. In 1960 she signed the "Manifesto of 121," urging military conscripts to refuse to serve. As the conflict dragged on, until Algerian independence was achieved finally in 1962, she experienced a deep personal conflict that mirrored the divisions within France. Her sense of identity was undermined by her shame and distress over French conduct in Algeria, for which she held the middle classes responsible, and she came to feel so much anger against the latter and to find the atmosphere so poisoned that her resentment lasted until well after the war and contributed to an increasingly radicalized position.

In 1955 Beauvoir visited China, where her impressions were favorable. In 1960 she and Sartre traveled to Brazil and, twice, to Cuba. The trips, recounted in detail in *La Force des choses* (1963; *The Force of Circumstance*), were an invigorating personal and political experience. During their weeks in Cuba they were, predictably, utterly seduced by Castro's reforms and projects; the island nation seemed to have brought to realization the promises of socialism, which, Beauvoir conceded, had been distorted and betrayed in the Soviet Union. Brazil offered a cornucopia of visual, auditory, and gustatory experiences, plus new friends and copious information. In a nation marked by class polarization, with very few possessing most of the wealth and the rest indigent, Beauvoir was not so much dismayed by what she saw—although she was far from indifferent to the misery of the populace—as encouraged by what she interpreted as signs of social change, especially the presence of socialists among the wealthy.

This trip was followed by others. Beauvoir and Sartre went to the Soviet Union on several occasions, including a long trip in 1963 and other visits in 1964, 1965, and 1966. She visited Japan in 1966, where her welcome was tremendous. During most of her visits she gave lectures, met writers and intellectuals and sometimes government and opposition leaders, but was also able to sightsee, usually in both city and countryside. In 1967 she traveled with Sartre to Egypt and then Israel on a semiofficial visit arranged by a newspaper; Lanzmann accompanied them. She met with Nasser and other officials, then with highly placed figures in Israel. As a friend of Lanzmann's, she was particularly interested in that state; moreover, she and Sartre had a history of friendships with European Jews and support for Zionism. She was not, however, without understanding for Egypt, which she had long wished to visit and where social matters interested her especially. She was bold enough to raise with officials the issue of women's rights, pointing out that, official policy to the contrary, custom still deprived women of most rights, in practice, and left them in the condition of subjection that had always been theirs. When she was awarded the Jerusalem Prize in 1975, it was doubtless a reflection of her support for Israel, especially in its ongoing quarrel with UNESCO for supposed anti-Israeli prejudice, although the motive was officially her support for individual rights. At that time she specified in the press that she did not support *only* Israel; she wished for a solution that would allow Jews and Arabs to live in peace in Jerusalem.

The Last Decades: Political and Personal Struggles

Throughout this period Beauvoir became more and more politicized, and her outlook grew increasingly internationalist, on a par with, but not solely because of, her growing fame. The American presence in Indochina, which struck her as an abomination, increased her violent dislike of the United States, and although in a stable Europe the French enjoyed prosperity and prestige, superpower rivalry still meant a politically and ideologically dichotomized world in which her sentiments went always to the proponents of socialist revolution. With Sartre, she participated in the Russell Tribunal, an international committee that was meeting in Sweden and Denmark and whose self-appointed role was to judge the United States for war crimes in Vietnam. Dashing the hopes of the Prague Spring, the Soviet repression in Czechoslovakia in August 1968 appalled Beauvoir, especially since she and Sartre had met some of the intellectuals who had attempted to liberalize the nation. Thereafter, her political sympathies turned increasingly to China and Maoism, preached by militant followers in France. She supported a variety of causes abroad, such as those of socialists in Chile, Basque separatists in Spain, and free emigration for Jews from Russia.

During the May 1968 student revolts in Paris, Beauvoir attended meetings at the university and supported attempts to demolish the academic bureaucracy; she was disappointed when the uprisings did not turn into full social revolution. Her feeling of solidarity with radical students (including Maoists) led to her assuming in 1970 the editorship of two radical newspapers, *La Cause du peuple* and *L'Idiot international;* chiefly, however, her antiestablishment activity was limited to signing petitions and participating in demonstrations.

In the area of women's rights Beauvoir was similarly active. Drawn to the urgency of women's issues, she participated in demonstrations, signed petitions, and served on committees; in particular, she signed in 1970 the "Manifesto of 343," whose signees, in an attempt to legalize abortion so that the procedure could be performed under favorable conditions, declared that they had undergone abortions. She declared herself formally to be a feminist, published testimonials from women in *Les Temps modernes,* and by 1974 was named president of the League of Women's Rights. Her stance at first was the one she had held since 1949: that only within a radically altered social order would the phrase "women's rights" have meaning. This position was, however, modified when Beauvoir came to recognize the need for immediate change as an interim measure; her willingness to give priority to women's concerns marked a distinct departure from her previous views and, from the feminist vantage point, an advance. Beauvoir was also concerned with conditions of employment for workers of both sexes, employee safety, and other labor-related issues.

After the success of *Les Mandarins,* Beauvoir considered writing again about Zaza's tragedy. Finding that her attempt to give life to the story failed, she turned instead to writing about herself; the first three volumes of her memoirs appeared within the space of five years (1958–63). She wished also to return to fiction. Her last novel, *Les Belles Images,* appeared in 1966, with very high sales figures. It was followed by *La Femme rompue* (1967; *The Woman Destroyed*), three stories on associated themes. A plan to write a novel about old age proved fruitless (Bair, 531); instead Beauvoir published her documentary exposé on the question, *La Vieillesse* (*Old Age*), in 1970.

Beauvoir's mother died in 1963. Hélène and Simone, who were both in Paris and stayed close to Mme de Beauvoir's bedside during her last illness, remained close friends throughout their adulthood, but, as Simone insisted, theirs was a bond of choice, not one imposed by blood. Beauvoir's circle of friends underwent some changes, with the death of Giacometti, for instance, but remained remarkably cohesive. One new friendship was added—a surprise for Beauvoir, who again had supposed that nothing new would happen to her. Sylvie Le Bon entered her life when, as a student, she wrote to Beauvoir in 1960. Gradually, despite the age difference, the two developed a close friendship based on shared interests and pursuits (Sylvie became a professor) and certain common elements in their pasts. They came to treat each other as equals, sharing many experiences, including travel; finally Beauvoir adopted Sylvie, chiefly to ensure that the younger woman could have legal charge over her—thus sparing Hélène—in case she became incapacitated.

This relationship has been seen by some as quasi-maternal, by others as quasi-lesbian. Although Beauvoir wrote that homosexual feeling exists in masked form in nearly all women, this assertion is suspect in general and almost surely does not reflect her own tendencies, despite claims of some that she was a closet lesbian (Bair, 510).[22] It is true that Beauvoir's letters to Sartre, published in 1990, reveal that she did on occasion have physical contacts with young women; in these relationships she appears to have lent herself passively to the caresses of a series of admiring schoolgirls who had passionate crushes on her, including Olga. These same documents make it amply clear, however, that she did not initiate the contacts and that she had no taste for them.[23] Similarly, to see Sylvie as a substitute child is an oversimplification, especially since, in Beauvoir's view, the mother-daughter relationship is by its very structure unsatisfactory, at least under the present form of social organization; she explicitly denied looking on Sylvie as a daughter (Dayan, 72). The relationship is reminiscent of those she had formed earlier with other students, relationships in which she acted alternately as friend, mentor, and even substitute parent to the young woman. One could argue, however, that this relationship replaces what would have been her commitment to her children, had she had any; her students and young friends, while not ersatz offspring, provided her with the experience of being both a part of and separate from another generation, one to whom one's efforts are directed. Finally, it must be noted that Beauvoir's friendship with Sylvie, which parallels Sartre's with Arlette El Kaïm, may have been an unconscious revenge against him for letting other women take her place; her feelings of resentment were deepest toward Arlette, who finally became executrix of his estate.

In the last decade of Sartre's life (1970–80), Beauvoir's relationship with him became strained; she was obliged, reluctantly, to yield to the ascendancy assumed over him by Arlette and other young disciples, including Pierre Victor (pseudonym of Benny Lévy). Sartre made outbursts against her, though those may have been due to his illness more than to true annoyance. Yet Beauvoir shared the burden of caring for him, and she was constantly concerned for his health. What have been called the "conflicts within the Sartrean family" became increasingly obvious and, finally, public after Sartre's death, when as executrix Arlette began publishing his manuscripts and disposing of his things in a manner designed to irritate Beauvoir.[24]

Beauvoir's last years were saddened by the death of her brilliant companion on 15 April 1980. For a month afterward she was hospitalized with pneumonia and fatigue, exacerbated by her abuse, for years, of alcohol, tranquilizers, and other drugs, and she long remained too weak for much activity. Sylvie took care of her and urged her to reduce her reliance on stimulants and depressives. Resentful of Arlette's attitude and haste in publishing Sartre's unfinished texts, Beauvoir decided to bring out his correspondence with her—citing it as evidence of *her* importance in Sartre's life (contrary to Arlette's claims), although in fact it helps destroy the myth of a perfectly united couple (Francis and Gontier 1987, 353). Eschewing still the approval of the conservative and centrist French, Beauvoir nevertheless cared about her image, as her work with her biographers showed. She continued criticizing the government and refused the Legion of Honor, which President François Mitterand wished to confer on her. But she did accept the Sonning Prize for European Culture, awarded by the Danish government. She remained titular director of *Les Temps modernes* and read many manuscripts, although Lanzmann and others did the daily work. She was delighted when a film version of *Le Deuxième Sexe,* comprising four episodes and produced entirely by women, was shown on French television in 1984 (Bair, 610).

Having regained some strength, in 1983 Beauvoir took a trip with Sylvie to the United States, a country that continued to fascinate her, its politics notwithstanding. In early April 1986 she was taken ill with what was diagnosed as pulmonary edema and several complications; she died on the fourteenth, before her sister could return from California, where she was inaugurating an exhibit of her paintings. Beauvoir was buried in Montparnasse Cemetery, next to Sartre's grave; her body was later cremated.

Chapter Two
Beauvoir and the Situation of the Woman Writer

As understood by the French existentialists, a writer's situation, like other human situations, is a given, in the sense that the writer is historically situated by circumstances beyond individual control, including social, linguistic, and political circumstances, and is characterized by facticity—that is, embodied as man or woman, of a certain race, in a world of material objects. Yet the idea of situation as a given entails also that of response: one cannot refrain from responding to circumstances, rejecting or accepting them, working within or attempting to remake them, and, ultimately, choosing oneself on the basis of circumstances. This is the existentialist understanding of freedom: not an abstract, limitless power but the exercise of choice within the framework of given factors, toward a freely chosen end. To assume one's situation by going beyond it toward meaningful action is the essence of existentialist morality and the contrary of bad faith (flight from responsibility). What is meant by the term *situation* in this chapter, then, is the totality of circumstances and response. This definition is close to what Sartre meant by the term when he gave to his series of literary, aesthetic, and political essays the title *Situations*.[1]

Beauvoir's position as a woman writer was thus at once dictated by circumstances and defined by herself. It is related to otherness, insofar as, in a society based on the individual and not the collectivity—that is, all contemporary Western societies—one is always *other* with respect to competing individuals and groups; as Beauvoir argued in *Le Deuxième Sexe,* this is particularly true for women, defined both biologically and socially as *other* to men.[2] Beauvoir's position is also dialectical, since action (that is, the pressure of circumstances) produces counteraction, which then alters circumstances, leading to a synthesis. It will be shown later how readers' reactions affected Beauvoir's work. Chance, as she understood it (*TCF,* 18), had made her a woman and placed her in the twentieth century. However great the importance of early childhood in her view, she was convinced that she chose to be a writer as a way of assuming her condition. The synthesis of chance and choice produced, in her case, a very interesting woman, one who was a feminist before the modern feminist movement existed in France and yet who can be defined to some degree as nonfeminist.

Women Authors and French Literary History

Despite strong and legally supported patriarchal traditions in French society, there have been successful and gifted women authors from the beginning of French literature, some of whom have stressed their difference or even alienation, while for others the matter has been inconsequential. Women troubadours composed lyrics in Provençal in the late twelfth century; in the same period, roughly, Marie de France proved herself to be an expert narrator of Celtic tales, perhaps as a way of asserting herself and setting herself apart as a feminine writer.[3] More than two centuries later, Christine de Pizan dealt with matters of particular interest to women. During the Renaissance, Marguerite de Navarre, the sister of François I, was a major prose writer (her *Heptaméron* is an outstanding collection of tales) and the author of moving devotional poetry. Louise Labé and Pernette du Guillet wrote verse of high quality. In the seventeenth century Marie de Gournay, the editor of Montaigne's *Essais*, published a treatise on *Egalité des hommes et des femmes*. In the same period a number of women excelled in the novel—for example, the anonymous author of *Lettres d'une religieuse portugaise*, Madeleine de Scudéry, and Mme de Lafayette, the author of one of the finest psychological novels in French, *La Princesse de Clèves*. In the eighteenth century, when, as Sartre noted,[4] writers were for the first time widely dependent on neither throne, aristocracy, nor church, many women took up their pens as novelists, sometimes also presiding over salons that brought together the greatest luminaries of the age. Among these women authors of the Enlightenment, some supported positions that would now be recognized as feminist; an example is Madeleine de Puisieux's treatise *La Femme n'est pas inférieure à l'homme* (1750).

Many American readers are acquainted with the major woman novelist of the nineteenth century in France, George Sand, but other authors too are worth noting: the poet Marceline Desbordes-Valmore, the critic and novelist Germaine de Staël, the diarist Eugénie de Guérin (whom Beauvoir read), the feminist social critic Flora Tristan, the autobiographical writer Louise Michel. Beauvoir, who studied English in school, was also acquainted with American and British women novelists such as Louisa May Alcott, Jane Austen, the Brontë sisters, and George Eliot, whose *Mill on the Floss* brought her to tears. By the early decades of the twentieth century in France, the number of women literary figures had multiplied, although only Colette was widely known. It should be amply clear, then, that Beauvoir would not have seen herself as a pioneer. Rather, to be a writer was to assume a status that had already been defined by numerous predecessors.

This perspective does not mean, however, that for women the status of writer was unproblematic or that assuming it was without difficulty. From the beginning, the woman writer was an exception and was inevitably, if unfortunately, identified as a *woman* author. Moreover, during the eighteenth and nineteenth centuries a touch of scandal had accompanied certain famous women writers in France, some of whom had written anonymously or adopted pen names, and Colette gave further excuse to associate women novelists with immoral topics and scandalous personal conduct. (In the Beauvoir milieu, where much modern literature was considered immoral, women writers, painters, and so forth would have been considered vulgar and probably subversive.) These factors tended to accentuate the separation already assumed by readers between the woman writer and her contemporaries, by implication if not in fact, and to give her an autonomous, if often criticized, status. In other ways, women writers tended to be more subjected than men. A number of them were partially or entirely dependent on husbands or lovers, and this dependence was often a trammel to their development. In addition, women writers relied largely for their subject matter on the couple. (This was true for men also, to a considerable degree—French literature has been greatly concerned with the topics of passionate love and marriage as an institution—but was less so for men than for women.) Novels by Mme de Lafayette, Germaine de Staël, George Sand, and Colette, as well as many works by Marguerite Duras, focus on relationships between men and women, sometimes highly eroticized ones.

Moreover, with perhaps few exceptions, French women writers from the beginning had, consciously or otherwise, placed themselves in the literary world of men. They generally used literary forms that had been created by male writers, the social and moral framework in their works was usually derivative, and their literary language, however well used, reflected the language devised by men.[5] If, as some would argue, they historically showed greater sensitivity than their counterparts to women's problems and portrayed female characters more truthfully, they still tended to do so obliquely, and their writing, even when subversive, rarely represented a direct attack on male-dominated institutions. Until the 1970s, when the French publishing house Editions des Femmes was founded and a number of journals devoted to women's writing were created, to be an author was to belong to what radical feminists of today would consider a male, hence oppressive, establishment. It might be argued that, in some cases, this very oppression, if such it was, served to motivate and shape women's writing; the dynamics of writing within a male world lent shape to their work and energized it, often in the form of powerful women characters. As Gide argued, art lives on constraint, both aesthetic and psychological.

Beauvoir's Position as a Woman Writer

To some degree, it would seem that Beauvoir's evolution as an intellectual and hence as a writer was enhanced by her position as a woman in the male-dominated intellectual world of the Sorbonne, the lycées, Paris of the intelligentsia, and, finally, the entire literary tradition. Her father had told her that she had a man's mind. Sartre said she had the intelligence of a man, joined to the sensibility of a woman.[6] This masculine intellect meant, it turned out, that she could compete with men on their terrain; it did not encourage her to redefine that terrain. Furthermore, her relationship with Sartre, while not problematic to herself, she affirmed, casts on her career a particular light. Like writers such as Colette, she was for a time somewhat financially dependent on a man; until she won the Prix Goncourt, the purse she shared with Sartre was refilled more often by him than by her. In particular, his generosity enabled her to devote her full time to writing after the war (dismissed by the university under the Occupation, she had been reinstated but resigned). While his recommendation did not suffice to persuade Gallimard to publish *Quand prime le spirituel* in 1937, support from Sartre in the early 1940s was probably useful when Beauvoir submitted the manuscript of *L'Invitée*. After they achieved fame, moreover, their role as a public couple, which understandably annoyed her at times, nevertheless shaped her conduct and her writing; she often chose, for instance, to eschew treating certain topics (notably philosophical and political ones—among those which would traditionally be considered man's purview) because she considered Sartre more qualified to treat them.

The result is that, to many recent feminists, Beauvoir is only halfway one of theirs, perhaps even not at all, since she is a product of a literary tradition and a set of social relationships that they condemn as irremediably distorted.[7] Moreover, she did not always see her status as problematic. Just as François Mauriac observed that there was a distinction between being a writer who was a Catholic and being a Catholic writer,[8] Beauvoir implicitly distinguished between being a writer who was also a woman and being a "woman writer." She stated late in her career that, for a writer, sex might make little difference: "I do not think there is a difference between living one's life as a woman writer and living it as a man writer" ("Je ne pense pas qu'il y ait de différence entre vivre sa vie en écrivain femme ou en écrivain homme"; Dayan, 79). In particular, she admitted not having sought to develop a peculiarly feminine language, noting that she used techniques employed by everyone and was influenced by Hemingway as much as Colette. This statement, among others, shows that Beauvoir identified and defined herself in contradistinction not to men but rather to other women: *not* a wife, *not* a mother, *not* a socialite or patron of tearooms, *not* (at least not always) a follower of fashion; instead, an *agrégée,* a philosopher, a writer, like a man. That is, she did not assume herself as woman but as more-than-woman and less-than-woman. Given that contemporary feminist theorists and critics, from Monique Wittig and Marie Cardinal, among those who write in French, through Gloria Steinem, Kate Millet, Sandra Gilbert and Susan Gubar, and countless other American figures, are primarily concerned with distinguishing themselves from men, it is clear why they are of two minds with respect to Beauvoir.[9] She represents the type of feminism Julia Kristeva calls insertion into "men's time," as opposed to "women's time," with its refusal of male categories and insistence that women be recognized for their difference.[10]

Yet in some ways, Beauvoir wrote from within her feminine situation and toward others in the same situation. Though as a student of philosophy she was firmly grounded in the Cartesian tradition and was influenced also by Hegel's concept of universals, she was typically existentialist in valorizing the concrete over the abstract, the individual mind over the universal mind, and the reasons of situation over analytic reason as a whole. As she looked over her career, she was pleased to realize that she had often written for women, preferring that to having worked on an abstract, universal level. If she did not feel what Harold

Bloom has called the "anxiety of influence," or the "anxiety of author-ship" (Sankovitch, 1)—in the sense of being fearful of working on a generally male terrain—she was certainly *aware* of herself as a woman writer. It is this dimension of her work that makes her decision to become active in the French women's liberation movement in the 1970s consistent with her previous career. Moreover, she had a subject matter to problematize that men do not have—her otherness, that is, herself as a *negative* of, or opposite to, the male norm. (The existence of a modern literature of virility, represented by Malraux and Montherlant in France and Hemingway in the United States, does not invalidate the observation that, when men problematize their condition, they usually do so with respect not to a woman antagonist but rather to fate, society, or some other force that affects human beings as a whole.)

Beauvoir's writing for women entails several elements. One can be called that of the personal example: she showed that the life of an intellectual and a writer is not inconsistent with being a woman, and that a woman can handle concepts and words as competently as her male peers. She did note the incompatability of her career (and, by extension, perhaps that of women intellectuals in general) with mother-hood. The choice not to have children was a personal one but was dictated in large measure, if not entirely, by her image of herself as being a writer above all. Noting that others had often reproached her for this decision, much more frequently than they chided Sartre and other childless male writers, she concluded that most people assume a woman writer to be essentially a dilettante, one who lives by ordinary feminine occupations and writes for distraction, whereas they identify male writers wholly with their profession, as they identify men gener-ally with their work. Beauvoir's aim of illustrating a woman writer's life thus necessarily meant defending it: "It is the whole of a life that is structured by and on writing" ("C'est l'ensemble d'une vie qui est structurée par et sur l'écriture"; Dayan, 80). She insisted that women in general should become identified with their work just as men are, so that their status, in a world that judges action, would be identical.[11]

Another element of Beauvoir's writing for women is the way she structures into fiction her vision of the traps laid for women by them-selves and by social institutions, and women's failures in avoiding those traps. From *L'Invitée* through *Les Belles Images,* she creates situations that lead women into denying their own freedom through bad faith—retrenching behind commonplaces, using their sex as an excuse, lying blatantly to themselves, and blaming others. Their relationships with men—husbands, lovers—and other family members are distorted by this bad faith, with the result that their situation worsens and, at the extreme, they become so alienated from others that their action can have no meaning. Such is the case in *Les Mandarins* with Paule, based partly on Renée Ballon, a teacher whom Beauvoir knew in Rouen and who, under the delusion that André Malraux was in love with her, became unable to carry on a normal life. Numerous other characters of Beauvoir have a distorted sense of themselves in relation to others, or they take refuge in half-truths and lies to conceal the reality of their failures. Beauvoir was explicit about wanting to use her work to illustrate such errors. Her work does not, however, deserve the term *didactic,* for rarely are solutions given; rather, fiction is the exposition of a situation in which the characters are assumed to be free and on whom no solution should be imposed by the creator's hand.

Another element of Beauvoir's fiction that can be interpreted as directed toward women consists in its peculiarly feminine quality.[12] That this quality exists might be questioned, and, even where it can be distinguished, it would be difficult to find critical agreement on it and its importance. Certainly little or nothing in her work resembles Colette's treatment of motherhood, gardens, domestic animals, seduction, and other topics that most readers would consider eminently feminine. Beauvoir's work sometimes appears just as masculine as that of male novelists, perhaps more so than some: her early work includes dominant heroes as well as heroines, and in *Les Mandarins* there are three major male figures to one principal female figure. Yet it is hard to imagine a male novelist having composed *L'Invitée,* with its excessively long analyses of the heroine's psyche and relationships with the other characters; the fact that commentators on this novel are overwhelmingly women may bear out its distinctly feminine slant. And Beauvoir's last stories and novel, artistically perhaps her best, have women as the central consciences and are dominated by these characters' particular concerns as wives and mothers.

It would be more difficult to demonstrate that Beauvoir's own literary sensibility is predominantly a feminine one. Her interest in the experience of sexual love is no more peculiarly feminine than a man's would be, and her style as a whole is characterized by both sensibility and intellect—qualities shared by all distinguished artists. Yet she herself believed that she had portrayed women as only a woman could,[13] and this factor suggests that she had the advantage not merely of knowing a woman's situation and reactions from the inside but also of possessing the literary means necessary to render these and distinguish them from the situation and reactions of male characters. And it might be argued that Beauvoir's ability to render concrete experience—the smells, sights, and sounds of a foreign city; the touch of a blanket; the feelings of abandon; a sense of *taedium vitae*—is characteristically feminine, although this ability is shared by male writers, including Sartre.

What Beauvoir did not attempt to produce was what is now called *écriture féminine,* not just writing *for* women but a particular use of language that is seen as counteraction to male language, or "discourse controlled by the phallus,"[14] and that has been defined as "inscription of the female body and difference in language and text" (Showalter, 249). Since the term does not refer simply to the theme of women, exactly what feminists have in mind is unclear, unless one takes the matter to the extreme, as Monique Wittig and Sande Zeig have done,[15] and invents new words as rivals to "male" nouns and verbs. In any case, there seems to be in Beauvoir's work, despite sensitivity to the body (as in the abortion episode of *Le Sang des autres*), little effort to give to expression a peculiarly feminine cast. Unlike some current writers, Beauvoir does not attempt self-consciously to reinterpret history or myth in feminine terms; nor does she give particular weight to what are, according to both traditionalist male writers and radical female ones, *feminine* values—love, desire, emotion.[16]

A final element of Beauvoir's work that is directed toward women consists in explicit treatment of women's questions in *Le Deuxième Sexe* and elsewhere. One should not suppose, of course, that women alone compose the audience for these works: false myths concerning women's situation are, Beauvoir shows, a creation of men and women both, and since men are greatly responsible for perpetuating them, given their evident self-interest in doing so, it was they as much as women readers whom she tried to reach. In essays in *Les Temps modernes* and in interviews, prefaces, and other public statements she addressed issues of importance to women in Europe, America, and the third world, ceaselessly returning to major points she had already made in *Le Deuxième Sexe* and showing how they applied in particular situations. It has been remarked that Beauvoir, when visiting Egypt in 1967, criticized the failure of Nasser's government to put into practice the sexual equality that had been decreed by the constitution but that Egyptian men, steeped in Muslim law and tradition, resisted vehemently. In Israel, she observed how Israeli women, who had been made equal partners in fighting against the British and Arabs, were, in peacetime, relegated to menial jobs or the most tedious of domestic work, with lower salaries or none, and how they generally cooperated in this new, but retrogressive, division of labor (*TCF,* 426–27).

Readers' Reactions

A part of the woman writer's situation not to be overlooked is Beauvoir's reception by readers, notably women, who approach her works from a specifically feminine point of view that men, however interested, cannot fully adopt and who expect a reading experience that differs from that offered by male writers. To a considerable degree, Beauvoir has not disappointed her women readers.

Several distinctions need to be made, however. Her early novels and play were certainly not directed toward a specifically female audience. As noted earlier, they contain strong male characters; moreover, except for *L'Invitée* they deal predominantly with issues—such as war, resistance, and the importance of historical action—that have traditionally appealed to men more than to women. Beauvoir long saw herself as belonging to the class of writers in general, along with her male friends such as Sartre and Nizan, with the question of her sex being of secondary or no importance. It was after she decided to study herself specifically—a decision that led first to *Le Deuxième Sexe* and then to the memoirs—that she became cognizant enough of the problematics of women to wish to give them a privileged place in her work.

Beauvoir thus attracted an increased feminine audience, one that looked to her experience, as recorded in her memoirs and fiction, for insights into their own. In the prologues to *La Force de l'âge* and *La Force des choses* she attributes her decision to continue her memoirs beyond the first volume to the favorable response of women readers, who wanted to know more about her life after appreciating the account of its beginnings. Here, readers' reception, which Hans-Robert Jauss and others have shown to be a major factor shaping the "meaning" of the text, played a concrete role in directing the author's subsequent career—an illustration of its dialectical development.[17] Letters she received later bore out, to her eyes, the pertinence and importance of her writing on women: whether from successful women in command of their own lives or from those who were without meaningful work, unhappily tied to men whom they could not love or respect, enslaved by the family structure, or rejected by lovers, the flood of unsolicited responses to her writing showed how many women had been touched by her self-portraits and her exploration of women's situation. Such a response was also material in directing her fiction, in the last part of her career, toward the questions treated in *La Femme rompue* and *Les Belles Images*.

It is important to observe that this interest in the women's question arose in the context of Beauvoir's keen historical awareness as it developed during and after World War II and of her concern for far-reaching social reform; for years she insisted that the task of redefining women's position and remaking women themselves could not be separated from the wider task of remaking society as a whole. She stated that, were she to rewrite *Le Deuxième Sexe,* she would give it a basis in *rareté,* that is, the economic scarcity Sartre identified as fundamental to human relationships.[18] Thus, what have been called the radicalizations of Beauvoir[19] must be considered in connection with her political positions in general: her hatred of the capitalist-based institutions that dominated France in her youth and were revived after the war, her particular dislike for the bourgeoisie, her Marxist conviction that work should not be alienated from the worker, her wish for a full-fledged revolution in France and a classless society. Nevertheless, in the 1970s, when she became active in the Mouvement de libération des femmes, she came to separate the feminine question from social revolution as a whole, and to affirm, contrary to her previous opinion, that women's liberation had to come first. This change brought her position more nearly in line with that of orthodox women's liberation on both continents.

The type of audience for Beauvoir's writing on women has thus varied somewhat; feminists writing in North America and Europe in the 1960s tended to find her early positions, despite their solid foundation, too global and not close enough to their own concerns, such as day-care centers, working conditions, and equal pay, whereas sympathetic third-world readers well understood that in their society, at least, feminism had come from and remained associated with the socialist revolution. When Beauvoir began speaking out on concrete issues, notably abortion, she gained a wider audience, one that came to include large numbers of feminist-oriented critics. Later, paradoxically, she was criticized for falling short of radical feminism; her positions were also attacked by Marxists as being insufferably middle class.

In addition to the response of ordinary readers—a reaction of the sort that many authors are not in a position to know—a writer's situation includes public critical reactions, whether favorable or unfavorable, because these, like other given elements, must be accepted, rejected, or modified. This is true even if the artist has helped to shape the critical reaction. A quick glance at almost any recent list of studies on Beauvoir shows that the authors are overwhelmingly women, and that most recent commentators have adopted a markedly feminist approach to her work. It could be argued that *Le Deuxième Sexe* was a crucial factor in the formation of such a body of criticism by women, not because it gave credibility to women—they had had credibility as critics as well as creative writers for at least 150 years—but because it showed women's condition as problematic. By the time this large body of feminist criticism developed, Beauvoir's career as a creative writer had drawn to a close (though she continued to speak out on issues), and so it had no effect on the development of her work. Because of these critics, however, and because of the interest her work still arouses among women commentators in the 1990s, Beauvoir's current situation as a writer can be defined in considerable measure as that of a feminist.

One thus encounters a paradox that she would have understood well: the writer who began her career as a woman in a man's world, with no special interest in women's condition as a whole, now belongs preeminently to a world that women critics are claiming for themselves, one where women's condition is being redefined. The young intellectual who was so concerned with rebelling against her family and milieu, at considerable emotional cost, had long been inattentive to the generalizations she might have drawn from her experiences; current readers, with the benefit of hindsight and the categories of analysis proposed by her own work, go back to her individual experience to make the generalizations for her. Although Beauvoir noted that her life was problematic ("L'histoire de ma vie elle-même est une problématique") and offered no solutions, she did not deny that, based on it, conclusions could be drawn (Dayan, 75).

Chapter Three

Early Fiction and Drama

When the 15-year-old Simone de Beauvoir decided that she wanted to become a famous writer, it was apparently creative writing she had in mind, for, as she later explained, she distinguished the writings of a scholar ("l'œuvre d'un spécialiste"), directed toward a small audience, from novels ("les livres"), which touch the imagination and which everyone can read (*MJF*, 142). That is, she envisaged expression and communication as ends in themselves, rather than a tool for advancing knowledge, and fiction, by its popularity, provides the opportunity for communication with many. Such an attitude is not surprising in an adolescent; it was, moreover, consistent both with the high value academic and literary circles placed on the masterpieces of French fiction and with the popularity of novels among almost all classes in France.[1] Sartre himself began by writing fiction, then abandoned it. The young Beauvoir recognized also that a fictional character was a projection or re-creation of the self, and that having such alter egos would be an enrichment of her life. She understood too that literature was a kind of absolute that could replace the religious absolute she had lost when she ceased believing in God. Dreaming, she later noted, of being her own cause and end, she saw that imaginative writing afforded the artist the opportunity to create *ex nihilo* and direct this creation toward ends that are absolutes. Like Roquentin in Sartre's *La Nausée* (*Nausea*), she would thus justify her existence and at the same time serve humanity (*MJF*, 143).

What she did not yet realize was that fiction might also lend itself particularly well to the exposition of problems in human conduct, as she would later conceptualize them. She was to make excellent use of stories and novels to illustrate aspects of her philosophical positions and especially her fundamental conviction that human beings choose themselves in reference and response to a situation. Whether her fictional works are outstanding achievements in their genres, however, remains to be considered.

Quand prime le spirituel

Beauvoir's first literary efforts were "Les Malheurs de Marguerite" (Margaret's misfortunes) and "La Famille Cornichon" (The pickle family), composed between 1914 and 1916. These were followed by serious attempts in the 1920s to write novels, works that she found inadequate even as she was composing them but that she had neither the technical sophistication nor the maturity to improve. In 1932 she finished a novel but recognized it as poor, partly because it was too exterior to herself. In 1933 she completed another, concerning a brother and sister, but realized that it had degenerated from its promising beginnings into "an enormous mess" ("un énorme fatras"; *FA,* 229); certain elements from it reappear in later work. She continued experimenting with techniques of narration, partly under the influence of American novelists then becoming known in France, especially Hemingway and Dos Passos. From 1935 to 1937 she composed a group of five stories, originally entitled "Primauté du spirituel" (Primacy of the spiritual). When they were finally published in 1979, they were called *Quand prime le spirituel,* since the first title, borrowed from the neo-Thomist philosopher Jacques Maritain, had since been used for one of his books. The reference to the spiritual is, of course, ironic, since the author's concern was to show the damage done to families and individuals by those middle-class French who claimed to give primacy to religious and moral considerations—"spiritual hocus-pocus" ("mystifications spiritualistes"; *FA,* 230). The two publishers to whom she submitted the manuscript in 1937—Gallimard and Grasset—rejected it as immature, despite some good qualities. Gallimard's decision to publish it in 1979 obviously reflects Beauvoir's fame and the consequent assumption that readers would be interested in her apprentice work. If one believes the preface, Beauvoir herself thought the work had more than historical value.

Her description of the stories (*FA,* 230–32), quoted on the cover, shows discrepancies from their published form and suggests editing for publication. Long enough to be called novellas, the stories all bear a woman's name—an early indication of Beauvoir's concern with the feminine and her determination to give it full attention. Although the word *roman* is printed on the cover, the five pieces are only loosely tied together by some recurring characters; these characters furnish complementary perspectives on people and events. The preface states that the

stories are based on the author's experience or that of her friends; apart
from Zaza and a few other models in *La Force de l'âge,* the critic cannot
identify all the borrowings, but a great deal of the material plainly
reflects Beauvoir herself. The milieu is that of the proper bourgeoisie,
especially its schools for girls.

In "Marcelle," the heroine is first presented as a child. Sensitive,
given to religious feeling, she imagines she will marry and inspire a
man of genius. Her conviction that destiny descends on one, rather
than being created day by day, is an error Beauvoir frequently criticizes.
Although Marcelle Drouffe then loses her faith, she evolves into an
idealistic, if shallow, young woman, one given to romantic reveries.
She is employed at a dispensary in a working-class neighborhood and
helps establish a cultural center there. Early enthusiasm wanes as she
discovers social realities. She abandons her first fiancé, a pious and
unimaginative engineer, for a poet. After their marriage, the husband
she had taken for a Rimbaud proves to be an indolent parasite and
philanderer. She does not have the courage to insist on a separation, but
he leaves on his own, having found a generous mistress. Abandoned,
Marcelle imagines in a pseudoepiphany that her destiny must be not to
marry a genius but to be one.

Beauvoir thought that the satire of the stifling atmosphere of
middle-class values and its false idealism was timid, but it is closer to
heavy-handed. The work is laden with the vocabulary of the very
spiritualism she wanted to satirize, and her critical intelligence does
not come through sufficiently to attract the reader's complicity. Yet
"Marcelle" is not entirely without literary interest. The perceptive
description of the heroine's wedding night could occupy a place in an
anthology of such scenes from much more practiced writers, such as
Mauriac. The portrait of Denis, the husband, is more effective than
that of Marcelle, where shading is lost in excessive exposition. The
girl's realization, at a young age, that she is "not like others" (a phrase
that echoes Gide's cry of anguished separation, "Je ne suis pas comme
les autres") could have led the heroine to discovering her real self,
hidden under the clichés of her milieu; in subsequent fiction Beauvoir
would be able to manipulate more skillfully the contrast between characters' potentiality and the inauthenticity to which most fall prey.

In "Chantal," the second story, the language of the heroine's diary,
which constitutes two sections, pleased the author when she reread it;
these sections succeed in revealing the "distance from self to self that
constitutes bad faith" ("la distance de soi à soi qu'est la mauvaise foi";

FA, 231–32). The eponymous heroine, based partly on a friend, Simone Lebourdin, but very like Beauvoir, is in her first year as a *lycée* teacher in a provincial town. She is treated critically, showing that Beauvoir was acquiring the ability to create a character who was at once a projection of herself and a negative mirror.[2] The contrast between the two narrative points of view, first- and third-person omniscient, with the focus either on the heroine or on a pupil as the central intelligence, shows how Chantal appears to others; Beauvoir was learning to handle perspective to effect.

One of Chantal's errors, well conveyed by the pretentious style of her diary, is her aesthetic approach to experience. To see and evaluate things and people as if they were art objects is a serious error because it confuses the moral and the aesthetic, the *real* with what Sartre called the *irréel,* that is, images. Chantal likes small-town fairs because of Rimbaud; she appreciates the provincial city because it is quaint, like a scene out of Balzac or Dickens. She tries to give her life artistic value by surrounding herself with the beautiful and marvelous. When she has read a few pages of Proust, sipped some tea, and browsed in the streets, she imagines her life as something out of a painting. Such an aesthetic posture leads to role-playing: the denial of one's free self through creating a pseudoself. Essentially, she wants to live her life as a story seen from the far end.[3]

Chantal's second flaw is the need to see herself through others in order to acquire value in her own eyes. Her diary reveals her concern for creating the persona of the liberated Parisian; she at once disguises and unmasks herself. She is preoccupied with (a) how she will prove to a friend that she is not to be pitied for teaching in the provinces and (b) her dress, calculated to appeal to the students and shock her colleagues. She cares even more about the way a pupil's parents see her. At the end of the school year, she imagines that her own image will be left behind in others' eyes, a legendary (that is, aesthetic) form of herself.

The third flaw, a consequence of the others, is Chantal's indifference to the possible moral consequences of her acts. Having broken down the barrier between instructor and pupil with two girls who interest her (one looks like a Virgin painted by Fra Lippi), she treats them as an audience, encourages their confidences, and even favors a clandestine romance between one of them and a young man who reminds Chantal of Alain-Fournier's hero in *Le Grand Meaulnes* (*The Wanderer*). But when the girl becomes pregnant and wants an abortion, Chantal takes a moralizing position and refuses to help, thinking only of how she could be dismissed for her role in the romance. The irony, though perhaps somewhat forced, is handled better here than in the first story. The young author also showed that she could write dialogue and that she had learned the effects that can be achieved by manipulating points of view, to match her phenomenologist's conviction that human reality, like reality in general, is perspectival.

Like "Marcelle" and "Chantal," "Lisa," a somewhat shorter story, is set in a milieu familiar to the author. The heroine is a boarder and teaching assistant at the Institution Saint-Ange in Auteuil. She resents having to earn her living by selling her mind and feels only dread and loathing at the idea of spending her life as a professor. The school is so depressing, and the rules so strict, that she seeks escape in an almost-pathological cultivation of her imagination, an action leading to a distortion of reality. The young man to whom she is attracted (the brother of Marcelle Drouffe) takes no interest in her; friendship with Marcelle's sister, Marguerite, proves unsatisfactory; and reality constantly gives the lie to her expectations. Only the belief that an older woman can mistake her for her husband's mistress and that a middle-aged dentist can be attracted to her offers Lisa a self-image that is not wholly negative. These discoveries are not incidental; they are related subtly to a self that she recognizes poorly, one for whom the physical is more important than the pious directors at Saint-Ange imagine. The ending shows how much Lisa is preoccupied with her body.

"Lisa" is not so substantial an achievement as "Chantal." The exposition is well done, however, and there are good moments, such as Lisa's confrontation with the irate wife, the evocation of the dentist's office, and the description of his hands. Beauvoir succeeds in creating, with nice ironic touches, both the ambience of a Catholic boarding school and a young woman whose future appears as dreary as her present and who seems trapped by intellectual and religious expectations she cannot share, the only remedy to which is fantasy. The focus on the conflict between the ideal and the real, expectations and realizations, is doubtless related to the young writer's own persistent idealism (the "schizophrenia" of which she later spoke).

Evaluations of "Anne," the fourth story, will vary according to the lens through which it is read. Beauvoir herself later judged it (*FA*, 231) as one more failure in her series of attempts through the 1930s to base a successful piece of fiction on Zaza's death; in particular, Beauvoir found the motivation weak. But she may have underestimated her achievement. The story succeeds in stigmatizing the hypocritical and narrow-minded Catholic bourgeoisie, preoccupied with appearances and social success. The author shapes the facts in such a way that the family responsibility for Anne Vignon's tragedy is shared by her suitor, Pascal Drouffe, who is portrayed as an unwitting accomplice, and, to a slight degree, by her friend Chantal. If one knows nothing of the facts behind it, the denouement may appear excessive: dying of love or in reaction to parental severity no longer seems plausible. If one is acquainted with the facts, to which the story is basically faithful, its value as fiction may be judged secondary to its documentary value.

The four parts are all told by an omniscient narrator, but the focus is often on a central intelligence—Mme Vignon, Chantal, or Pascal. Within the third-person-omniscient narration are embedded passages of interior monologue by Mme Vignon. The narrative technique thus shows how different characters interpret identical situations in radically different ways—that is, the subjective quality of reality. Anne herself is almost never seen from inside. The consequent impression she gives of being passive suggests the abrogation of her freedom and paralyzing psychological conflict; still, the work might have gained in strength had Anne been portrayed differently.

Mme Vignon's opening monologue, in the form of a rambling prayer at mass (interspersing standardized formulas with her own running thoughts), reveals her bourgeois prudence and preoccupations, including her desire to control Anne and a firm intention to marry off her eldest daughter. As the author observed, Mme Vignon reveals herself in her truth and her falsehood alike (*FA*, 231). When Anne and her mother quarrel over the former's relationship with Pascal Drouffe, it is decreed that the association will end. At the close of part 1, Anne deliberately cuts her foot with a hatchet—a gesture Zaza had carried out (Bair, 80)—so that she will not have to accompany her sister to visit a suitor's parents; revealing her sense of hopelessness and her distaste at the false and oppressive courtship rituals imposed by her society, the gesture foreshadows Anne's final madness.

Part 2 is seen through the eyes of Anne's friend Chantal, suspect to Mme Vignon because she is an intellectual. Chantal needs Anne's admiration and gratitude to maintain her self-image, despite the superiority that her professorial career affords (she is pleased to show her tasteful clothes in a milieu where earlier she had felt dowdy—a reflection, perhaps, of the writer's memories of being shabbily dressed when she visited Zaza). She also expects to woo Anne farther away from her mother; she will consider it a personal triumph if Anne marries Pascal.

Part 3 is centered first on Pascal, then on the young couple, during a farewell conversation before Anne is sent away to England. He is a less ardent lover than one has supposed; he seems to welcome the pretext offered by his sister's illness to postpone an official engagement. His empty idealism, coupled with his selfishness, are signs of bad faith. He explains his lack of commitment by his supposed inability to love well, while enjoying Anne's complete devotion. If one reads this story as a projection of how Beauvoir saw Zaza's fiancé before she learned the entire truth, one will conclude that she blamed Merleau-Ponty for his pusillanimity.

The last part is told by the omniscient authorial voice. The author handles with skill the scene of the heroine's madness, based on the episode when Zaza, already physically ill and deranged, confronted her suitor's startled mother with wild accusations. Beauvoir's ability to write dialogue for situations she could visualize strongly is apparent in the scene. Anne's death does not, however, conclude the story. Rather, Beauvoir ends it by studying the effect of Anne's death on the others, all of whom draw some advantage from it—a prefiguration of the existentialist tenet that death is the affair of the living. Mme Vignon turns her daughter into a kind of saint, publishing pious selections from her diary and almost praying to her in sacrilege. Pascal similarly idealizes Anne, since he is now safe from entanglements. Chantal's grief is less tinged with triumph than Mme Vignon's, but even she is a vampire, sucking life from her deceased friend, whose story, beautiful and tragic, will, as she says, belong to her forever.

The last story, "Marguerite," was in the author's eyes the most successful by far. Readers probably agree;[4] both plot and characterization are well handled, and there is less implausibility. Recounted in the first person, it is highly autobiographical, with a minimum of invented material. The author adopts toward her fictional self an attitude that is at once ironic and vaguely complacent—a tone characteristic also of the first two volumes of memoirs. The strengths of the story reappear in Beauvoir's later fiction: a persuasive psychology, drawing its truth from personal experience, and a style that comes close to fulfilling Stendhal's ideal of the best style as that which is both unobtrusive and clear. The story also illustrates a permanent weakness of Beauvoir's: her very limited ability to invent from whole cloth convincing characters and situations—that is, her lack of fictional imagination.

Marguerite Drouffe's upbringing at home and at the Institut Joliet resembles the author's own, dominated by moral and religious proscriptions and an attendant idealism, assuming vaguely mystical and ascetic forms. Marguerite's loss of belief leads to the discovery of the absurdity and nothingness of life: "I felt all hollow and soft, as if I were going down through thicknesses and thicknesses of emptiness" ("Je me suis sentie toute creuse et molle, comme si je descendais à travers des épaisseurs et des épaisseurs de vide").[5] Her loss of faith, provoked by her discovery of the discrepancy between the Absolute of God and the commonness of His representatives on earth, is paralleled by, but not explicitly associated with, her discovery of sexuality, an important theme.

To offset the emptiness left by her loss of faith, the heroine pursues frenetic intellectual activity, accelerating her studies and enclosing herself in her own mental world. She remains vulnerable, however, especially to the prestige of others (the ontological replacement for God and human authority based on moral law). Like her sister, Marcelle, Marguerite falls victim to idealized love. At first her feeling toward Denis, Marcelle's husband, is simply girlish admiration for his apparent intellectual sophistication and his freedom from bourgeois constraints. Thanks to him, she is initiated to a wider intellectual world and also a social one, when he takes her to a Montparnasse bar. (The descriptions of his behavior and some of his remarks largely parallel those of Beauvoir's cousin Jacques in the memoirs.) When Denis leaves his wife, Marguerite loses sight of him but does not forget his admonitions to live freely, advice that loosely reflects the precepts of the surrealists, Gidean *disponibilité,* and the gratuitous act. She continues to frequent bars, where she endangers herself by her imprudences.

When Marguerite by chance meets Denis again, he is living with Marie-Ange, for whom he left Marcelle in the first story. He cannot devote himself to any useful daily activity, whether from weakness of character and indolence or, as he airily claims, from a noble dissatisfaction with crass reality. Marguerite attempts to assuage his mysterious romantic melancholia. The plot takes a surprising turn when Marie-Ange, who resembles Beauvoir's lesbian colleague in Marseilles, attempts to seduce Marguerite; the latter's refusal of the woman's advances precipitates a crisis, and Denis is thrown out. Rather than work, Denis returns to Marcelle, who agrees to forgive him.

The story does not end, however, with this predictable turn of events, because it is Marguerite's story, not Denis's. How she handles his reconciliation with Marcelle shows the changes that have taken place in her. Gazing along the boulevards of Paris at what the naturalists called slices of life, she realizes that her devotion to Denis has distorted her views on things (making her, in existentialist terms, inauthentic). She has a near-epiphany when things break through what she calls their "allegorical cloak" ("manteau allégorique"; *QPS,* 348), but, unlike Roquentin in *La Nausée,* she sees in a positive light the richness and inexhaustibility of things, at whose center she finds her consciousness. Later she concludes that such a spiritual conversion (as she puts it) was less important than she supposed, since what she needed was to get rid of the spiritual. The fact remains that the dazzling presence of things, replacing the symbolic function they have had for her, serves to reveal her moral freedom, as her consciousness becomes aware of its freedom to accept or reject the world. At the end, Marguerite reveals that Chantal has since married a rich doctor, that Pascal is successful as an archaeologist (that is, working with dead cultures), and that Marcelle has published a booklet of poems; as for herself, denying ready-made values, she prefers to know the world as it is.

Connoisseurs of modern stories will find little to praise in these; the weaker are characterized by florid prose, too little dialogue, and underdrawn portraits, and even the stronger have neither the forceful characters nor the powerful sense of reality that can make a story memorable. Decades later, Beauvoir showed in *La Femme rompue* that she could utilize the long story—a somewhat difficult form to handle—to go deep into a character and probe the most complex family relationships. But *Quand prime le spirituel* is not without merit as a document on the French bourgeoisie of the 1920s, and it foreshadows the author's subsequent work, particularly its autobiographical basis, its dependence on philosophical notions Beauvoir shared with Sartre, and its focus on women characters. It is characteristic also in its negative content: like Sartre and Mauriac, to take two examples, Beauvoir would almost always focus critically on the problems and misuses of human life, instead of inviting her readers to share a powerfully affirmative vision, whether political or aesthetic, like that of Proust and Malraux.

L'Invitée

To judge by scholarly attention, especially in recent years, Beauvoir's first full-length novel is her most admired, or at least the most challenging to many readers—despite what some view as its tediousness.[6] It has attracted those interested in both philosophical and psychological fiction, as well as those concerned with imaginative transpositions of autobiography. To some, it may seem quite contemporary, partly because the dominant character is a woman, one greatly concerned with herself. Although from the beginning there are references to the 1938 Munich agreement and foreshadowings of the ensuing world conflict, the novel is not visibly historical; much of it suggests separation from the wider world, even confinement.[7] This hothouse quality may, however, be seen precisely as reflecting the period obliquely, or at least the author, who, as she later confessed, maintained an ostrichlike attitude, refusing to admit to herself that European peace was gravely endangered. In retrospect, one may conclude that the work is as "schizophrenic" as she. The heroine does not believe that war is coming: "Those things happen only to others" ("Ces choses n'arrivent qu'aux autres").[8] The book thus seems lacking in timeliness, next to other works composed in the immediate period—Nizan's *La Conspiration* (The conspiracy), Malraux's *L'Espoir* (*Man's Hope*), Saint-Exupéry's *Pilote de guerre* (*Flight over Arras*). This aspect is surprising, because although the book had taken shape earlier, Beauvoir continued it after war broke out; it was finally published in 1943.

Dedicated to Olga Kosakiewicz, the novel is the transposition of the drama of the trio Beauvoir-Sartre-Olga, a drama that, in fictional form, strains credulity. After the appearance of *La Force de l'âge,* it became apparent, despite the author's partial disclaimers, how closely the fictional version followed experience. Some conversations echo those recorded elsewhere; Pierre, the Sartre figure, is especially close to his model. The parallels with reality are closer than readers of the memoirs realized, since Beauvoir omitted from the latter her love affair with Bost, a relationship that found its way into the novel. The most striking case of divergence between the real and the fictional is the ending, when the heroine, Françoise Miquel, kills Xavière, an act that has no parallel in Beauvoir's biography.

The novel's chief concern is the dynamics of human relationships, characterized by conflict and ultimately by violence. Embodied in the plot by mental and physical actions, human relationships are also expressed in psychological and especially philosophical terms by the characters, in a vocabulary that is roughly the early Sartrean, as elaborated in *L'Etre et le néant* (*Being and Nothingness*), published the same year.[9] Fallaize (26) notes that the oscillation between the human, or psychological, dilemma and the philosophical perceptions creates ambiguity, the philosophy sometimes seeming like an elaborate rationalization for the concrete experience. The epigraph from Hegel, "Each consciousness pursues the death of the other," posits as fundamental the same hostility that Sartre saw in all human relationships, at least in terms of the present social context.[10] Yet this conflict is associated with freedom because the characters are seen as creating themselves rather than conforming to moral or ontological models: "One freely makes oneself what one is" ("On se fait librement ce qu'on est"; I, 253). The story ends with the word *chosen;* the heroine has freely decided.

Yet because each consciousness feels itself as absolute, total subjectivity, to which others are objects, one encounters the dilemma of the determined freedom, the absolute self that is nevertheless objectified and enslaved by others. Whereas the absolute of self is threatened by other absolutes, each depends for its self-image, or ratification, on the image others give back, whence the paradox that the inner self feels empty, though it lives itself as an absolute, and the others on the exterior—the judges—are dense. This ontological drama is experienced by Xavière, who cannot accept being judged by others; by Françoise, who is most often in the foreground, whose point of view dominates the book, and who feels herself to be a negative to Pierre's "positive"; and by Françoise's friend Elisabeth, Pierre's sister, who lives solely in function of her efforts to make herself so necessary to her lover that he will change his life—that is, to dominate him. The drama of the empty self is connected to the theme of bad faith, when characters deny their own vulnerability, trying either (a) to pretend that they cannot be objectified by others or (b) to *use* others, or imposed values and verities, as absolutes, thus avoiding the evidence of the empty self.

Significantly, the characters least associated with the theme of determination are men, doubtless because they are rarely seen from the inside; the very fact that the author portrays them as *other* to her women characters suggests that, for her, men sense themselves as freer than women, less objectified, more nearly approximating the ontological ideal of being on the inside what one is for others, without fissure between being and appearance. Pierre practices what is clearly masculine imperialism, wishing, for instance, to dominate Xavière's consciousness to the point where he alone will matter to her. He has what the author calls a "maniacal need" ("besoin maniaque") to impose himself on others (I, 171).[11] This imposing of self can be achieved through a dominant gaze (looks in the novel convey fascination and power, that is, a masochistic impulse and a sadistic one) or through other manipulations, including sexual ones. Indeed, power dictates sexual behavior much more than sensuality does.[12] Sartrean ontology makes no sexual distinctions in its analysis of the nothingness of consciousness, but, socially speaking, Beauvoir's novel suggests that women are much more vulnerable to the judgments of others, that their freedom is more easily eroded. In *Le Deuxième Sexe,* she took it on herself to explain why this is so.

The point of departure of the plot is simple. Françoise, a writer, and her friend and sometime lover Pierre Labrousse, a theater director, decide to bring to Paris the young Xavière, who has been wasting away intellectually and emotionally in Rouen; their idea is that there Xavière will be able to pursue her philosophical studies, free from pressure to take up a useful career and free from other constraints. They promise her a "golden existence" ("une existence toute dorée") in what they see as an extension of their own relationship (*I,* 38). Françoise and Pierre base their union on freedom and the conviction that legal contracts and social usages, which dictate others' relationships, specifically marriage, are pointless for them, since by choice they support each other in a commitment neither would question. Equality in giving and receiving appears to underlie their intimacy; in philosophical terms, they ratify, or justify, each other. This dependency on another subjectivity is a variety of bad faith, although entire reciprocity, without either misrepresentation or violence, would signify an authentic relationship. In fact, the relationship is *not* equal: Françoise depends much more on the nearly autonomous Pierre than he on her.[13]

What has been a satisfactory two-way relationship is tested nearly to the breaking point with the entry of Xavière. The unwelcome third in a romantic triangle is a standard ingredient of both French boulevard comedy and less frivolous literature. In *L'Invitée,* the treatment of the triangle has neither dramatic concision nor the light touch that characterizes the theme, at its best, in the works of Jean Giraudoux and Jean Anouilh. Here, as often in existentialist literature, a stock situation is subtly analyzed in a quasi-philosophical vocabulary. Yet the situation is not really transformed dramatically, and the drawn-out analysis of actions and motivations becomes tedious, despite considerable thematic interplay.

Françoise feels threatened not in her feminine role with respect to an admired male figure—for she has been used to Pierre's sexual liberties—but in her very being. The trio constantly disintegrates into pairs, relegating the third consciousness to nothingness because it is no longer acknowledged, or justified, by the others. If these other consciousnesses were indifferent to Françoise, there would be no story, but she has invested in both of them her self-image—in the older affective vocabulary, she *loves* each—and to be excluded by them is an acute denial of the self. The pairing off changes in melodramatic reversals; even Pierre can be left out. Any new alliance creates a new enemy, as the left-out third tries to reintegrate itself. Neither Françoise nor Xavière can endure this ontological jealousy; even Pierre is not immune to it.[14] To act as an intermediary in mending a quarrel or reestablishing complicity is risky: one can end up hated by both others and assuming the position of the excluded one.

The relationship between the two women sometimes resembles the traditional older sister–younger sister bond; elsewhere, Françoise (who bears the name of the author's mother) is like a mother—she speaks of her adoptive daughter (*I,* 276)—but she is an ambiguous mother who, assuming no genuine authority over the girl, can additionally play now the role of friend, now that of rival (thus giving a vaguely incestuous quality to some passages). Such flexible and apparently free relationships suggest revenge by Beauvoir against the traditional maternal-filial relationship of the middle class. At best, however, Françoise's attitude is maternalistic, even imperialistic: "Xavière belonged to her" ("Xavière lui appartenait"; *I,* 19). Elsewhere, there is full-blown rivalry between the two, a bond no better, certainly, than generational hostility within a family.[15] Sometimes Xavière assumes a dominant role, turning the tables on her mentor figure. Beauvoir's skill in handling the constantly shifting relationship and its subtleties can be considered one of the young author's chief achievements in the novel.

The role of Xavière, while crucial, is open to the criticism of implausibility. She is, to be sure, a telling illustration of some of the book's thematics—the most extreme case of bad faith and of a consciousness that paradoxically feels itself to be both everything and nothing, both free and determined. In that sense, she may be the book's most successful portrait, and credit is due to Beauvoir, even though she had a live model. But if one reads for more than the philosophical implications, the situation may appear unsatisfactory and the character unconvincing. That two intelligent and mature intellectuals would let someone in late adolescence dominate them as Xavière does stretches credulity, the more so because she is portrayed by Beauvoir as insufferable: vain, capricious, petulant, tyrannical, indolent, petty.[16]

Xavière does have the prestige of youth; she is unattached, free; she is quintessentially "other" because she appears to be ontologically self-sufficient (certainly not financially or practically so, however). But this is an illusion, for she more than anyone else is concerned with her appearance (literally and figuratively), while resisting the claims on her that such an appeal to others implies. "When people talk about me," she says, "it seems to me that they acquire superiority over me" ("Quand on me parle de moi . . . il me semble qu'on prend une supériorité sur moi"; *I*, 15). Her acts of rebellion are rarely interesting. Her gesture of burning her hand with a cigarette at a nightclub—an episode that parallels the scene in Sartre's *L'Age de raison* (*The Age of Reason*) in which Ivich cuts herself—is one of the few occasions where her refusal of others and self becomes dramatic. Elsewhere, her gestures, like her conversation, range from dull and vacuous to exasperating. Like Ivich, she is loath to eat and sleep, because doing so means surrendering to the claims of the body: "It disgusts me when I feel natural needs" ("Ça me dégoûte quand je me sens des besoins naturels"; *I*, 67). Ontologically, Xavière's loathing of bodily functions is the revolt of consciousness at its facticity. Psychologically, this loathing is the refusal to identify wholly with her body because she is not ready to accept her sexuality. When Xavière does consent to sexual contacts, they become not a solution but new obstacles to accepting herself and others, since her ambivalence toward the body becomes self-loathing. At the same time, however, she flaunts her sexuality by visible flirtations with male figures.[17]

The plausibility problem is not the only one. The relationships are overly drawn out, and by the middle of the book a reader may well wish for the author to see the plot quickly to its denouement. It might be thought that the very nature of the trio precludes a conclusion: when the balance is upset—that is, when one duo begins to dominate—the excluded third intervenes and creates a new pair and a new outsider. Such is the case in Sartre's *Huis-clos* (*No Exit*), an even more claustrophobic work built around one man and two women, to which *L'Invitée* compares somewhat unfavorably.

Beauvoir changes these dynamics by introducing two other characters. One is Elisabeth, who serves as a challenge and a foil to Françoise (Beauvoir called her "un repoussoir"; *FA*, 350, 557). She is the portrait of a failure—what the heroine does not want to become. An aspiring painter, Elisabeth is unconvincing as a potential artist, either because Beauvoir wanted to portray failure or because she was unable to draw the portrait of any artist except herself, projected onto Françoise. Elisabeth is other-oriented, always concerned about the impression she makes, outwardly aggressive but filled with self-doubt. In a classic illustration of bad faith, she attempts to fool herself into believing that her lover, Claude, who no longer even desires her, will divorce his wife.

The other character outside the triangle is Gerbert, an attractive young actor (based on Bost) to whom each of the women in the triangle is attracted. Xavière's complete inability to know herself according to the Socratic precept, and to accept the existence of other consciousnesses who pose a threat to hers, leads her to sleep with him and thus to complicate her precarious relationships with the others. Gerbert also has with Françoise, during a camping trip, what is as close to an idyll as anything in Beauvoir's work, told in persuasive and fresh terms.

The outbreak of war in September 1939 precipitates the denouement. After Pierre's departure, Xavière, feeling left out, becomes obsessed with the letters he writes to Françoise. Stealing the key to the latter's writing desk, Xavière discovers letters from Gerbert that leave no doubt about the warmth of his feelings for the older woman. Her reaction is jealousy, but a subtle one that adds deep-seated self-doubt to resentment. What in the hands of another writer could have prompted outbursts of jealousy and perhaps violence is handled differently by Beauvoir. Xavière's reaction is to yield to her agoraphobic impulses, which she has cultivated to Françoise's annoyance, and break all contact with her friend, who, in Pierre's absence, has resumed her role as a mother figure. This behavior itself would not lead to murder, however. What makes Françoise kill Xavière is that the latter will not forgive her—that is, will not wipe out from her mind the image of a Françoise who is treacherous, jealous, and vengeful; moreover, Xavière has shared this image with Gerbert. Xavière has the power to annihilate Françoise's view of herself and impose her own.[18] When, earlier, characters were unable to endure others' unfavorable images, they had the recourse of the third, with whom they could form an alliance that would, by turning the tables, extinguish the negative one. Without Pierre, Françoise cannot assume the offensive, because there is no audience for *her* version except herself: in terms of the plot, she has been totally dominated. Her only recourse is murder, the denouement that motivated the entire book (*FA*, 349).[19]

Although it would be erroneous to suppose that Beauvoir was uninterested in moral issues, the ethical question of murder is not directly confronted; the act stands out as morally neutral and ontologically, even socially, affirmative. Some critics have read *L'Invitée* as an adventure of the self, wherein a woman accustomed to leaning on another—

Pierre—and to accepting *his* image of her and the world finally liberates herself from him (during his absence, it will be noted) by eliminating a consciousness that has a claim on him and thus asserting herself over him (Fallaize, 27; Keefe, 154). The work appears in this light as the bildungsroman of a late bloomer, the discovery of ontological and moral independence. It is difficult, however, to read a murder as the culmination of a process of self-fulfillment unless limitless personal affirmation or solipsism (enclosure within the self) is the ideal.

The progress the author had made in storytelling since her early attempts is visible in *L'Invitée*. Thanks perhaps to Sartre's influence, Beauvoir had a sense of what technique could contribute to her fiction. To suppose that every plot element and each narrative device were consciously chosen for their narrative effect or philosophical meaning is, however, probably to suppose too much. The fact that two initial chapters, relating the heroine's childhood, had to be excised, on an editor's advice, suggests that the craftsmanship in the manuscript was not perfect. The episode of the heroine's illness is apt. While it can be read as an ingenious escape mechanism, it so closely parallels Beauvoir's own that one senses it was inserted chiefly because the fiction was still very close to the author's experience. Similarly, the affair between Gerbert and Françoise suggests a cherished experience more than calculated composition. Whereas some readers have seen the episode as demonstrating the heroine's self-emancipation (she desires him earlier but only toward the end allows herself to make advances), that interpretation makes the act one of sexual infidelity, with the traditional value of revenge. More in keeping with the tone of the passage is to read it as an achievement of *liberté à deux* (freedom for two), a freely granted and shared equality through sexual communication, and thus a positive counterweight to the repeated negative image of relationships elsewhere. Françoise does, however, later turn the episode into a sort of triumph over Xavière, who remains ignorant of it until the denouement.

Françoise is generally the central intelligence; in a few chapters, Elisabeth is central, and, once, Gerbert. While this change of focus affords exterior viewpoints on Françoise, it seems arbitrary. Although strictly speaking, the narrative point of view is omniscient, Beauvoir ordinarily restricts the observations to what the central intelligence can know. The third person prevails, with considerable *style indirect libre,* or free indirect style—the reporting of a character's voiced thoughts in the third person instead of the first but in past tenses and without authorial tags.[20] Without warning, however, first-person thoughts are inserted into the others, a switching Beauvoir would exploit later and Sartre would illustrate in *Le Sursis*.

The argument for limited omniscience is plausibility, or enhancement of verisimilitude: one thereby reduces the godlike foreknowledge and manipulation of characters—the sort of fiction Sartre criticized in his 1939 essay on Mauriac (*Situations,* vol. 1). (Beauvoir's switching of focus to different narrators, however, somewhat undermines the heightened verisimilitude.) The technique also increases dramatic effect, since the reader knows what the central intelligence knows but must discover the rest as the characters do, subjected to the same misapprehensions, distortions, and surprises as they. The technique can be the source of excellent ironies, when the central intelligence does not see its own errors. In addition, it enhances the sense of characters' subjectivity, an effect that fits perfectly with the emphasis in the novel on subject versus object. Those characters not seen from the inside—Xavière, the topic of endless speculation, and Pierre—remain almost opaque.

The limitation of the technique is that, without authorial comment, there is no corrective vision except other characters' remarks, for which the narrating voice is the authority; reality is limited to one perspective. The distortions brought about by Françoise's vision are challenged only in quoted material (for what it is worth) and the few cases in which Gerbert and Elisabeth offer other viewpoints; this lack of correction means either that the reader feels vaguely that the picture is incomplete, or better, that the distortions themselves are the subject of the novel. To read the novel thus as a phenomenological study in intention and consciousness is seductive but is probably not what the author had in mind, despite her philosophical training; she seems, rather, to have thought of the book as a narrative working-out of her own problems, a catharsis, like that Gide had in mind when he observed that he was not Michel in *L'Immoraliste* but could have become so. Beauvoir admitted having freed herself from Olga by the act of writing, thus illustrating for herself the existentialist tenet that literature is bound up with the project to be free.

Le Sang des autres

Beauvoir knew that her second novel, set during the Resistance, could not appear until the German occupation of France ended. Begun in 1941, published in 1945, it reflects her personal experiences and her increasing sense of involvement with her time, brought home first during the Munich crisis, then more strikingly when war broke out in 1939 and France fell the next year. The political questions the novel raises had been at the forefront of French political consciousness, and the book, which sold well and was favorably reviewed, was greeted as a Resistance novel. This fact annoyed her, for she wanted it to be taken instead as a major statement on the human condition. In fact, despite implausibilities, excessive ideological baggage, and other deficiencies, this novel, like much of her writing, constitutes a striking expression of the metaphysical in concrete, historical terms. As Keefe observes (164), there is "great strength in the middle sections of the book, which give pointed embodiment to many of the theoretical problems raised in her moral essays." The book is probably the most openly philosophical of her novels; page after page contains observations that would not be out of place in her own or Sartre's existentialist treatises, and the tone is often frankly didactic. The plot is invented but incorporates countless details from Beauvoir's experiences and those of her friends.

Le Sang des autres has an elaborate narrative structure marked by dualities. The narrative focus alternates between the two main characters, Jean Blomart and Hélène Bertrand. The story is told by either an impersonal omniscient narrator, using the third person and adopting in alternate chapters the point of view of the main characters, with considerable use of free indirect style, or, in chapters focused on him, from the hero's point of view, in the first person.[21] Switching is sudden and frequent, resulting in a blurring of the narrative voices, and Jean seems sometimes to assume the status of omniscient narrator, telling things that he could not have known. This violation of strict narrative verisimilitude does not weaken the story, which is too long to be felt by the reader as a mental whole; in any case, entire chapters narrated by the impersonal omniscient voice and centered on Hélène keep the embedded retrospective narrative from seeming just a reminiscence. Yet the fact that Jean's point of view, often in the first person, dominates means that the story represents his rendering of the past; the perspectives of other characters, including Hélène, are visible only through quotation and insights given by the omniscient narrator and, rarely, a first-person thought.

The contrast between *je* (I) and *il* (he) suggests the division of the self—on the social plane, the separation between the Jean who is born into the bourgeoisie and the Jean who wishes to espouse the cause of the proletariat, and, on the ontological one, the separation of reflexive consciousness from itself that is fundamental to existentialist phenomenology. Speaking of himself, Jean says, "Now I see him" ("Maintenant, je le vois").[22] This *je* is often paired with a *tu* (you)—not another narrative voice but the narratee (*narrataire*), that is, Hélène, whom Jean addresses as she lies dying, as if to call on her collaboration in his mental processes.

There are two narrative lines, a framing story, set in occupied France, and the embedded flashback. Both narrative points of view (the impersonal narrator and Jean) are heard in each. Scattered throughout the flashback are scenes that return to the framing story. In addition, passages in italics present momentary returns—usually affective reactions. Some of these refer to events not yet narrated in the framed story—what Gérard Genette calls *prolepses,* in contradistinction to flashbacks, or *analepses.*[23] Past and present thus form two chronological foci. The verb tenses, however, are used in such a way as not to support this chronological duality but rather to subvert it: the historical past opens the novel, while some sections of the framed retrospective narrative are told in the historical present. To these dualities are added pairs of characters—the two men with whom Hélène is involved, Jean's two lovers, and the two friends for whose death Jean feels responsible.

The framed story develops from Jean's recollections, as he spends a night in anguish prior to making a decision concerning a terrorist act members of his Resistance group propose to carry out. The story constitutes a means to a decision; the past allows one to know the present in such a way as to be able to move to the future (*FA,* 558). This does not mean that the agent lacks the freedom to decide what form the future will take; Jean sees his acts as ontologically brand-new, growing out of freedom, not determination. His hesitation concerning the planned act of sabotage arises from the fact that earlier he was responsible for sending Hélène on the terrorist mission during which she was critically wounded. The blood of others of the title is thus first of all Hélène's and that of the other activists who risk their lives. Since as leader, Jean does not ordinarily participate in the attacks, he does not risk his life to the same degree. This theme of the anguished responsibility of leadership creates an ironic counterpart to the theme of elitism, as he criticizes it in the bourgeoisie, represented by his father.

Jean is born into the ownership class, and, like Sartre's Hugo in *Les Mains sales* (*Dirty Hands*), feels guilty when he discovers the difference between his family's living standards and those of workers, a difference his father dismisses as integral to a stable social organization. The death of their servant's child in a miserable room, with its double blow—the metaphysical scandal of death, the social scandal of inequity—nauseates Jean.[24] Turning against his father, he joins the Communist party. His friend Marcel, a painter (modeled on Giacometti), explains to him in vain that a bourgeois can never fight for the proletariat as a worker does, because the bourgeois remains an outsider, a worker by choice, not birth; the outcome of a struggle is inevitably colored, as Hegel showed, by the origins of the struggle. When Marcel's brother, Jacques, is killed in a scuffle with the police, after Jean had encouraged him to become a Communist militant, the latter feels responsible.

Jean's feelings of guilt arising from his privileged background and Jacques's death become a generalized culpability and a dread of unforeseen consequences, and they are a primary motivation in the rest of the novel. Withdrawing from militant action, Jean moves to trade unionism and a resolute pacifism, the topic of discussions with his friends, who represent different shades of opinion concerning growing European fascism. Gradually, however, he realizes that not to act is itself a form of action (a fundamental tenet of French existentialism); this point applies particularly well to the appeasement of Hitler's expansionist policies. Jean also discovers the phenomenological principle that what is called the world is created by human perspectives on it: "I recreate it at each moment by my presence" ("Je le recrée à chaque instant par ma présence"; *SA,* 166). He is persuaded to help his erstwhile lover, Madeleine, be smuggled into Spain to join the Republicans, and though he asserts that fascism anywhere in Europe should be the concern of the French, he does not himself resume activism until the Occupation, when he becomes head of a clandestine group.[25] His uncommitted stance is somewhat paralleled by his reluctance to become involved with Hélène, although to see an identical motivation in his pacifism and his coolness toward her is to overlook the complexity of relationships between the sexes. When he finally makes himself overstate his affection for her, it may be out of a sense of responsibility, or it may be from inertia. Only at the story's end, when Jean and Hélène undertake a common action, does he realize he truly loves her.

Hélène, who comes from a family of shopkeepers, gives voice to many of the author's attitudes toward the world and, later, toward political action. But Hélène is a strange self-projection. Whereas Jean is likable—almost implausibly so—Hélène is another of Beauvoir's exasperating women, one whose mental dramas are frequently boring. Selfish and capricious, she shares with other Beauvoir heroines the need to possess totally the consciousness of others, and her affection is cumbersome and oppressive. Although her denial of solidarity with others and her intransigence and romanticism resemble the author's, some of her unattractive features were borrowed from Nathalie Sorokine, to whom the novel is dedicated. Hélène becomes interested in Jean, a friend of her longtime suitor Paul, and tricks him into stealing a bicycle for her. Jean appeals to her because he is solid, dense; he seems to be self-sufficient. He valorizes things for her; she feels she shares in the reality of the world around him, and her sense of being is enhanced. But her demands are great, and, to feel utterly justified, she would require his enslavement to her and her needs. When Jean resists her advances, she turns to another man and becomes pregnant by him. The gruesome scene of her abortion, at which Jean, through a sense of responsibility, agrees to assist her, is marked by reactions of metaphysical disgust. The scene echoes the death of the servant's child and foreshadows the roundup of Jewish children toward the end of the novel, as well as a tardy wish Hélène expresses to have a child by Jean, even though he says creating another existence is meaningless. That the blood of others is also that of an aborted fetus and its mother gives to the title another possible meaning, although Beauvoir does not pursue its implications and Hélène shows no signs of guilt. Commentators sometimes blame Jean, at least by implication, for the suffering Hélène endures because he rejected her—a specious interpretation that ignores her free will and the element of revenge in her action.[26]

During the 1939–40 "phony war," Hélène succeeds in having Jean assigned to Paris, against his will, since he feels solidarity with the soldiers stationed in vulnerable border posts. She later becomes involved with a German officer and plans to leave for Berlin. Whereas one is not surprised that Jean, with his sense of responsibility, is drawn into the Resistance, Hélène's evolution from selfish indifference to patriotic acts of sabotage is unconvincing, notwithstanding foreshadowings, as when she assists others during the June exodus from Paris in 1940 (modeled on the author's experiences). Her conversion—for such it is—comes when she sees a mother and child separated, as Jews are being rounded up for deportation and her closest friend is in hiding. She reflects, "I watched History going by! It was my history [or story]" ("Je regardais passer l'Histoire! c'était mon histoire"; SA, 315).

Marcel and his wife, Denise, furnish a classic example of a demanding artist and an uncomprehending spouse. They too, however, come to recognize their responsibility to the collectivity and thus contribute to the thematics of the novel. He is concerned only with his painting, which he assumes to be an absolute, ontologically separate from the human gaze. His indifference to ordinary concerns creates ceaseless problems for Denise. Though their domestic arguments could easily have remained trite, Beauvoir heightens their interest by relating them from different points of view. Denise attempts to escape, first by writing a novel, then through paranoia and other delusions. Ultimately, history impinges on both of them. When Marcel becomes a prisoner of war, he discovers solidarity with his fellow captives and, in painting frescoes for a reading room, learns that art, like other human enterprises, is not invested absolutely with meaning but acquires it only when spectators and readers freely grant it. He returns, to participate in Jean's resistance group, with Denise.

The existentialist themes of the work are numerous, from the theme announced by the epigraph (borrowed from Dostoevsky), "Everyone is responsible to all for everything," through anguish, freedom, solitude, the role of consciousness, and the meaninglessness of existence. One is responsible for one's choices and yet can often do nothing. There is no ground, no justification for existence, which is rotten; life is "an absurdity responsible for itself" ("une absurdité responsable d'elle-même"; *SA*, 146). Consciousness feels empty, in contrast to the being of the rest of the world, and even the body is penetrated with this nothingness; Hélène, looking at her body, compares it to an oyster, soft and grayish (*SA*, 59). Absolutes (what Beauvoir, after Voltaire, calls the point of view from the star Sirius) are a lie; all values, or reasons for living, are created by human beings (*SA*, 98, 209).

As Beauvoir argued in her philosophical essays of the 1940s, it is action that creates these values. The origins of human acts are multiple and their consequences far-reaching, going beyond what one foresees and desires in a "fatal chain" ("chaîne fatale"; *SA*, 12).[27] There is no "right," or innocent, action, since every act impinges in some way on the freedom of others. Yet there is no way to avoid acting, and, as Jean says, "We exist only if we act" ("Nous n'existons que si nous agissons"; *SA*, 256). The constraint that every subject exercises on others is especially marked in personal relationships, as the various pairs of lovers show.

Political, notably terrorist, action poses a particular problem. Two arguments are given to justify sabotage and other forms of resistance against the occupants, despite the inevitable reprisals. The first is the ontological and moral leveling of all action to the same plane: "The blood one spares cannot be expiated any more than the blood one sheds" ("Le sang qu'on épargne est aussi inexpiable que le sang qu'on fait verser"; *SA, 257*). This argument recalls the emphasis of Kierkegaard on generalized guilt,[28] and it foreshadows the conclusion in Sartre's *Le Diable et le Bon Dieu* (*The Devil and the Good Lord*) that there is no clean action and all means to the proposed end are justifiable. The argument can be understood in dialectical terms by seeing that, since all actions lead to reactions and all ends produce what Beauvoir called counterfinalities (*FC, 76*), which destroy individual initiative, no act can be separated from its contrary and all ends are constantly subverted.[29] One has to act, as Jean discovers, without a guarantee of either success or justice. The second argument is the pragmatic one, often made in connection with terrorism and war: sacrificing a few lives will save many. Jean argues that reprisals are even *desirable,* because French blood must flow for a politics of collaboration with Germany to be considered unacceptable.[30] To the objection that the just end is distorted by unjust means (such as the sacrifice of innocent hostages), Jean replies that one cannot avoid such injustices, even by doing nothing.

Another major existentialist theme, announced by the title, is otherness. Beauvoir later stated that she had wanted to define proper human relationships ("notre juste rapport avec les autres"; *FA, 622*). One aspect of the theme is ethical (responsibility for others); the other is ontological. What Sartre calls the *pour-autrui,* or being-for-others, is connected to the *pour-soi,* or being-for-itself, that is, consciousness as it perceives itself. To deny the validity of one's appearances to others and their judgments on the grounds that one "is not" what one seems is to misunderstand human reality, composed of the sum of one's appearances or "profiles" (including actions) instead of some pregiven inner essence. Moreover, one is always other to oneself in the sense that the self is mediated through others;[31] with them also the relationship is irreducibly that of alterity, "the curse of being another" ("la malédiction d'être autre"; *SA, 140*). This idea is brought out particularly well between the lover and the beloved, who, as Jean realizes, can neither possess each other fully nor reduce each other to the image they would prefer. These two aspects of otherness join to create the political moral of the novel: because one's reality is mediated and one is always responsible for others, there is no singular destiny, despite feelings of solitude. As Jean reflects, "Precisely, my life is made up of my relationships with others" ("Ma vie est justement faite de mes rapports avec les autres hommes"; *SA, 165*).

The rhetoric of the novel leaves the reader little doubt about what the denouement will be; inevitably, Jean decides to order the sabotage, in full knowledge of the risks and consequences. His existential angst gives way to taking responsibility for shedding others' blood. Hélène herself reclaims full responsibility for what she has done and thus helps to relieve his sense of guilt: "I shouldn't wish to have had another life" ("Je ne voudrais pas avoir eu une autre vie"; *SA,* 325).[32] They achieve a tardy unity through their common action, after she has joined his clandestine group; they have succeeded in establishing what Beauvoir calls "translucid relationships" ("des rapports translucides"; *FA,* 555) from one liberty to another. In what is patently a reply to the conclusion of *L'Etre et le néant,* Jean decides that, if he can further for anyone the cause of freedom—the supreme good—his passion will not have been useless.

Critical assessments of the novel have varied but tend to be negative. Beauvoir herself ultimately judged it to be less satisfactory than *L'Invitée* (*FA,* 558). Maurice Blanchot offered the key to its weakness when he called it a thesis novel, not because it deals with meanings— he recognizes that all serious fiction does—but because it shows less than it states and because its statements form a single, closed conclusion that imposes itself on the reader.[33] Beauvoir also criticized its abstractions and the characters' flatness, and she found the motivation weak, especially for Jean's sense of guilt. While some commentators have found her judgment too harsh, others have agreed with her that it represents regression from its predecessor. Maurice Nadeau complained that the ideological strings pulling the characters were too obvious.[34] Yet the novel has a broader scope of concerns than its predecessor and a more suggestive chronological structure; it gives a sense of the importance of human action that is not found in *L'Invitée.* Victor Brombert praised it as the existentialist novel that focuses most sharply on the problem of involvement.[35] And as Keefe observes, it "by no means fails to achieve [the] main objective of illustrating the true complexity of human relations" (169).

Tous les hommes sont mortels

Despite a good title, an original idea, an interesting historical background, and some fine storytelling, *Tous les hommes sont mortels* (begun in 1943, published in 1946) was not the success the author hoped for and is probably the least admired of her novels today, although it was translated into 11 languages. Beauvoir had supposed it to be the strongest of the three she had yet published, a fact that points to the well-known difficulty authors have in evaluating their own works and predicting their success. In fact, the book was received with indifference or hostility. Unlike her other novels and stories, all situated in a period roughly contemporary with the writing, it is, at least in part, a historical novel or, better, a historical fable. It is also a political exemplum and a philosophical tale, with the main part structured on the adventures of one character, like the philosophical tales of Voltaire but much longer. By what the author called "a lengthy wandering around [the topic of] death" ("un long vagabondage autour de la mort"; *FA, 621*), it confronts directly the crucial metaphysical problem of mortality that had become keen to Beauvoir with her adolescent loss of faith and that continued to haunt her. But instead of treating the problem in essay form, as Camus did in *Noces* (*Nuptials*), or, like Hemingway and Malraux, creating characters whose actions lead them to the brink of death, Beauvoir invented a character who cannot die and who thus poses in reverse terms the perennial philosophical problem of mortality as well as that of human action.

Dedicated to Sartre, the work can be thought of as an existentialist parable, the moral of which (at least in part) is that for human action to have meaning or value it must represent commitment and risk—not necessarily danger, but the risk of failure and loss. Since an immortal can make no lasting commitment (he will outlive that to which he devotes himself) and can risk nothing essential, his acts are gestures, as theatrical as on a stage. According to Beauvoir's existentialism, meaning follows commitment, rather than preceding it: his acts are without meaning. Others can be affected by what he does, but he is separated from them because he does not share in the defining relationship between these actions and time. Cut off from the most telling fact of the human situation and from the consequences of his own deeds, he is a type of impostor, the quintessential alienated man.

In the early 1940s Beauvoir had become interested in chronicles of the Italian Renaissance by Leonard Sismondi (*FA, 602*); they furnished the point of departure for the historical plot line. She also read extensively concerning the period of the Hapsburg ruler Charles V and on the New World during the period of exploration and early settlement. She has her protagonist, Raymond Fosca, born in the late thirteenth century in Carmona, a fictitious Italian principality. The novel does not, however, begin with his earliest adventures. Rather, Beauvoir uses a frame narrative structure in which the opening and closing sections (called "Prologue" and "Epilogue," although the first is nearly 70 pages long), set in modern France, enclose the story of Fosca's life (which has lasted more than 600 years), as he narrates it to Régine, the woman who has become fascinated with him. The story is thus partly hers, and, as in *Le Sang des autres,* there are two protagonists, male and female; there are, moreover, two narrative voices, since the framing sections are narrated in the third person, chiefly from Régine's point of view, while the rest is told retrospectively in the first person. The reader shares with Régine the position of narratee (*narrataire*) and thus by implication is drawn into the central *diegesis,* or plane of action, of the novel, though at the end of each section of Fosca's narrative, when he and Régine comment briefly on what he has related, and in the epilogue, the reader again becomes external to Régine's story.

The narrative is permeated with implicit historical irony. First, Fosca as retrospective narrator knows the outcome of the episodes he relates; this factor is a function of the distance between his narrating voice and the Fosca who acts in each episode. In some cases, the reader too has foreknowledge of the outcome, as with Fosca's doomed efforts to help Charles V combat the power of France and the Reformation. Such knowledge can cast a negative light on Fosca's acts on behalf of progress: one remembers, for instance, the bloody French Revolution at the close of the Enlightenment. There is also philosophical irony, since Fosca as narrator realizes that, of all his involvements, none has lasting meaning for him or for the world; they are specters of memory. Even the occasional corrections he brings to his earlier view of things in the course of the narrative—one of the interesting effects of telling one's tale—cannot be considered significant, for there are no grounds for taking them as definitive. His disillusionment is even built into the story, as his actions in later centuries are conditioned by bitterness growing out of earlier actions. He often deplores the uselessness of human initiative: "Nothing is useful to man because he has nothing to make of himself" ("Rien n'est utile à l'homme parce qu'il n'a rien à faire de lui-même").[36] The very notion of progress (actions that change things) is threatened by the irony of hindsight, with its concomitant sense of repetition and futility: "I don't believe in progress" ("Je ne crois pas au progrès"; *TLH,* 275). History thus appears to be a giant joke in the face of human demands for meaning.

Suitably, Régine is an actress, another of Beauvoir's artists—like Elisabeth in *L'Invitée* and Paule in *Les Mandarins*—who live permanently in bad faith, seeking to persuade themselves that they could fulfill themselves artistically were the circumstances different. Like

Anny in Sartre's *La Nausée,* Régine was probably based on Simone
Jollivet, but in her absolutism she resembles Beauvoir herself. For
Régine the theater represents a temporary immortality through the
creation and imposition on others of a new self, all the more dissatisfying because it cannot last. She is ambitious, jealous, demanding, even
sadistic; she looks on others, including Fosca, whom she meets by
chance at a hotel, as objects to be dominated or manipulated. At the
outset, she is fascinated with Fosca because he does not resemble others:
handsome but blasé and passive, he has no visible desires and exerts no
will. His secret, when he discloses it to her, transforms him into a
unique lover who could give her a special metaphysical status by loving
her as he had loved no other—the perennial dream of romantics—and
by giving immortality to her through his memory. To be thus loved
and remembered would represent considerable progress over what
Régine achieves by acting (including playing, in real life, the part of an
actress), and, in a theatrical gesture, she gives up the stage before an
audience composed of her startled friends, who seem to her like
anthropophagi sucking her life through her mouth and eyes (*TLH,* 73).
Although he knows the inevitable outcome of his involvement—he has
had other love affairs, and all have ended—Fosca lets himself be moved
by her but soon realizes that, in his detachment, he cannot love her as
an ordinary man could, and that his love is harmful to her. He tells his
story by way of self-justification in order to show her the futility of her
dream.

As a youth in Carmona, Fosca participates in a plot to overthrow a
tyrannical ruler, and later himself becomes ruler. His concern seems to
be at first for the people of the city, who have suffered every kind of
oppression. But he is really interested in political power and in what it
can achieve—the Nietzschean challenge, "What can man do?" He
drinks the potion offered by a beggar because he sees in immortality—
that is, invulnerability to death—a means of solving military and
political problems and leading Carmona to glory. The lengthy accounts
of his struggles to consolidate and extend his power throughout Italy,
by means of alliances and wars, emphasize their difficulty; the human
cost of his early successes—his alienation from women, the death of his
first son in battle—is considerable.

In part 2 of the narrative, Fosca is at the court of Charles V, as a
counselor.[37] Having discovered in Italy that controlling the peninsula is
impossible, he hopes to achieve on the stage of the whole of Europe his
ambition to totalize history, using Charles, who wants to reconstitute the

Holy Roman Empire. He even urges Charles to establish a world empire by extending Spanish hegemony through the Americas. Fosca's policies, however, are again negated everywhere by counterfinalities, such as the influx of gold and silver into Spain from the New World, which upsets the economic balance, and by the free choices of human beings, such as French and papal hostility and Martin Luther's stand against the Roman Church: "The machinery was set up, the wheels were in gear, and they were turning immutably" ("La mécanique était montée, les rouages s'engrenaient, et ils tournaient immuablement"). "The salvation of the world" ("le salut du monde"), which Fosca promised he would help the young Charles attain, proves utterly impossible (*TLH,* 164, 185). When Fosca visits the New World, plundered for European power, he discovers the dreadful exploitation—even genocide—of the Indians by the Spaniards and realizes that Charles's aims of humane colonization have been thoroughly undermined.

Part 3 of Fosca's tale centers on North America, where he meets an explorer, Charlier, whose career resembles Jacques Cartier's; Charlier's aim is to find the great river that will provide a passage west across the continent from the Great Lakes. Fosca's attempts to assist him in reaching his goal end in failure. This enterprise is clearly different, however, from the political manipulations in which Fosca had previously engaged in Europe, and one may read the episode as an investigation of the value of private action—in this case, an action for which Charlier pays with his life—or as a suggestion of what the New World might mean for the old. (This interpretation is supported by the depiction, in part 2, of an egalitarian, communal society in South America that could be considered a model for human social organization.)

The episodes of the fourth and fifth parts take place in France in the eighteenth and nineteenth centuries. In the France of the Enlightenment, Fosca marries Marianne de Sinclair, a learned woman—perhaps modeled partly after the historical Julie de l'Espinasse—who devotes her energies to the advancement of science and education in order to effect social change. When an enemy of Fosca's betrays him by revealing his secret to Marianne, their relationship is forever changed; she feels betrayed, since his love was not on the same footing as hers: she was his for life, whereas he would go on to other women, other lives. In the nineteenth century a descendant of Fosca and Marianne, Armand, who participates in the uprisings first against the Bourbons and then against the Orléans monarchy, discovers that his contemporary Fosca is also his ancestor. The contrast between the world-weary Fosca, who has already seen the fall of too many regimes and the failure of too many hopes for improving the human lot, and the committed, energetic Armand is played out against their physical resemblance. The section ends when Fosca says good-bye to the small group around Armand who have struggled to help bring about the Second Republic. In the epilogue one learns that Fosca then slept for 60 years and subsequently spent 30 more in an insane asylum, just before meeting Régine.

In the early parts of his story Fosca tries to achieve permanent historical change, chiefly through his own ambitions; in the later parts he has abandoned such ambitions, and when he acts it is for causes that, according to the system of values in Beauvoir's writings, are good. Yet he cannot be considered a hero. His participation in Marianne's progressive university is reluctant. At worst, he is a sadistic manipulator, at best, a stranger, as he says to his fellows, who may pay for his decisions with their lives. Although the protagonist, Fosca appears in some ways unreal in comparison with the figures of Charles V, the Lutheran monk who will be burned rather than recant, Charlier, Marianne, and Armand, whose action represents them fully. The ninety years spent in sleep and internment constitute renunciation of life, and Fosca has wished ardently that he might die as others do. Even the love affair with Régine is a failure, since the whole point of his narrative is to show her that he is incapable of sharing her situation. A dark pessimism thus colors the novel as a whole.

One should not conclude, however, that this pessimism is unqualified. As a concurrent but reverse plot to Fosca's disenchantment and Régine's bitterness, the novel offers evidence of a slow historical progress—the expansion of rationalism and scientific knowledge as opposed to medieval obscurantism, the toppling of the monarchy, more liberal social ideas—that results in the creation of the modern world. This progress is the result of the rise of individualism. The religious revolution of Lutheranism puts religious authority in the mind of the individual; the rationalist and scientific revolution of the eighteenth century puts the world in the mind of the individual (through the mind's ability to acquire and apply knowledge); the liberal revolution of 1848 puts political authority in the mind of the individual. These achievements all represent the erosion of institutional oppression over the individual and the growth of freedom—precisely the supreme value Beauvoir claimed for herself and others.

In contrast to these achievements, which Fosca witnesses, are other historical factors that act as a counterbalance to implied progress—

Charles V's efforts to consolidate the power of the church and empire, the extension of European political oppression over American natives, the repression of popular uprisings in France, and the threat represented by science. As a political exemplum, the novel is not clearly an apology for democracy, although not for tyranny either, despite Fosca's nostalgia for the power and individualistic spirit of Renaissance princes. Rather, it offers a lesson in the limits of political power, even when supported by force; both human freedom and counterfinalities create currents of political action that cannot be controlled. One must take cognizance also of the context in which the novel was written, surely one of the most somber periods of modern history; Beauvoir pointed out that the present was no better than the bloody epochs she described in the novel (*FC,* 76). Yet the implied progress, incarnated in its last stage by Armand, Fosca's descendant, and his friend Garnier cannot be entirely discounted.

Perhaps it is this subcurrent that led one critic to speak of the implied presence in the novel of "the myth of mankind finally unified which Hegel bestowed on Marxism."[38] To read the novel thus, however, is probably to misunderstand it. Beauvoir was never strongly influenced by Hegel; his totalizing idealism was alien to her sense of the concrete and the present. Moreover, the Marxism to which she would be attracted from the early 1950s on was less the eschatological vision of history deified than a practical blend of materialistic philosophy with economics and social thought, plus dialectical reasoning. Beauvoir herself said that she had attacked in *Tous les hommes sont mortels* the Hegelian and Communist illusion of history as a monolith (*FC,* 77). Fosca reflects, "The universe was elsewhere, always elsewhere. And it is nowhere; there are only men, men forever divided" ("L'Univers était ailleurs, toujours ailleurs! Et il n'est nulle part: il n'y a que des hommes, des hommes, à jamais divisés"; *TLH,* 212).

Further, at least as much emphasis is given to Fosca's personal drama as to the historical one. Meaningful action depends on one's committing oneself to a goal in a concrete situation that then defines the agent; this idea includes relationships with others. Goethe's statement "My field is time" points to the crucial fact that the goal means nothing if time is limitless, and to be suprahistorical is to be separate from history. Garnier's words to Fosca are a reply to the latter's demand that action be ratified by the future, that is, by eternity: "It's not our business to wait for the future to give a meaning to our actions; otherwise, all action would be impossible" ("Nous n'avons pas à attendre que

l'avenir donne un sens à nos actes; sinon toute action serait impossible";
TLH, 326). Régine's failure to profit from this lesson does not invalidate it. In fact, one way to read the novel is as the failure of a woman to
accept herself. The cry Régine utters in the last sentence—a protest
against the thought of mortality, certainly, and perhaps against the
futility that marks Fosca—is not the conclusion of the tragic hero
(Oedipus' saying "All is well" or Camus's "One must imagine Sisyphus
happy"); it is the cry of the unreconciled 15-year-old rolling on the
carpet in her parents' apartment.

The novel has several problems. For the story to hold any interest,
one must, of course, grant the author the original premise of Fosca's
immortality, although the blend of realistic narrative and fable is not
entirely successful. Despite its use of the first person, the narrative is
often close to the tedious style of a chronicle. The psychological com-
plexities of Fosca's character are not sufficiently delineated; one does
not understand, for instance, the mixture of humane concern and cal-
lousness that marks him, as when he speaks of taking pleasure in
destroying and humiliating others. Furthermore, other characters in his
past are seen only through his eyes and, except for a few, lack both
roundness and definition; a striking exception is Charlier, who is as
central as Fosca to part 3 of the narrative. Moreover, the events are often
lacking in color and texture; the inclusion in Fosca's account of scenic
presentation (acting out, as opposed to summary) does not sufficiently
offset his dominant voice. This weakness is, fortunately, less marked in
the later sections, where the characters' concerns for developing knowledge and democratic government are more familiar to readers than
medieval plagues, wars, and the fortunes of city states, and thus take on
greater reality.

There is also the problem of Régine, whom one first sees after a
performance—so egotistic and shallow and in such bad faith that it is
difficult to be touched by her concerns. The numerous phrases attributed to her in free indirect style that are marked by Beauvoir's own
philosophical vocabulary seem out of character. That an ordinary actress
should be dissatisfied with her career, wish for more adulation, and
dread aging is plausible, but it is less so that she should reflect, "They
[men] became transparent and hollow" ("Ils devenaient transparents et
creux"), or, Xavière-like, "When people live, when people love and are
happy around me, it seems to me that they are killing me" ("Quand des
gens vivent, quand des gens aiment et sont heureux autour de moi, il
me semble qu'ils m'assassinent"; *TLH,* 14, 16).

The dual plot line raises questions. Is this novel primarily the story of Régine and her concern to impose herself on others and thus achieve a sense of ontological plenitude? It is she with whom the novel opens and closes, and she reappears briefly at the end of each section of Fosca's narrative. But if hers is the main story, its scope and meaning are limited to what she learns—that an immortal cannot love her as she would wish, cannot guarantee her immortality by loving her beyond the limits of her life—and to what she does not learn—that her mortality is integral to herself. Or is the novel chiefly the story of Fosca, whose eternal youth proves to be his damnation and who, like Sartre's characters in *Huis-clos,* can only continue a senseless round of gestures? Or is it the story of humankind or at least Western man between the late Middle Ages and the time of the nineteenth-century liberal revolutions? It has been shown that, to some degree, the novel is all these.

But then, what is one to make of the relationships between historical change and the individuals who dominate the novel, whose actions seem futile and meaningless, in one case because he is immortal, in another case because she is not? The progress suggested by historical events seems to be of no value to Régine, if she uses her modern freedom purchased by immense struggles in the past only to wish to destroy others' freedom by a self-apotheosis. And Fosca is convinced of his failure to achieve anything—that is, to stage history as he should have liked, in an integrative fashion by which all human activities would have been directed toward unifying goals, rather than clashing and contradicting each other; he represents the powerlessness of the individual.

Beauvoir noted that she had no philosophy of history and that her novel concluded with none; nor did she have any definitive point of view (*FC,* 77, 79). If these related stories are to be unified, it must be as parts of an existentialist parable, for all three plot lines—the stories of Régine, Fosca, and Western man—can be related to dominant existentialist themes: action, happiness, freedom. Fosca said he wanted to *make* others happy; he learned that only they can do so. Régine's cry of anguish can be understood in light of Sartre's maxim that life begins on the far side of despair. The heretical monk's statement—"There is only one good, and that is to act according to one's conscience" ("Il n'y a qu'un seul bien, c'est d'agir selon sa conscience")—implies both individual freedom and responsibility. Values, which define the acting subject, are created singly, according to situations and individuals and "the fire that burns in their hearts" ("le feu qui brûle dans leurs cœurs"), and, as Fosca concludes, "Their welfare depends only on them" ("leur bien ne dépend que d'eux-mêmes"; *TLH,* 213).

Les Bouches inutiles

Beauvoir's only drama was written in 1944, before she finished *Tous les hommes sont mortels,* but was inspired by the same readings that had furnished the point of departure for her third novel. She had wanted to write a play since seeing on stage in 1943 Sartre's *Les Mouches (The Flies)*; the way his ideas took on flesh and speech in the theater impressed her deeply. In Sismondi's Italian chronicles she discovered her topic when she read about the sacrifice of "useless mouths"—children, women, the infirm—during a siege. *Les Bouches inutiles* was produced in November 1945, shortly after the war ended, and the ethical problem involved in sacrificing some, whether soldiers or hostages, to save others was not indifferent to audiences. Yet the stage run was only moderate (50 performances). Sartre thought that, while not a complete success, it did have good qualities, whereas Beauvoir did not like the production and was discouraged by the unfavorable critical reception. She later decided that, while she wrote effective dialogues in fiction (those in *L'Invitée* had been admired), the language in her play was not successful, perhaps because she tried to make it both spare and dense. Moreover, the drama is too clearly a demonstration of ethical points, a result of what she called her moralism (*FA,* 602–3). Lacking the complexity of characters and force of Sartre's plays, it cannot be considered the best of existentialist theater. [39]

Dedicated to the author's mother, the play (which could be called "The Bread of Others") is in two acts, subdivided into eight tableaux: although it adheres roughly to the classical unities of time, place, and action, the traditional five-act structure is abandoned. The cast of characters is large, standing for a whole city. The action is set in fourteenth-century Flanders. Vaucelles, whose citizens have rebelled against the Duke of Burgundy and founded a democracy, has been under siege from the Burgundians for a year, and, with grain supplies rationed, the people are near starvation. Jean-Pierre Gautier brings from the French King the message that he will come to the aid of Vaucelles, but only some months hence. Louis d'Avesnes, one of the governors, offers a position on the governing council to Jean-Pierre, because the people trust his judgment and harsh measures must be taken. Jean-Pierre refuses, however, because he wants to keep his hands pure: "Our acts go and burst, far from us, with strange faces" ("Nos actes vont éclater loin de nous sous des figures inconnues").[40] This dread of consequences, coupled with a belief in freedom and yet a generalized sense of responsibility toward others, shows Jean-Pierre's kinship to Jean in *Le Sang des autres*. At the end of act 1, the council reluctantly decides to expell from Vaucelles the old people, women, and children so that the able-bodied men can have their rations and endure until spring, thus preserving the city's independence.

Beauvoir was interested in not merely the ethical problems raised by such a decision but also its effects on those who make it and on its victims. Their reactions are played out along with a number of sub-plots, concerned with the building of a new belfry (which represents the future) and the relationships between the sexes. Catherine, Louis's wife, who is a strong feminine force in the play, perceives the council's decision as treason both against the women, who have been reduced to instruments serving men's will, and against themselves. It was the common undertakings of wives and husbands that gave their lives meaning because these undertakings established each couple's relation-ship with the world: "If a man and a woman have thrown themselves with the same spirit toward an identical future, in the work they have built together . . . in this whole world that their common will has modeled, they become united indissolubly" ("Si un homme et une femme se sont jetés d'un même élan vers un même avenir, dans l'œuvre qu'ils ont construite ensemble . . . dans ce monde tout entier qu'a modelé leur volonté commune, ils se retrouvent confondus d'une manière indissoluble"; *BIn,* 56). Their past now becomes a lie. To preserve future freedom by exercising violence and coercion on the present is a contradiction. Louis, on the other hand, argues that in this case crime is preferable to innocence, because crime will mean survival for the city, whereas innocence means starvation.

The theme of free choice is also illustrated through the topic of sexual choice. Louis and Catherine's daughter, Clarice (played by Olga, under the name Olga Dominique), an insolent, proud, and intransigent girl, is in love with Jean-Pierre but will not admit so, through pride, so long as he denies any commitment. She refuses the match her father is arranging and prefers suicide for herself and the child she is carrying. Her brother, Georges, one of the play's villains, covets her sexually, while also trying to force his affections on Jean-Pierre's sister, Jeanne, who finally dies from his violence. The refusal of these young women to yield to unwanted affections—that is, to let their freedom be alienated—dramatizes on the individual plane the integral connection between life and liberty.

When Georges tries to embrace Clarice, justifying his incestuous desire in the name of the rule of force, Louis discovers that no morality is possible if the council's decree is carried out, since moral standards have been shown to be expedient. Jean-Pierre likewise recognizes that he can no longer refuse to take a stand: "There is no longer a city, but torturers and their victims" ("Il n'y a plus de ville, mais des bourreaux et leurs victimes"; *BIn*, 93). Jean-Pierre decides to try to persuade the men of Vaucelles to reject their leaders and make a sortie against the Burgundians, an action that may fail but will constitute a free and united action. He even consents to love Clarice, since to separate his destiny from others' by denying affective ties is unauthentic. His first attempt to sway the citizens fails, but when Catherine's eloquent protests bring home to Louis the personal consequences of his position, he too argues before the council that the sortie, even if it fails, is preferable to a policy of expediency. The project of freedom will, then, be a collective one. His arguments are rebutted by François, a young man who has plotted to seize power, but the latter, with Georges, is proved to be a traitor. In the final tableau, the populace prepares to move against the Burgundians.

The play's themes include most of those in Beauvoir's other works written under the Occupation and some new ones. They are all related to the underlying question of human welfare and happiness. Human beings are responsible for their own good, and indeed for the whole world, in the sense that their projects fashion inert matter and give meaning to it. Recurring topics include freedom, responsibility, solidarity, anguish, and the problem of the end and the means, the most fundamental one. There is identity between means and end. Tyrannical means create tyranny, whereas the exercise of free choice creates freedom. Denying freedom to any citizen undermines its value, since it is whole and cannot be qualified: "You can't make a place for oppression" ("On ne fait pas sa part à l'oppression"; *FA*, 603). This conclusion is slightly different from that in *Le Sang des autres*, in which Jean chooses to violate the freedom of potential hostages without their knowledge and consent. The historical differences can explain this variation, since the restricted scale of the struggle in the play allows all the citizens to be parties to the final decision.

Two associated themes are those of government and will. Will can be seen as another form of the human project, which, freely chosen, shapes the future. This concept is illustrated by the marriage of Catherine and Louis—altogether one of the most satisfactory sexual relationships in Beauvoir's work—in which each partner recognizes in the other's will what he or she desires. Extended to all citizens, this union of wills is implicitly the basis for a truly democratic society. Though no clear reference is made to Rousseau, Beauvoir may have had in mind his concept of the general will as the source of authority; the play shows clearly that the popular will cannot be alienated without the undoing of the basic political pact.

This view of will is to be distinguished from the Nietzschean one, which characterizes the superior man. The play seems to criticize fascist rhetoric, in which the idea of will is associated with absolute power, which denies freedom to others in the name of freedom. François, the traitor, wants to hold absolute power, abrogating others' wills for their own good. "I wished for power," he admits. "But it's also true that it was for the good of Vaucelles. Never will your weak hearts be capable of giving it the destiny of which I dreamed" ("J'ai souhaité le pouvoir. Mais il est vrai aussi que c'était pour le bien de Vaucelles. Jamais vos faibles cœurs ne seront capables de lui donner le destin que je rêvais pour elle"; *BIn,* 130). This argument destroys itself in terms of the play, for to choose an end for someone else is fundamentally impossible, the goal being precisely that end which is freely chosen by the individual. *All* must want the same welfare for Vaucelles; to sacrifice some to others' view of the good is to deny good, whereas for all to choose to risk their lives in the name of freedom makes freedom triumph.[41] The people are the best, indeed the only, judge of what is suitable because they live the situation in their very flesh.

Les Bouches inutiles has attracted little critical attention of late. Some of the plot is needlessly melodramatic (Georges embracing his sister, Catherine trying to stab Louis to prove their solidarity), and the characters' changes of heart are not all convincing. But the work deals in concrete terms with a moral problem that remains timely, and the fabric of ideas, while lacking in subtlety, shows the drama at the heart of existential choice. For those who do not care for the belabored psychology of Beauvoir's novels, *Les Bouches inutiles* furnishes an accessible example of the way she put ideas into human form.

Chapter Four
Later Fiction

After completing *Tous les hommes sont mortels,* Beauvoir briefly turned her attention away from imaginative writing, concentrating instead on journalism, essays, and documentary studies. But by 1949 she was ready to begin another novel. In it and in her last two volumes of fiction—all published in the 1950s and 1960s—the phenomenological and existentialist elements that strongly mark the early novels are no longer so prominent; instead, social questions are in the foreground. The author's situation, too, had changed: from the unknown writer who published her first book in 1943, she had become a public figure. Her personal experience continued to feed her fiction; the autobiographical element, obvious in *Les Mandarins* (1954), remains important, if indirect, in the two volumes of the 1960s, *Les Belles Images* (1966) and *La Femme rompue* (1967).

Les Mandarins

The winner of the Prix Goncourt, Beauvoir's fourth novel, which has been translated into 15 languages, sold extremely well even before the prize was announced; and shortly the author's name and photograph were displayed in almost every literary magazine and bookshop. Running to about 570 pages in small print, the novel may seem excessively long today; however, when memories of the immediate postwar period were still fresh, readers found in *Les Mandarins* much that was familiar and meaningful. A factor contributing to its popularity may have been that readers thought they recognized some well-known writers—Beauvoir herself, Sartre, Camus, and others. Beauvoir insisted the book was not a roman à clef, that is, a portrayal of real figures. The fact remains that she projected an enormous amount of herself into Anne Dubreuilh, the main woman character, and Henri Perron, a journalist, who also resembles Camus somewhat; indeed, Beauvoir said she divided herself between them, giving Henri the more active and creative self—he is a writer—and attributing to Anne the emotional side and what she called the negative aspect of her experience (*FC*, 287–88). Robert, Anne's husband, bears many similarities to Sartre; their daughter, Nadine, has features of Nathalie (but also recalls Olga); and Arthur Koestler appears under the guise of Scriassine. Lewis Brogan is a barely disguised Algren (to whom the work was dedicated).

The title, which was proposed by Lanzmann (*FC*, 321), is not to be taken in the pejorative sense one might suppose.[1] The mandarins are the French intellectuals of the postwar period, a group—almost a caste—to which several main characters belong. Far from suggesting that they compose a parasitic class that has lost touch with reality and serves only its esoteric interests and traditions, the author shows the best of them immersed in their time, attempting to take responsibility for it by acting on French public opinion through writing and activism. Thus, one way to read *Les Mandarins* is as an answer to the question of what it means to be an intellectual. The decision to make her characters members of the French intelligentsia reflects Beauvoir's wish to write about the period through what she knew best; it also allowed her to make the work into a novel of ideas. In fact, for those who like explicit ideological and political discussions in fiction, the work is a rich find. Despite their commitment to their time, however, the intellectuals Beauvoir portrays form a very small world, one that seems more marginal than central to global concern, especially since, as Robert realizes, France has fallen to a subordinate position between two world powers; in addition, the inability of the major characters to bring about significant historical change suggests that the word *mandarins* may after all have a pejorative sense.[2]

With a complicated plot and a wide range of personal and ideological questions to treat, Beauvoir wisely chose, again, a varied narrative structure, with both third- and first-person narration.[3] In the third-person sections, the narration is omniscient but tends to adopt the point of view of either Henri or Anne; both summary and free indirect style are used. In the first-person passages, the voice is always Anne's. Her text varies between expository and retrospective (recounting what has happened, either recently or at some distance, such as her first acquaintance with Robert) and meditative and simultaneous (a monologue in the present tense). No attempt is made to justify the first-person narration within the overall structure, and there is no explicit narratee. A nearly even distribution of the narration occurs between these two points of view, and some material is presented twice. The novel thus furnishes correcting and complementary perspectives on reality, illustrating the phenomenologists' insistence on its subjective quality. Anne, however, has the last word, since she narrates the final chapter. A great deal of scenic presentation is used; the dialogues are often among the best passages. The third main character, Robert, who links the other two, is never the central intelligence; he retains the opacity and prestige of "the other." (He is often referred to by his last name, and Anne addresses him by the formal *vous*.)[4] Throughout the novel, men appear as more dynamic and active, capable of leadership; women are highly dependent on emotional satisfaction for a sense of self. Whether this aspect represents a criticism of the sexes, an attempt to portray matters realistically, or the author's own inclinations cannot be determined.[5]

Les Mandarins deals with both political and personal choice, that is, action. What sort of action should one pursue, given the historical circumstances, and on what grounds? What are the limits and the ultimate value of action? Beauvoir stressed (*FC,* 290) the role of preferences, by which she meant relative choices that *create* value, as opposed to a "universal morality" ("une morale de l'universel").[6] The novel is an object lesson in the difficulties of practical politics, yet politics is not always the principal concern. The events take place against the background of the recently ended Occupation, during which widely diverging groups, including Communists and non-Communist Catholics, had joined in an effort to drive out the Germans. Their cooperation and eventual success had created a sentiment of national unity on which many hoped to build a new French society in the postwar period. This optimistic hope, soon put to the test, ignored the deep divergence between those who were simply patriots and the Communists, whose official (and usually real) goal had been to liberate France but to whom that action constituted only a means toward the greater end of moving France into the Soviet sphere and organizing a Communist government at home.

What to do amid the confusion of postwar political struggles is the main concern of Robert, Henri, and others. For this aspect of the novel, Beauvoir drew liberally on her own thinking and on Sartre's relationships with the Communists in the cold war period, relationships that went from very hostile (on the Communists' part) to moderately cordial by 1952, when Sartre took up his pen in their favor. Some episodes reflect events that occurred after the work was begun; contemporary developments fed it as it went through its multiple versions, and there are anachronisms. Conflicts between former *résistants* and former collaborators, Communists and non-Communist leftists, the Left as a whole and the Gaullist right—these are not only a topic of discussion but the impetus to much plot development. The *épuration,* or punishment of former collaborators, is a particularly sensitive issue; involving clandestine activity and even death, the episodes connected with it make this a novel of action as well as ideas.

Beyond the questions of internal politics is a wider scene of Europe and the world. The sense of historicity (the insertion of the individual into the collective and the pressure of historical forces) is strong. Beauvoir noted in her memoirs, "Not only did I not weave my own life, but its face, the face of my time and everything I loved depended on the future" "(Non seulement ma vie, ce n'était pas moi qui la tissais, mais sa figure, la figure de mon époque et de tout ce que j'aimais, dépendait de l'avenir"; *FC,* 289). When she began *Les Mandarins,* the cold war already dominated European politics. Sartre was involved in the non-aligned Rassemblement démocratique révolutionnaire (the model for Robert Dubreuilh's movement), attempting to promote socialism and keep France independent of both the United States and Russia. In the novel the philosophical differences between East and West are an ever-present concern, especially after the explosion of the atom bombs over Japan. The preference of most characters—excepting Scriassine, portrayed as slimy and rabidly anti-Stalinist—goes against the United States and the capitalistic imperialism for which it stands. A major topic, however, is the attitude one should adopt toward the abuses of Stalinism.

A contrast and necessary complement to politics is the world of personal dramas. Despite her keen awareness of the relationship between the individual consciousness and the world, Beauvoir did not have the ability to suggest the psychological or metaphysical anguish of a character in memorable ways. Nor, with exceptions, does she create in *Les Mandarins* what existentialists call "limit situations," extreme circumstances that force difficult and radical choices on characters. Rather, she sets up common situations to which characters react in ordinary ways and which may help explain the novel's popularity. These situations include unhappy relationships between men and women, financial pressures, friction between mothers and daughters, the manipulations of ambitious women, rivalries between men, and so on. Between them and the wider concerns are woven many ties, however. As Henri realizes, "The truth of his life was outside of him, in events and . . . things" ("La vérité de sa vie était hors de lui, dans les événements, dans les gens"; *M*, 255).

To those just noted are added the themes of sexuality and love, friendship, the function of literature and its pertinence in a changed world, the value of psychiatry (Anne is a practicing psychiatrist), and the feminine question. (Beauvoir wrote that a number of things she wanted to say in the novel were connected to her situation as a woman [*FC*, 284].) The scene of the action is usually in or near Paris, but some scenes take place in the provinces, Portugal, Italy, and North America. The time span is late 1944 to 1948. Numerous plot threads are followed in a parallel development, a technique Beauvoir had earlier borrowed from American novelists.

The complex plot is both linear and circular; that is, some changes represent obvious progress, whereas others bring the characters back to their point of departure, although with different perspectives and understanding. Beauvoir compared this structure to the Kierkegaardian idea of repetition (*FC*, 289). The opening chapters are divided into two sections, one focused on Henri, the other on Anne. In the remaining chapters the narrative focus alternates. The initial episode, a Christmastime celebration in 1944 that serves to introduce the principal characters, is first told from the point of view of Henri, a leftist writer and Resistance leader; Anne then renarrates it. Henri lives with, but no longer loves, Paule, a former singer who ostensibly gave up her career for him but in reality did so to avoid responsibility for her own choices; she is "radically alienated to a man, tyrannizing him in the name of this servitude" ("radicalement aliénée à un homme et le tyrannisant au nom de cet esclavage"; *FC*, 285). He suffers her smothering affection. Henri's friends include the Dubreuilh couple and their daughter, Nadine, an unpleasant and often-ignoble adolescent. They praise the American liberators and share the optimism born from the Liberation, while realizing that their private and public lives are about to take new turns.

Henri, for instance, is to leave for Portugal (a trip based on Beauvoir's own). In chapter 3 the discovery of that nation's misery, behind the facade of plenty, will lead him to question the role of literature as he has practiced it, a personal and aesthetic enterprise. He has already realized that underground activity against the Nazis is one thing and politics another, and that many of his prewar assumptions must be discarded. Nadine persuades him to take her along on the trip—he agrees partly as a way of declaring his independence from Paule. Nadine's brutal sexuality, aggressiveness, and other maladjustments can be blamed on the wartime death of her lover, Diégo (modeled on Nathalie's lover, Bourla), shot by the Germans; Beauvoir introduced her into the novel partly to indicate the difficulties of growing up and coming to maturity in the war and postwar periods. Nadine's difficult personality has also arisen from her unsatisfactory relationship with her mother. Since Beauvoir was convinced, as *Le Deuxième Sexe* shows, that mother-daughter bonds were condemned either to overpossessiveness (as displayed by her own mother) or coldness and indifference, it is small wonder that she makes the relationship between Anne and Nadine one of resentment: Anne acknowledges that she does not love her daughter enough, although she meddles in her affairs while giving her almost free rein; Nadine is resentful of both the coldness and the meddling.[7]

Anne, meanwhile, is preoccupied with herself and her relationship with Robert, on whom she is intellectually and emotionally dependent. She experiences in great anguish her own mortality, as adolescent fears resurface, heightened by the war. She does not entirely believe in psychiatry anymore, since the very notion of a cure is problematic, and even more the question of what to do with one's life after a cure. Robert, a writer some 20 years older than she, is concerned with how to achieve his political goals after peace returns to Europe. He is willing to abandon his creative writing: literature is made for men, he says, and not men for literature (*M,* 41). He considers the old humanistic goals that supposedly underlay the failed Third Republic to be utterly bankrupt and knows that the values and aims of the Resistance, so clearly focused, will not suffice to organize the postwar period; even so, he will experience difficulty in consenting to the implications of his commitment to activist socialism and will withdraw from writing and public life before ultimately returning to activism.

Robert participates in founding a political movement, the SRL, which aims to unite all non-Communist segments of the Left and create a third force; he wants Henri to make his Resistance newspaper, *L'Espoir,* its official organ. Henri has come to believe that the United States no longer stands for freedom, since it has become an imperialistic power. Yet he hesitates to make the paper subservient to a movement, even one with which he sympathizes. These hesitations are heightened by the inevitable problem of cooperation with the Communists (for which Lachaume is the principal spokesman), who accept allies only on their own terms.

Henri does finally agree to cooperate with the SRL, but he does so only to find that he is being maneuvered in various ways. He is also faced with material problems—paper and money; he is unwilling to accept subsidies, since they destroy a paper's independence.

When Henri receives from a Russian refugee evidence of organized exploitation on a vast scale in Soviet labor camps, politics and ethics come together in a way that reflects Beauvoir's increasingly Marxist thinking. Henri's position, which is consistent with the liberal humanistic ethics that inspired much Resistance activity, is that such revelations must be published, in the name of truth. Robert, on the other hand, argues (to a skeptical Anne) that their objective truth is immaterial: what matters is their effect, and in this case the Left would be demoralized and further disunited by them, while the reactionary Right, including the United States, would triumph. In a longer perspective, millions of oppressed people would lose hope in the Soviet Union; to destroy this hope would be a violation of the new collective morality that must replace the old individualistic one. Even if violence has been used against the Soviet proletariat, it is justified by the goals. This dilemma dramatizes the conflict between principle and expediency, theory and praxis, and analytic and dialectical thinking, a conflict that justifies force in the name of practical results (see *M, 336*).

Anne shares her husband's political convictions, but her daily cares are more personal. Her sense that her life is at a standstill leads her to consent to a brief and unrewarding sexual affair with Scriassine that foreshadows, negatively, her liaison with Lewis (in the Dubreuilh marriage, each partner is free; Robert, who often seems like a disembodied intelligence, has little interest in sex and no relations with Anne). Meanwhile, Paule tries desperately to deny that Henri no longer loves her; she reconstructs reality by means of personal myths, especially that of muse to the great writer (Henri). Henri, in contrast, tries to let her know the truth, and does so in every manner possible except the direct one. Each is, as Sartre said in *Les Mains sales,* part victim, part accomplice in his or her own enslavement. As Elaine Marks has observed, it is impossible, despite Beauvoir's disclaimers, not to see here a reflection of the conflict between Camus and his wife, Francine.[8] When Henri finally breaks with her enough to move out, Paule is devastated but denies that anything significant has occurred. Through Paule the novelist is criticizing the traps into which women fall, particularly the temptation to stake all on love. Paule's self-deception turns to delusions

and schizophrenia; like Beauvoir's deluded friend in Rouen, she ultimately invites Anne to a dinner party at which there are neither guests
nor food (*FA,* 173, 178). Only Anne's intervention prevents Paule from
poisoning herself.

Anne's reputation as a psychiatrist brings an invitation to lecture in
the United States. Her visit there proves momentous when, in Chicago,
she meets Lewis, whose leftist politics match hers and whose contacts
with the sordid side of the city lead her to see an America she would not
otherwise have known. (The portrait of the city is, however, simplisti-
cally drawn, though not lacking in warmth.) The attraction between
them is powerful, and Anne feels rejuvenated, or, as she says significantly, "freed from myself" ("délivrée de moi"; *M,* 422). The love affair
follows very closely, but with condensations, the accounts of the affair
between the author and Algren. (The latter was not pleased by the
account; he felt his privacy had been egregiously violated.) The account
of Anne and Lewis's meeting, their visits to bars in the city, their trip
down the Ohio and Mississippi rivers to New Orleans and then to the
Yucatán, their subsequent visit to New York, and their stay by Lake
Michigan—these give to passion and feeling what is perhaps their
rightful place in a novel that is otherwise greatly concerned with politics.[9] The affair's conventionality should not, however, be overlooked;
nor should its parallelism, in a different key, to the Henri-Paule affair,
since Anne also develops a tremendous emotional dependence on Lewis.
The affair cannot endure; ultimately, Anne is obliged by the evidence to
recognize that her life is established in France: "That was my spot . . .
my place on the earth" ("C'était ma place . . . ma place sur terre"; *M,*
331). And Lewis's understanding of love precludes sharing her with
another. Anne's psychological conflict is dramatized in episodes of
quarrels, reunions, and bitter departures.

In France, Henri, having abandoned his novel, has written a play
about the Resistance. A director agrees to produce it if he will accept
for a lead role a lovely actress, Josette. Like Nadine, she is a victim of
her mother, a manipulating, ambitious woman who uses Josette as an
instrument for her own ends. The acquaintance soon turns into a liaison, leading to complications typical of the period. Josette's mother,
Henri discovers, collaborated with the Germans, and Josette had an
affair with a German officer. For those who know these facts, Henri is
ripe for blackmail. To avoid having Josette's past publicized (and to
avoid the risk she might be punished), Henri finds himself giving false
testimony at the trial of a collaborator, contradicting the testimony of

witnesses who had been victims of the Nazis. This distasteful episode makes him more vulnerable still to exposure.

It also brings to the forefront an important secondary theme of the novel, justice. What justice should be is particularly difficult to determine in the case of suspected collaborators.[10] While the principal characters all consider them loathsome, summary, execution-style justice meted out to them no longer seems acceptable; the standards of the war are gone. Henri, who is drawn into the fringes of the matter, is forced also to acknowledge differences among sentiment, economic collaboration, and denunciations of others. When near the end a traitor is killed on the Dubreuilh property and Henri finds himself obliged to help dispose of his body, he has no sense of triumph; the individual justice that seemed important earlier is swallowed up in larger considerations.

Robert and Henri, who have quarreled publicly over the issue of the Soviet prison camps, thus breaking up the SRL, are reconciled; Robert uses the Josette incident to argue that individual morality is impossible in the post-Resistance era. As he says, in a curved space one cannot draw a straight line (M, 489). Robert's position helps Henri recognize the inevitable compromises that must be made, whatever one's principles. This has proved particularly true for someone who tries to adhere to a middle position; all sides have attempted to annex Henri, and when he will not yield, he is considered, "objectively," as his Communist opponents say, a traitor. Ultimately, both Henri and Robert, who emerges from his fatalism, agree to work with the Communists, despite their differences—preferring the Soviet Union to the United States; the alternative is to do nothing at all. Henri, who has lost control of L'Espoir, publishes in Robert's review, Vigilance, an exposé on colonial abuses in Madagascar.

By the end of the novel, Henri, who breaks with Josette following the trial, and Nadine have married after she became pregnant. It is a surprising turn: her wanting a child is strange, in view of her own filial experience, and Henri's character would not seem to lend itself to domesticity. Doubtless the child represents hope for the future, even in the world of the cold war; critics have noted Henri's abundance of optimism and energy at the end, as well as his affirmative image of himself, which makes him decide after all not to move to Italy but rather to stay in France and write.

Anne's affair with Lewis has concluded, and her old fears of mortality and the futility of everything haunt her again. She falls into a depression so deep that she comes close to suicide (she thinks of swallowing the very poison she has taken from Paule). This rather melodramatic episode can be seen as a variation on the romantic cliché by which tragic love leads to death, but it can also be read in terms of modern theories—including psychoanalytic ones—of the relationship between mind and body or as a criticism of what women have allowed themselves to become. In any case, belief in curing the human condition, whether by psychiatry or politics, is not meaningful enough to save Anne—a pertinent lesson in this novel of ideas. Ties with others can do so, however; although death would mean liberation to her, she realizes it would torment those close to her. She has thus returned to her point of departure—a sense of dependency, little faith in her own accomplishments, and the prospect of old age. The novel ends on a note of anguish, moderated by the thought that Anne might be happy again.

"We write for our own time," said Sartre.[11] *Les Mandarins* was clearly a novel for the early fifties. Henri's description of the sort of book he would like to write—a novel reflecting his time, bearing witness—fits Beauvoir's own work. The Communist press was generous toward it, perhaps in recognition of the positions Beauvoir and her friends had taken two or three years before and perhaps seeing in it an exoneration of the exercise of violence under Stalin (all the main characters finally accept this point of view).[12] The moderate press received it even more warmly, finding much in it that reflected very badly on the French Communist party and the left wing in general. Unfortunately, what made the novel so timely in 1954 is partly responsible for its decreased interest decades later. It is an extremely intelligent book, by a perceptive writer, but some areas of its intelligence—the matters of the cold war and collaboration—are no longer directly pertinent, and because action is in the end dictated by praxis and not principle, the present-day reader may find little of interest behind the complicated politics. Such a view would be shortsighted, however: there is still much to be gleaned from Henri's reflections and Robert's comments on the conflict between thought and action. With respect to women, Beauvoir would go farther in her last two books of fiction, surpassing even the scenes of Paule's ravings, Nadine's neuroses, and Anne's near-paralyzing depression.

Les Belles Images

When Beauvoir's last novel, published in France in 1966, appeared in English, its title was deemed untranslatable. The phrase *les belles images,* which recurs throughout the text, has a number of references.

Some readers have supposed that, since the heroine, Laurence, works for an advertising agency, the chief meaning of "beautiful images" or "pictures" is advertising copy—the complex of graphic elements and words destined to provoke desire. This meaning, however, is only the most immediate one. Applied variously to tourists' photos, televised scenes of violence and disaster, preconceptions, social and behavioral patterns, and people themselves, the phrase refers fundamentally to mental constructs, those "images" which Beauvoir, with Sartre, assumes to be a crucial form of mental functioning. In Sartrean phenomenology—one way of understanding the novel—imagination is to be distinguished from perception. Since the image exists only unreally, it is radically different from the object of perception, although their essence may be the same (imagined or painted versus real dog). *Les belles images* are thus by definition what is unreal.

It is not, however, a matter of condemning imagination, which is a fundamental and morally neutral function of mind, a form of intentionality (that is, a way of "intending" or confronting the world). But Beauvoir's novel shows that others' freedom can be abrogated by an appeal to their imagination, which becomes alienated. The moral onus is thus not on images themselves but on their quality and the uses to which they are put, or what can be called, following Michel Foucault and others, the "discourse" of a society, which Beauvoir said she wanted to reproduce (*TCF*, 139). As in the more patently existentialist works of the 1940s, individuals are shown as being responsible for creating values, even if they do so in a serial fashion, by imitation.

Despite this existentialist moral, at first glance *Les Belles Images* is such a radical departure from its predecessors that, as critics claimed, one does not recognize the author's hand. No character in the novel speaks for Beauvoir throughout, and one has to read between the lines for a positive meaning (see *TCF*, 139). The tone is detached. The wartime and postwar Europe visible in Beauvoir's earlier fiction has been replaced by a technocratic society, or what the heroine's husband, Jean-Claude, calls a world culture. Earlier political choices have made of France a fully, conspicuously capitalistic society. While history is evoked sometimes as a backdrop—Hiroshima and the Algerian war are mentioned—and large-scale problems, especially in the third world, such as the American war in Vietnam, famine in Asia, refugees, and civil conflicts, impinge on public consciousness, no life-or-death choices need be made. The characters' concerns are much like those of prosperous Americans at the same period, and even a quarter-century later they seem entirely familiar—almost stereotypes. Their cliché-ridden language recalls Flaubert's "received ideas," those common-places that are now the currency of a mass-culture society. Beauvoir had made a study of the dominant discourse in books and magazines relat-ing to contemporary society, in order to constitute a *sottisier,* or list of stupidities (*TCF,* 139).

The novelist chooses her characters among the privileged bourgeoi-sie, concerned chiefly with money for its symbolic value, operating by means of secondary signs (expensive cars, country houses). These signs serve to ratify the self because others recognize them tacitly as indica-tions of worth. The code is mostly arbitrary—there is little true superi-ority in most style—but is nonetheless real, since among other things it is connected to power. Within this social context Beauvoir does what countless writers, from Jane Austen through Balzac, Proust, and Fran-çoise Sagan (to whom she has been compared), have done before her: pierce and dismantle the mechanisms—images, in this case—that are crucial to the functioning of the society. Unlike many other social novelists, however, Beauvoir has a ferocious dislike for the class she portrays. Her early hostility toward the French bourgeoisie had been exacerbated by its postwar resurgence and in particular by the Algerian war, during which the majority of the members of the bourgeoisie had supported French repression in North Africa, and this hostility pro-duced a sardonic portrait of the class. *Les Belles Images* is not a great social novel, to be sure, and most of its characters are deplorably shallow, without those charming eccentricities that redeem many fig-ures in other novels of manners. Although its sales in France reached some 120,000 copies, critics generally found the novel inferior to Beauvoir's previous work.[13] But it has merits, including a welcome concision, a coherent thematic and metaphoric system, and scenes that have been called brilliant (Keefe, 203). In fact, some commentators have considered it the most "literary" of Beauvoir's fiction, for its technique, design, and thematic structure.[14]

The work is particularly concerned with the feminine condition, a timely topic in the mid-1960s, shortly before the French women's movement was founded. It points to the author's continuing interest in the topic, after *Le Deuxième Sexe.* As in *L'Invitée,* a woman is the principal character, and others are much in evidence. Topics such as sexual stereotyping, maternity, marriage, and women in the professions are central. The mother-daughter relationship is especially important. Women, Beauvoir suggests, are particularly vulnerable to images because reality for them has been mediated through men; they have been the recipients rather than the creators of values: "Women are much more susceptible, because they are completely oppressed by men; they take men at their word and believe in the gods that men have made up" (Jardine, 232–33). Three generations show how women can imitate others to a self-destructive degree, interiorizing the image others present. Beauvoir also shows, however, what other feminists have emphasized: that this inauthenticity affects its agent; the male characters too have alienated themselves.

The narration is divided between (a) the third person, with limited omniscience focused on Laurence and a great deal of free indirect style, and (b) first-person interior monologue, including verbalized affective reactions, reflections, simultaneous narration, and retrospective narration. The interrogative mode is frequent, suggesting self-doubt. The present tense is used freely in both, providing fluid transitions between the voices. There is even a second-person monologue, probably to be seen as a dialogue within the self rather than as an authorial address to the heroine or as a quasi-I.[15] Switches from first to third person are frequent—often within a sentence.[16] The effect is to divide the heroine (much as Jean Blomart is divided), the third person showing her at greater remove and suggesting a social self, the first person giving the subjective, repressed self. An expository scene in which the heroine's role as narrative focus only gradually becomes clear opens the novel; another scene closes it, and in between are many scenes in which the conversations reveal the speakers and their milieu as surely as a sociological treatise would, but more subtly. Indirect style, which Beauvoir had used in Le Sang des autres, serves often to report dialogue—a device that contributes to distancing speech from meaning.

In La Force des choses Beauvoir responded to Nathalie Sarraute, who had criticized her outdated technique and psychology, although she herself used indirect style. To the charge that she rendered reality—including speech, which Sarraute called "the prolongation of subterranean movements"—in a misleading manner, Beauvoir replied that, despite the problems dialogue poses for a novelist, not all fictional conversation should be embedded in a mental continuum or interior monologue, and that speech should be seen as principally exterior, an act (291). This position clearly separates her from Sarraute and from deconstructionists, with their emphasis on the inability of language to convey reality. Yet in Les Belles Images Beauvoir isolates sentences from their context; juxtaposes them in rapid succession, as one might hear them at a cocktail party; and thus emphasizes their shallowness and meaninglessness—an effect achieved by many of Sarraute's pages, whether of conversation or interior monologue.[17] On a related matter, Beauvoir criticizes through her main character excessive emphasis on description in fiction, presumably as practiced by Alain Robbe-Grillet; she clearly wanted to stress that she remained committed to a novel with a plot, dealing with ideas.[18]

The heroine's mother, Dominique, age 51, is almost totally alienated from her freedom. She has spent her life courting and imitating others. Having separated from Laurence's father because he had not made for himself a brilliant, that is, socially recognized, career as a lawyer, she has had a liaison with a multimillionaire, Gilbert Mortier, who has provided her with all the appurtenances of the chic rich; meanwhile, she has with great effort made for herself a career in radio and television, which, as an arm of the government, panders, like advertising, to class greed and myths of progress. The career means little, however, for when Gilbert leaves her to marry a 19-year-old (clearly an "image" that will prove to others his virility and charm), Dominique is totally at a loss. As she says, a woman without a man is nothing: *déclassée*. She fears most of all that the public image of her as desirable and charming will be replaced by that of an abandoned woman, solitary, aging, dependent on gigolos. Since to her this view would constitute her essential self, she desperately seeks an alternative, while plotting her revenge—again, for its public effect—and subsisting on tranquilizers. Friendships are useless—she has no true friends, only chic acquaintances; Laurence, who never calls her anything but Dominique, thinks of her as a stranger. Since to return to one's husband will not give cause for mockery, that is Dominique's strategy. Beauvoir is clearly criticizing here the woman who has invested everything in men and for whom even a satisfactory career cannot produce reconcilement with the self.

For Laurence also, torn between various moral authorities, truth has been mediated through others—her father; her mother, who raised her despotically and shaped her into the successful social woman (or "image") she now is; and her husband. The last, a successful architect who has charm and is attentively affectionate, has been Laurence's principal authority since their marriage, replacing the oppressive influence of Dominique. He is a meliorist whose historical determinism is no less monolithic than a Marxist's: he predicts the disappearance of want and conflict by 1990, yet designs government low-income housing that will have no private bathrooms. Unpleasant truths of the moment he rationalizes away or ignores. The ideals in which he believes and which Laurence's mother held up for her—money, success, style—are part and parcel of Laurence's work in advertising; she knows that one sells not a product but an idea. The ideals have lost some of their appeal because Laurence sees through their "mystification" (*BI,* 195), but she does not know what to put in their place. She is both a victim and a party—an accomplice, the author calls her (*TCF,* 139)—to her own alienation, which produces, finally, deep doubts about the self. She compares herself to Midas: "Everything she touches turns into an image" ("Tout ce qu'elle touche se tourne en image"; *BI,* 25–26).

Only her father (never named) seems to propose a different set of values. His modest standard of living and pursuit of what Laurence considers, thanks to him, the "real values"—books, music, art, history—constitute a yardstick of judgment: "His loyalties are to himself and not to objects" ("Ses fidélités sont en lui, non dans les choses"; *BI,* 154). For all her admiration, however, Laurence feels she lacks what enables her father to cultivate and rely on his inner self—his "secret"— and her equilibrium is constantly threatened. As an escape, she has indulged in a liaison with a colleague from the agency, but, as their co-worker Mona says, he resembles her husband, that is, proposes an identical image. Mona too is a mirror, but a negative one, a quiet antagonist. Coming from a different class, she judges the world of exploitive capitalism while working for it.

Beauvoir's interest in mental illness, which dates from at least the mid-1930s, when she visited an insane asylum, and which appears in the portrait of Paule in *Les Mandarins,* is evident again, as mental alienation is associated with the main character herself. The clinical depression into which Laurence fell some years before the novel opens, when she learned that French authorities had used torture in Algeria, shows how she has resisted the glossing over of want and conflict and the suppression of an authentic self. Her literal sickness can be read as a psychosomatic manifestation of the sickness of the public body. Her way of curing it has been to take up a career and to deny the cause of her malaise; she reads almost nothing that deals with concrete problems of the present. A contrast to Laurence is furnished by her sister, Martha, who has alienated her freedom not to materialism or others around her but to religion and its *belles images* of security and certitude. In this strategy, God is the absolute other, one who reflects back on the believer a mediated image of the self, ratified and guaranteed. Laurence's rejection of the alienation of belief for herself and especially for her daughter represents a first step in reclaiming her own authority.

The case of Catherine displays the author's interest in the education of children. The girl is threatened with the same victimization as her mother. For fear that unpleasant realities will disturb her, her parents forbid her to read newspapers and have any other access to what is happening outside her closed circle. But an older, less sheltered classmate provides Catherine with graphic evidence of misery, specifically a poster campaigning against hunger, which, as she correctly senses, the progressive global civilization praised by her father does little to relieve.[19] Her reaction is to put the metaphysical question she had asked—Why exist?—into a social context—What can my existence do to or for others? Jean-Charles's reaction to the symptoms of trauma she shows is to end the friendship and send Catherine to a psychologist. When Laurence ultimately insists on the more difficult path of allowing Catherine to confront reality, the role of clinical psychology in contributing to a healthy self is called into question.

All the changes of the plot, which adroitly joins interior and exterior drama, affect the heroine, whose position is pivotal. When Gilbert leaves Dominique, Laurence has to endure her fits of rage at the same time that Catherine is having nightmares, a development that leads to disputes between the parents. Realizing that what he gives her is not essentially different, and that he is keeping her from her family and perhaps something else, Laurence decides to break off with her lover. Then, to avoid hitting a careless cyclist, she wrecks the family car, an accident for which she is callously rebuked by Jean-Charles, especially irritable because he has changed jobs.

The most momentous change is that Laurence comes to see her father in a new light. During their trip to Greece, the sort of trip she had long dreamed of, she makes the jolting discovery that his supposed authenticity is as dishonest as Dominique's frank dependence and Gilbert's materialism. He feigns sympathy for the Greek Communists, yet denies the reality of misery, insisting that the scarcity in which Greeks live is a sign of a healthy antimaterialism. He mentally collects "images" from museums and temples on which to feed his sense of the past and its supposed greater authenticity. Hie aestheticism is fraudulent, a deliberate escapism, blinding him to the present world. On the heels of this discovery, Laurence learns that he and Dominique are reconciled and that he has agreed to participate in a radio program, after having attacked government institutions as corrupt. He who had said, "I have always tried to have my life and my principles agree" ("J'ai toujours essayé de mettre ma vie en accord avec mes principes"; *BI,* 46), consents to the very political and personal compromises he had deplored in others. He even takes sides with Jean-Charles concerning Catherine.

Laurence is devastated because she has lost the only mediating image that was entirely positive.[20] This devastation is not just the sign of an unresolved Electra complex (prefigured in their visit to the Mycenean ruins of Agamemnon's temple). Or rather, Beauvoir is less interested in the complex than in its implications in existentialist terms.[21] The father's inadequacies serve to make Laurence aware of her own bad faith, since she realizes that she drew from him the values she needed to combat the image of the self as ratified—in truth devoured by—its possessions. Her reaction is anorexia, which recalls thematically the mass hunger represented in the poster that had touched Catherine. She refuses to *swallow,* as she says, both others' truths and food. Jean-Charles proposes that Laurence see a specialist. Her refusal points to the author's conviction that the heroine's need to determine her own self is neither an illness nor an aberration, and that medical and psychoanalytic solutions alike would be inappropriate. Laurence does not content herself, however, with this passive rebellion. By an act of will directed against Jean-Charles and her parents, but also against her former self, she reasserts her freedom by exercising her own authority: henceforth it will be she who decides what Catherine will do; at least the child will have, as the ending suggests, a chance for a more authentic life.

It would be convenient if the reader could conclude that the solution to the failures of the society portrayed is to eliminate the role of mediating images. Unfortunately, as Sartrean psychology shows, the self is always mediated, from earliest childhood. Identity depends on difference: others are essential for the self to be cognizant of itself. The answer is not an extreme individualism that would deny the other; Dominique discovers that "others exist, on their own" ("Les autres existent, pour leur compte"; *BI,* 175). Rather, authenticity would have to come through acknowledgment of others' freedom and the elimination of the conflict that, as early as *L'Invitée,* Beauvoir proclaimed as fundamental. This means that all must be redeemed together; salvation is collective. Laurence's task is enormous: to bring all her intimates to a common recognition of freedom and creation of an authentic self. There is some hope that she can do so for and with Catherine. Ultimately, all of society, globally, would have to be reformed, and selves become transparent to each other so that mediation of self to other would be as self to self.[22] Then the "inner-directed person" and the "outer-directed"—terms Beauvoir had learned from the sociologist David Riesman (*FC,* 394)—would be the same.

La Femme rompue

Beauvoir's last volume of fiction, published in 1968, comprises three long stories, or novellas, loosely associated through the common themes of the feminine condition and aging, as well as a shared self-deception on each heroine's part.[23] There are also recurrent secondary themes, including the relationship of mother to children. The milieu is the bourgeoisie, and although intellectuals appear, social concerns are generally marginal. In each case, a woman's voice is heard, uniquely or preponderantly, and the narration is in the first person, either in a diary or simply spoken directly. Sartre considered the volume, which was dramatized on television in 1977, to be Beauvoir's strongest writing (Dayan, 28). The critics, however, were generally very severe, some of them treating the volume as trash. They were aware that the stories had first appeared in the magazine *Elle;* Beauvoir explained that she published them there to enlarge her audience, but she was also in need of money (Bair, 673, n. 35).

"L'Age de discrétion," the initial story, has connections with nonfictional works of Beauvoir's last period that deal with aging and its consequences. In Gide's *Les Faux-Monnayeurs* (*The Counterfeiters*), a character complains that almost universally novelists have neglected the elderly. Gide himself remedied the neglect slightly, but Beauvoir goes further. At 60, the heroine is not yet old and infirm, but she sees the ravages of aging in her husband and senses herself on the threshold of that "age of discretion" in which behavior is dictated by both social expectations—which, of course, one may choose to defy—and a body that is no longer obedient to will. To this central theme are added the topics of social justice, the past, and the other, especially communication and personal relationships. These themes are broached within the context of a domestic crisis. In fact, like much other Beauvoirian fiction, "L'Age de discrétion" is concerned with traditional psychological and social topics that often characterize women's fiction: the couple, maternity, the family. The novelist's technical control over her material and the intelligent manner in which the psychological drama is played out offset what would otherwise be a banal tale.

The heroine, for whom Beauvoir borrows many details from her own biography, is the first-person narrator. While the author may not have intended her as a classically "unreliable" or obtuse narrator in the sense Wayne C. Booth gave to the term,[24] in that the general direction of the story is toward self-enlightenment rather than self-deception, the absence of a correcting viewpoint renders her reporting of events suspect. There is no visible narratee, and no attempt is made within the narrative to justify either that fact or the changes in the time of narration, the latter characterized by analepses and prolepses: beginning in the present, it makes a retrospective loop, followed by a second one, returns briefly to the present, and then continues linearly in the past until it ends on a series of questions in the future tense. The distance between the action told and the telling expands and retracts; sometimes the heroine uses the imperfect ("used to . . ."), while elsewhere she anticipates by prolepses. This varying distance makes the past more or less present, mirroring the mental processes by which the heroine's reflections focus on the moment or seek to revive the past that produced it.

The crisis that gives rise to the *récit* is provoked by the return of the heroine's son, Philippe, from his honeymoon, and the surprise announcement that he has abandoned his fledgling university career to seek something more dynamic, with the encouragement of his wife and father-in-law, who come from the moneyed and worldly bourgeoisie (the one depicted in *Les Belles Images*), a contrast to the world of his parents. The heroine is a university professor who deems her career to be one of the few ways of remaining intellectually honest in a corrupt and unjust society. Her husband, André, a scientist, shares her political views, without her moral intransigence. That Philippe's decision constitutes a betrayal of his parents' ideological commitments as well as his own youthful ideals is made clear when he announces that he will join the Ministry of Culture, a branch of the loathed Gaullist government. The heroine also considers his decision a personal betrayal, for it was she who had molded him and directed him toward a university career. Indications both subtle and not-so-subtle of her maternal imperialism, which she is not ready to abandon, show how concerned Beauvoir was in this story to demonstrate again, as in her memoirs, how *not* to be a parent. The coexistence in the same character of this overly protective, despotic conduct and a highly valorized intellectual liberalism produces in the reader a certain malaise. André, who like Robert in *Les Mandarins* is a Sartre-like figure in his intellect, political activism, equitable temper, and good judgment, argues that the son must be allowed to choose for himself, and suggests that his mother's oppressive manipulation of him is responsible for making him the morally and intellectually mediocre person that in their eyes he is.

The drama precipitated by Philippe's decision has further repercussions, revealing how typically Beauvoirian the heroine is in her extremism. She feels betrayed by André, who does not approve their son's choice but, unlike her, has no wish to break with him completely; moreover, the physical passion that used to mend their quarrels is gone. The unfavorable critical reception of her most recent book casts doubt on the possibility for continued intellectual achievement and thus makes her retirement seem no longer fertile but instead the antechamber of the tomb. André's moroseness, fed by his own doubts about a scientist's ability to do useful work in old age and added to his old man's habits, sends her into such a depression that she finds jeopardized the fabric of a conjugal understanding established over decades.

The solution can be only tentative and partial, since a central problem is the loss of the vitality that enables one to go beyond betrayal and failure. Whereas Beauvoir's ethical writings of the 1940s argued that one may master a situation by free choices, the limits of this freedom are clearly visible in her later fiction. The heroine could rethink her attitude toward Philippe; one senses she may resume contact with him, albeit on a different footing. She can—and does—come to understand André's "betrayal" in a new light. Thanks to him, their lovers' quarrel, half real, half misunderstanding, is ended, and when André resolves to resist old age rather than surrender to its temptations, *she* feels its threat diminish. But as the title suggests, each age carries its own imperatives; her situation makes her, and she can only react.

No one in Beauvoir's fiction, not even Paule in *Les Mandarins,* reeks more of bad faith than Murielle, the speaker in the second story, "Monologue." While she shares some traits and obsessions with the heroines of the previous and following stories, her case is the most extreme. The entire 30-page text consists of her solipsistic ruminations in the first person, during the course of a New Year's Eve. The abrupt transitions, unexplained allusions, loose punctuation, run-on sentences, and irregular syntax create a stream-of-consciousness effect, but not all logic is abandoned. No other character is seen directly, but several are evoked, two during one-sided telephone conversations in which the other's words are echoed in the heroine's replies. The sounds of celebrations in the street and overhead, indicating the existence of others and impinging from the beginning on Murielle's consciousness, constitute a rival reality, opposed to her obsessive self-pitying and aggressive reinvention of the world suggested by the epigraph from Flaubert: "She takes vengeance by a monologue" ("Elle se venge par le monologue"). The writer's challenge, with an unreliable narrator and no major opposing voice, was to make the speaker both conceal the truth—for her bad faith requires that she deny to herself or rationalize away all her failures—and reveal it. The tone is one of aggression, befitting Murielle's generalized hostility; her coarse, even obscene language is obviously an offensive tactic.

The facts of Murielle's life come out gradually, through her manipulation and misrepresentation of them. Her anger springs mainly from those personal and family relationships which are traditionally woman's chief interest, and which have indeed defined most of Murielle's life, since she has no career, no other consuming interest. She resents her mother, who (if we are to believe her) preferred her brother and deprived her of needed affection; she resents likewise this same brother, the father who lifted him on his shoulders, her first husband, and, most recently, her estranged second husband, who has separated her from her young son, living elsewhere. Most of all she hates them—considered collectively—because, as she says, they killed her daughter, Sylvie. In fact, it becomes clear that Sylvie killed herself in despair, tyrannized by her mother's interference in her life—reading her diary, breaking up friendships and attempting to impose friends of her own choosing, alienating a professor Sylvie admired, and so on. As in the rest of her monologue, it is clear that Murielle's interpretations of events are so warped as to be nearly delusions.

Resentment takes the form not only of hostility but of paranoia and fantasies. Murielle imagines that both her young brother and her husband were seduced by her mother, that Sylvie's professor was a lesbian, that her doctor is a sadist, and that her family is trying to drive her insane, or simply have her committed. Her pan-sexuality, one aspect of the self-perversion that accompanies and, one could argue, springs from Murielle's self-deception, forms a counterreality—her answer to a world in which others have values such as love. Another offensive tactic is Murielle's frankness, an aspect of her supposed integrity that allows her to attack others on the pretext of telling the truth. She is also, or attempts to be, an expert manipulator of others. Saying that she was the best of mothers, she reveals to what lengths she went, or would go again, to mold her child to fit the image she has in mind. As Fallaize has pointed out (161), Murielle's monologue is a kind of mental dress rehearsal for the scene she anticipates the next day, when her son and second husband will pay her a New Year's visit and she will try to persuade them to come back to her; the methods she intends to use are foreshadowed in her ravings, not excluding her trump card—her threat to kill herself in front of the boy. Her phone calls are desperate attempts to anticipate the scene by enrolling her mother's aid and pressuring the husband. Like Daniel in Sartre's *Les Chemins de la liberté,* Murielle shows fascist tendencies, wishing, for instance, for others to disappear so that the air she breathes will be cleaner and there will be fewer vermin in the world. This desire to deprive others of their freedom for her own purposes reaches its pinnacle when, at the end, she asks that God be so that she can walk in paradise while her enemies roast in flames.

Such aggression, added to a web of misrepresentations and lies through which the truth appears only antiphrastically, leaves little room for the reader to sympathize with Murielle; unlike a number of Beauvoir's works in which the reader is drawn into a certain complicity with characters, here one is put off at every turn. The value of the story as a portrait of extreme self-deception, revealed from the inside, is considerable, however. By showing the pitfalls of a language used only for self-centered and self-deluding ends, the writer seems to suggest how integral speech is to an authentic relationship with the world— that is, how language must pass through others, involving them on the same footing as the self. As an exploration of the causes of inauthenticity, the story offers less, perhaps, than the other two in the collection. The few scenes glimpsed from Murielle's childhood cannot be considered a sufficient explanation of her distortions and hostility. In fact, although the existentialist tenet that one is responsible for the world is never expressed, it may shed more light on Murielle's example than a psychological or sociological explanation would.

One point needs to be made concerning the social context, however. In all three stories, but particularly this one, the relationships between mothers and children are called into question. Although Murielle's harassment of her daughter and son are extreme examples, in the other two stories an overly protective or overly manipulating mother is also responsible for a distortion of family relationships. These examples, added to those of Laurence in *Les Belles Images* and Anne in *Les Mandarins,* indicate that Beauvoir found the relationship between parents, especially mothers, and children to be as problematic, at least in the bourgeoisie, in postwar decades as she had experienced it herself. It has been observed that as late as 1979 Beauvoir was still suggesting that relationships imposed by the family, and especially those between mother and daughter, were rarely successful (Dayan, 73).

The connection between the last story and the rest of the volume is special. As the title story and the longest of the three, it occupies a privileged position, drawing attention to the most fundamental theme: women, as they are "broken" or "broken off with." The form is the diary, one that Beauvoir practiced herself and used for Anne in *Les Mandarins* and for her early heroine Chantal. One of the favorite modern forms, used to effect in France by Gide, Bernanos, Sartre, Butor, and many others, it is suited to the exploration of the self, one of the heroine's undertakings.

The diary is both exposition and event, stasis and process. It recounts a domestic drama but is itself a psychological drama, perhaps more disquieting than the other. Its formal interest lies partly in the ambiguity that inevitably colors it. Only the diarist's voice can be heard directly; all others pass through it and become suspect. Moreover, an inevitable distance exists between experience and its expression in words—even when the diary entry closely follows the event—and this aspect also creates distortion. Most important, the temptation for self-deception is enormous; words conceal as well as reveal, as "Monologue" well illustrates, and what is not expressed in a diary—what is deliberately cast aside as unimportant or shameful—may be the most telling element. Although the heroine gradually corrects herself, questioning what she has written before and bringing to bear different viewpoints, each new light shed on her experience is, of course, itself unreliable, and self-knowledge pursued through words appears elusive, a chain of false starts, errors, questions, and half-truths, never filled in.

The literary interest of the diary form can be contrasted with the triteness of the topic, straight out of the *courrier du cœur* (advice columns). The situation is the most conventional possible and explains the suitability of the story for magazine publication, as well as the number of letters Beauvoir received from women who said they recognized themselves in the story: Monique, a woman in her forties, learning that her husband is involved with another woman, younger and professionally brilliant, finds her world shattered, and in the course of some weeks goes through various stages in facing the drama and its implications for her future. The evolution of Monique's thinking and behavior is a function both of the changing situation—for the husband reveals only gradually the full extent of his commitment to the other woman

and evolves himself—and of the heroine's own linguistic and psychological enterprise, her attempt to grasp her situation and know herself.

Nearly everything reflected in the diary is a failure. Since it is now
disintegrating, Monique deems her marriage of almost a quarter-century
to be unsuccessful, although an observer might point to its achievements. She oscillates between accepting responsibility for its failure—
for only then can she continue to admire Maurice wholly—and blaming
him. She is not entirely innocent; the pressures she put on him—first to
marry; then to begin medical practice, sacrificing an internship; and
finally (unsuccessfully) to turn down a research position—represent
what Beauvoir seems to consider as unjustified interference with another's freedom. Admitting that one of her daughters has fled to the
United States perhaps to escape from her, and that the other has made a
disappointing marriage of which her husband disapproves, Monique also
questions her success as a mother, and what she reveals of her dealings
with them as adolescents shows that she was indeed an oppressive mother
who tried to impose, successfully in one case, her image of domestic
fulfillment on the girls. Since Monique has identified wholly with her
domestic roles, these failures represent the failure of the self, which leads
to self-blame and thus scission.

Beauvoir seems intent on showing in the remainder of the story how
the means to which people often have recourse when the stability of
their lives is jeopardized prove to be without value. Friendship is
almost worthless as a means of regaining a positive self-image; friends
serve merely as complacent mirrors, saying what is expected or repeat-
ing truisms. Nor can friends help one regain a disaffected partner, as
Proust's lovers know. Counselors and psychoanalysts are similarly useless; they either utter clichés or concentrate on complexes and traumas
(which explain nothing), whereas Monique's concern focuses on the
practical matter of saving her marriage. Her daughters are of no help;
they either cannot see or will not say the essential.

Even Monique's diary, undertaken in an attempt to assess her situation clearly and thereby win back her husband's love, is unsuccessful.
Its original questions—What is happening? Why? and How can I
remedy it?—lead to another, more perplexing one—Who am I? This
last question, directed to herself, cannot be answered by herself. Both
the retrospective and the introspective modes of seeking knowledge in
the diary seem inadequate, partly because the past is simply unknow-
able, crumbling away when one tries to seize it, and partly because
introspection leaves out an essential factor in the equation of the self:

others. The for-itself is also, it will be remembered, a for-others, and
the Socratic notion of self-knowledge has to be replaced by the recognition that relationships are crucial in defining the self. The diary and the
novella end with the heroine's panic at having to return to an empty
apartment; her final cry is one of fear.

Beauvoir's lessons in this volume—which is very clearly intended as
a warning—are not entirely negative. No solution is proposed, it is
true, to the fundamental problem of infidelity in marriage, or to the
particular problem of the male who, in midlife, turns to a woman who
by her youth gives him a more flattering, reassuring picture of himself.
The institution of marriage is not even questioned, although one might
conclude that Beauvoir is happy to expose its flaws. No positive model
for child rearing in a middle-class environment is offered, and to the
psychoses of Murielle the story can propose no solution. But in connection with the freedom and fulfillment of women there is one implied
course of action: work outside marriage. In *Le Deuxième Sexe* and countless articles and speeches, Beauvoir insisted on not only woman's *right*
to employment beyond housework and child care but her need for it, as
an expression of her freedom. While remunerated work is no guarantee
against error in dealings with oneself or others—the heroine of the first
story is a case in point—far better, one concludes, to have a profes-
sional life of one's own than be wholly dependent on men's *bon plaisir.*
Monique, in the last story, has not worked in the past, preferring to
devote herself to her husband and family, and she persists in this
position even as her marriage disintegrates, finding entry-level jobs
meaningless; Murielle's life has centered on lovers, and she has no
resources within herself other than paranoia. The stories illustrate
clearly Beauvoir's contention that women must assume equality with
men by building their lives around the principle of action, not that of
reaction.

Chapter Five
Philosophical and Political Studies, 1944–1955

Two Volumes on Existentialist Ethics

In recent decades, especially since the founding of the French Mouvement de la libération des femmes and the growth of American feminism, Beauvoir's fame as the author of *Le Deuxième Sexe* and a campaigner for women's rights has far outstripped her stature as an essayist on other topics. Elaine Marks (46) observes that "an interest in Beauvoir as a feminist thinker and writer seems to have obliterated any concern for Beauvoir as an existentialist thinker who wrote novels." Several volumes on Beauvoir's work published in the 1970s and 1980s barely if at all mention her philosophical writings. Yet her achievements in exposition and elaboration of philosophical problems and proposed solutions should not be overlooked, both for their own value and because they lay the foundation for her later activism. She entered the field with excellent qualifications. Her training was solid, and, through teaching, she had experience in expression, argumentation, and persuasion; moreover, for many years the continuous intellectual dialogue she pursued with Sartre frequently focused on philosophical matters—as the two commented on and critiqued their predecessors, elaborated basic definitions and concepts to which they could both subscribe, and drew conclusions. Her early studies on ethics and other problems still have merit.

Whereas Sartre was concerned in his philosophical writings of the 1930s and 1940s first with investigating the workings of the imagination and then with laying the ground for and building a phenomenological ontology—that is, a study of the philosophical problems of being, according to the method proposed by Edmund Husserl and to Sartre's own conclusions concerning the imagination—Beauvoir turned her attention to ethics. That she should choose this area is not surprising. She would not have presumed to redo or modify the ontology proposed in *L'Etre et le néant,* whose elaboration she had witnessed and doubtless contributed to; henceforth it formed for her the foundation of her understanding of human existence in the world. She did not have, moreover, an overriding interest in other branches of philosophy, such as epistemology and aesthetics, although theories of knowledge are crucial to some of her work and one can also draw from it elements of a phenomenological theory of art.[1] Furthermore, she came from a pious milieu in which misconduct was severely censured on both religious and social grounds; this upbringing marked her so deeply that, despite her later rebellion, she did not shake off her interiorized sense of moral imperatives. In addition, though capable of dealing with abstractions, she was characteristically drawn to the concrete, and the question, How shall I act, and for what good? is one of the most concrete and immediate that philosophy proposes. When Beauvoir published her first study, she had been a witness to the fall of France and was living under the Occupation, which posed, to the reflective person, constant ethical as well as practical problems; in addition, both then and later she was aware of the horrors of her age, from the Stalinist purges and labor camps (which, to be sure, she long rationalized as necessary) and the dreadful wide-scale cruelties of Nazism to the devastation of the atom bomb.

Beauvoir may have believed that ethics was an area in which she could make a substantial contribution. *L'Etre et le néant* ends with Sartre's disclaimer of proposing even the rudiments of an ethics. Adding that in a future text he would explore the *possibility* of a coherent ethics, he concluded with the oft-quoted and misunderstood phrase "Man is a useless passion" ("L'homme est une passion inutile").[2] Although years later he did indeed compose hundreds of pages of a treatise on morality, which remained unfinished and appeared only posthumously, he did not propose to pursue the topic in the 1940s.[3] Eschewing elaborate and abstruse grounding, Beauvoir took up the subject in *Pyrrhus et Cinéas* (1944). One of the first volumes published after the Liberation, it was very well received (*FC,* 23). It grew out of reflections on the period and on problems illustrated, but not exhausted, in *L'Invitée,* including the relationship between action and death, and relations with others. Less thorough, less rigorously argued than its successor, *Pour une morale de l'ambiguïté,* it can serve as a useful introduction to Beauvoir's ethical considerations.[4]

The author begins with the anecdote from Plutarch that furnishes the title. Pyrrhus recites his plans for future conquest: Greece, Africa,

Asia Minor, India. Afterward, he says, he will rest. Cineas replies, "Why not rest immediately?" This dialogue points to the principal focus of Beauvoir's concern: the justification of human action in light of its inevitable finality. An unnamed adversary is Pascal, whose judgment that human unhappiness comes from not knowing how to remain alone in a room is the classic expression in French letters of the quietist point of view, one arguing that action, or *divertissement,* is meaningless and even harmful because it detracts from concern for the eternal.

Throughout the essay, the author sees human beings as free projects, defined by their constant transcendence, or *dépassement,* by which they go beyond themselves. They belong neither to the instant nor to an eternity that they cannot conceive. Never identical to themselves, they exist as a negation of the present, transcending it toward the future. The classic problem of means and ends, which characterizes much ethical thought since Kant, is modified by Beauvoir's views on the ambiguity of finality: no ends are final, since each merely looks forward to a further one, and thus they are transformed into means. To refuse to act, on the pretext that this series of dialectically related means and ends proves endless and unresolvable, is inconsistent with human reality; it is, moreover, contradictory, since even doing nothing is an act. Only suicide is a consistent choice for those who will not accept this fundamental character of the human project. For those who live, action is the expression—indeed the sole expression—of their reality: "The only reality that belongs to me wholly is my act" ("La seule réalité qui m'appartienne entièrement, c'est donc mon acte").[5] The sum of these actions creates one's relationship to the world.

By "world" is meant, of course, both material reality and other human subjects. Whereas the environment and other aspects of material reality have recently come to be seen as an area of moral concern, ethics has usually dealt only with relationships among human beings; Beauvoir's considerations follow this pattern in treating actions with regard to others. She calls into question traditional moral guidelines for action, such as obedience to the Christian God, concern for others (one's "neighbor") or for universal humankind, and enlightened interest in a small sphere of action, represented by the garden to which Voltaire's Candide withdraws. She denies that ends can be pregiven or imposed from the outside, since they are defined by the very project that is directed toward them. To affirm preordained values—whether a so-called universal moral law or a more limited one, even one's own interests—as if the values were already in the universe like flowers to be picked is to adopt the "spirit of seriousness"—a sort of blindness and moral tyranny. Even the idea of cultivating one's garden, like Candide, is inadequate: how is it to be defined? ("Quel est mon jardin?"; *PC,* 11).

For instance, to the biblical question, Who is my neighbor? Christ did not offer a definition as an answer but instead proposed a concrete, existential example of an act that creates the relationship of "neighbor." Beauvoir contends that "one makes of another one's neighbor through becoming his neighbor by an act" ("On fait d'autrui un prochain en se faisant son prochain par un acte"; *PC,* 17). Humanity as a whole, both source and end of values for post-Enlightenment humanists, does not exist as a moral entity. The usual models for seeing it as such—organic or economic—are unacceptable; there is no way to confirm the whole, which remains an aggregate of individuals, and there is no way to judge whether an act is for the "good of humanity." The moral imperatives of Kant are abstractions that deny the individuality of each situation. As for God, Beauvoir argues on two grounds against His role as a source of moral authority. First, He does not need human obedience or complicity, since He is defined as the being that is ontologically complete, without lack or need. Second, data from comparative religion show that the claims of divine revelation compete in a mutually exclusive way and cannot all be true; in any case, the source of such revelation is always either a sacerdotal caste or individual conscience, which cannot be verified.

Acts, then, must be freely chosen by each subject and related to their ends by an integral relationship of identity that provides their meaning (the choice to subscribe to a fixed standard is an inauthentic one); they are also transcended by other acts, indefinitely. This transcendence means that they escape from the agent, both because the latter has already gone beyond the act toward a new project and because the act has a correlative in material reality—what Sartre calls the practico-inert, with its "coefficient of adversity"—that makes it thinglike, capable of being transcended by other freedoms: "What others create from my act is no longer mine" ("Ce qu'autrui crée à partir de moi n'est plus mien"; *PC,* 69). Acts, moreover, inevitably have an element of violence, in the sense that their consequences have a negating effect, if only indirectly, on both other projects and inert reality. Beauvoir's sense of the violence of human action was doubtless enhanced by the situation in which she wrote, but it goes beyond that situation to disclose the potential negative consequences on others at the heart of every action. Even gestures inspired by devotion are suspect, since devotion is often based on values (a particular idea of the good) that its recipient does not accept; such attention is then an imposition. To will for others is a contradiction: one would have to assume their liberty. To attempt to do so is tyranny. A genuine devotion is a risk, assumed voluntarily, taken in the hope that one is acting *for* another's liberty by offering "points of departure" for the authentic project of the other, not merely a momentary good (*PC,* 79).

Yet involvement with others is essential, for all that happens comes through them—starting with one's birth; they provide a sort of human facticity corresponding to the facticity of the world, which enables action. Such action is not only necessary but is the only possibility for achieving good, whether for oneself or others, "good" being identified by Beauvoir with a "struggle" ("lutte"). Attempts to deny the effects of violence are mistaken, including those which subsume it dialectically into the good. Beauvoir rejects specifically, for example, the all-encompassing good of the poet Claudel, whose variety of Christian dialectic emphasizes the biblical precept that all works for good for those who love God. Similarly, the Hegelian response—that every action is countered by a reaction and then subsumed in their synthesis, which prolongs the action by transcending it—is false, because the individual cannot relate to the theoretical totalization of human history toward which the Hegelian dialectic moves and which alone could justify his sufferings. Even to ask the individual to will this totalization is impossible; the universal is merely a concept, without relationship to existential reality.

Should violence then be justified on the concrete level in an ethics of the will to power? Beauvoir answers no. Genuine moral relationship with others is possible only in the form of an appeal to the freedom of others, for which one can be instrumental. Beauvoir gives the example of the artist, whose paintings, to be meaningful, require a freely granted complicity from the observing eye, which transcends the canvas in its own project. Similarly, in love one appeals to the freedom of others to acknowledge affection and return it freely; the idea of love imposed by violence is nonsensical. For these relationships and other authentic ones to exist (one could mention the relationship between teacher and pupil, writer and reader), each project must be able to respond of its free will; hence the emphasis in this essay, as in so much of Beauvoir's writing, is on the necessity for *liberating* human beings: "Respect for other's freedom is not an abstract rule; it is the first condition for the success of my effort" ("Le respect de la liberté d'autrui n'est pas une règle abstraite; il est la condition première du succès de mon effort") (*PC*, 112). Indeed, the ethical struggle alluded to in the foregoing discussions takes the form of this obligation to liberate. It also entails responsibility, in the sense that one is entirely answerable for one's choices as they relate to others. *Others* are free to relate to acts as they choose, but the agent is morally responsible for the act. Beauvoir quotes Dostoevsky's "Each is responsible for everything, before all," emphasizing that "motionless or acting, we always weigh on the earth" ("Immobiles ou agissant, nous pesons toujours sur la terre"; *PC*, 90).

The need for exploring further elements of an existentialist ethic became more evident after Sartre published in 1946 his Club Maintenant lecture of the previous year, *L'Existentialisme est un humanisme*, which had aroused a furor. Its skeletal treatment of certain principles of his ontology (such as "existence precedes essence") was accompanied by considerations on concrete ethical problems to which oversimplified solutions were proposed. *Pour une morale de l'ambiguïté* (1947) elaborated on the ethical assumptions in these solutions. Beauvoir wished especially to address Communist objections (*FC*, 80).

This work offers an argument for a humanistic ethics, that is, one having human beings, not God or any other absolute, as the point of departure and source of values. Taking as axiomatic Sartre's datum that human reality is grounded in freedom—the political as well as the philosophical watchword of the decade—with the consequence that there are no preordained laws or values, it investigates the way in which freedom can *found* values, while recognizing that, as will shortly be apparent, these values will always partake of ambiguity. These values, Beauvoir concludes, according to a circular reasoning that Sartre also used, must be consistent with freedom, since it is man's end as well as beginning: "The supreme end that man must aim for is freedom, alone capable of founding the value of every aim" ("La fin suprême que l'homme doit viser, c'est sa liberté, seule capable de fonder la valeur de toute fin").[6] That is, freedom is not some abstract value imposed or added from the outside; rather, it is the very foundation of the possibility to create *any* value. Thus each choice by every person must, if proper, both (a) recognize freedom in oneself and in others and (b) take it as its end: "To wish to be moral and to wish to be free are a single decision" ("Se vouloir moral et se vouloir libre, c'est une seule et même décision"; *PMA*, 34–35).

Beauvoir begins by setting up an ontological framework. The human situation is characterized by ambiguity—a term she prefers to the word *absurd,* used by such contemporaries as Malraux and Camus, and even by Sartre, but to her unsuitable, because it suggests no meaning is possible, whereas she argues meaning is not fixed but can be created (*PMA,* 180). Man, she quotes Sartre as saying, is the being that is not what he is, and is what he is not. He cannot be identical to himself; he is project, transcendence ("going-beyond"), always tearing away, separated from himself by his consciousness and projecting himself into the future. Seeking, nevertheless, to "be," the human project, constantly denying and negating itself through its transcendence, is one of bringing-into-being; it "unveils"("dévoile") being through consciousness. Put differently, it makes itself lack so that there can *be* something: "This end that man proposes for himself, in becoming lack of being, is in fact realized by him" ("Cette fin que l'homme se propose en se faisant manque d'être, elle se réalise en effet par lui"; *PMA,* 18). Ultimately, the human project is to exist absolutely, identical with itself—to be God, as it were. Of course this project is a failure, but it remains there, expressed by a series of lesser projects; man is condemned to a state of perpetual tension, neither wholly transcendent, like a god, nor wholly thinglike or factitious, like a tree or a stone. At the end of his project awaits the absolute wall of death.

In this ontological context, morality cannot be a given, only a creation. Were it not for the absence of God the guarantor, and the "failure" of human reality—its lack of identity with itself, its consciousness of the limits put on its projects, its failure to make itself an absolute—there would not even be any morality, which is a response to the ambiguous human situation. As Beauvoir showed in *Tous les hommes sont mortels,* death itself is essential for morality. What comes into existence through action is by definition what the human project, in its mortal condition, chooses to give value to; it is the way humankind brings the world into being and thus wishes the world. (Morality and will are thus closely allied here, as they are in Kant.) This creation of values through action must be done authentically; the human project must not deny its own inadequacies and ambiguities. Beauvoir writes, "To reach his truth man must not try to dissipate the ambiguity of his being but on the contrary consent to realize it" ("Pour atteindre sa vérité l'homme ne doit pas tenter de dissiper l'ambiguïté de son être mais au contraire accepter de la réaliser"; *PMA,* 20).[7] To acknowledge any exterior or absolute truth would be, clearly, to deny this ambiguity and live in bad faith. Beauvoir takes pains to criticize not only religious absolutes but those of Marxist dialectical materialism, in which, in principle at least, human freedom is abrogated in favor of ends imposed by historical necessity. (She argues that in fact Marxism leaves considerable room for freedom.)

Moreover, the human situation is complicated by a duality that is not the classic Cartesian mind-and-body duality but another aspect of ambiguity. Human reality is both interiority—the for-itself, the "incomparable monster that each is for himself and favors in his heart," as Malraux wrote[8]—and exteriority, the for-others, an existent in a world of other existents, including other people, with their own opposing projects; Beauvoir's fiction shows repeatedly how consciousness of self passes through the recognition of others: "The individual is defined only by his relationship to the world and to other individuals" ("L'individu ne se définit que par sa relation au monde et aux autres individus"; *PMA*, 218). Freedom is, in a word, in conflict with other freedoms; transcendence is arrested and made imminence by other transcendents, as the Sartrean gaze objectifies others. The theoretical difficulty of this position is obvious, not to mention the practical obstacles, for as Beauvoir showed pointedly in *L'Invitée*, subjects objectify others—in Hegelian terms, seeking the death of the other; in Kantian terms, making the other a means instead of an end. All action can thus be seen as a type of *asservissement*, or subjection, except the rare instance that deals solely with the inert and has no consequences for others. The solution is not a pseudouniversalist ethics that subordinates individual choice to some abstraction that supposedly serves all but instead denies their freedom—whence Beauvoir's opposition to the abstract Kantian and Hegelian ethics of the universal: "Absolute, universal man exists nowhere" ("L'homme universel, absolu n'existe nulle part"; *PMA*, 157).

To establish a concrete morality in the context of these unresolvable ontological ambiguities would seem impossible; Sartre even argued at one point that it was. How can one devote oneself to a project without alienating one's entire freedom to it? If each is transcendence and end to himself, how can there be general ends? Yet people do recognize common goals, which can support, rather than undermine, goals of others. Beauvoir is concerned with identifying at least some tentative guidelines for what she calls the antinomies of action, as well as rejecting certain untenable positions.

With respect to both individual and collectivity, freedom, although the foundation of human existence, must nevertheless be *assumed* authentically. Pure contingency (arbitrary, directionless action) is negative; freedom must be assumed by constructive action (hence the existentialist disdain for quietism and Stoicism).[9] A series of pointless fits and starts is the denial of freedom rather than its realization; actions must be coherent and reveal their meaning through time, the locus of freedom. This does not mean that there can be no changes of mind; nor does it mean that one must make lifelong commitments. It means simply that freedom is not itself until it is *engagé*. Beauvoir argues that senseless repetition of tasks, mechanical labor separated from enjoyment of the product, life imprisonment, or other situations in which a wall of absurdity is immediately placed before the human project are the hardest of all to bear, for they make existence itself meaningless. They are entirely different from the resistance of the world: the world supports human projects as air supports flight (*PMA*, 114).

Another essential principle is that freedom cannot remain purely interiorized; man creates meaning by projecting himself through action into the world of which others are a part: "To wish for there to be being is also to wish for the existence of those by whom and for whom the world is endowed with human meanings" ("Vouloir qu'il y ait de l'être, c'est aussi vouloir qu'il existe des hommes par qui et pour qui le monde soit doué de significations humaines"; *PMA*, 100). An ethics solely of the individual is thus a false notion; human liberty "cannot be accomplished except through others" ("ne peut s'accomplir qu'à travers la liberté d'autrui"; *PMA*, 218). Since each needs for others to be free, oppression and slavery oppress *all*, not just the immediate victims: "To want to be free is also to want others free" ("Se vouloir libre, c'est aussi vouloir les autres libres"; *PMA*, 102). Given that intentions count for nothing—one is only what one does—it is incumbent on human beings to act in accordance with this imperative of general freedom.

To do so, however, one must act *on* others and not just on inert nature. This is the crux of the problem; it means using others as things, objectifying them and thus denying *their* freedom. Such happens in war, for instance: the freedom and indeed the lives of some are sacrificed for a good that is supposed to be general. How, Beauvoir asks, can all freedoms be recognized? To deal with this issue she is obliged to have recourse to the notions of utilitarianism and proportion. Although morality is not quantifiable, since it is founded on an absolute, freedom, she recognizes the principle that action should, as much as possible, take as its end the freedom of human beings, in the greatest number (there being no "general man" that it could serve). This is true even though she denies, in the strict sense, that two men can have a more genuine project than one man, each individual freedom being unique and irreducible. To combat those she calls the enemy of man—those who oppress numbers of others—is legitimate. Thus great collective actions that however violent have as their objective the liberation of collectivities—such as popular uprisings, wars of liberation, and class emancipation—take on exceptional importance, as one would expect from an author who had been strongly influenced by Marxism and by her own experiences under the Occupation. Beauvoir acknowledges violence as built into the human situation and necessary. Yet subordination of the individual to the collectivity in principle is unacceptable: "If the individual is nothing, society cannot be anything" ("Si l'individu n'est rien, la société ne saurait être quelque chose"; *PMA,* 148). She denies the impossibility of using wide-scale injustice as a means toward justice, or founding a democracy on repression.

The question of evil in Beauvoir's framework is particularly interesting. In an ethics based on divine law, evil is clearly defined as disobedience to this law. In Kantian ethics and other humanistic versions that stress *will,* the concept of evil is less clear. If to *will* is to will good for oneself—the only coherent possibility—how, then, can evil arise except as some sort of error? This view clearly fails to explain what would seem to be *willed* evil. For Beauvoir the problem does not exist, because she sees freedom as a negative, not a positive principle, and thus does not have to assume it as directed necessarily toward the good. Only when it affirms itself as a value, in authenticity—that is, when human beings choose freely to recognize their ambiguous condition and accept its imperative of freedom—is there ethical coherence. Not to acknowledge freedom for oneself and others is to live in bad faith, or existentialist evil. This evil can be directed at oneself alone (a type of masochism), as with numerous characters in Beauvoir's imaginative works. Or it can be directed, subtly or overtly, at others (a type of sadism), whether a lover, a family member, or, on a vast scale, a whole class or group that one seeks to reduce to slavery.

Various types of bad faith are identified in Beauvoir's essay. They include the "serious" man, who believes in ready-made values and alienates to them his freedom and others'; most women, who alienate their freedom, usually to a man, whether naively or from cowardice; the adventurer, who denies responsibilities toward others while living out *his* freedom;[10] the sub-man, who consciously abdicates his project and vitality in favor of fear and inertia; and, at the extreme, nihilism. Strangely, the spirit of seriousness and nihilism meet, as Nazism showed; both are a refusal of the potentiality and obligations of human freedom. Opposed to these types of inauthenticity is the creative artist, to whom each work is ontologically and aesthetically whole and justifies itself, transcending the artist, yet who recognizes that his total artistic project is never complete, always *à venir,* to be pursued. Similarly, the scientist experiences freedom by devoting himself to an always-incomplete project of knowledge. Both are to be distinguished from the aesthete, who takes as an absolute value beauty or knowledge or the past (like Laurence's father in *Les Belles Images*) and uses it to escape from the burden of freedom and responsibility toward others.

Another positive example is the person who takes others' good as his aim on a concrete plane, acting toward others in such a way that both the immediate and the long-term welfare of the person are considered in proper proportion. Here, Beauvoir's ethics joins Christian and Kantian morality to the degree that others' welfare becomes an aim, but the absolute religious good is missing: "The welfare of an individual or a group of individuals deserves being taken as an absolute aim of our action; but we are not authorized to decide on this good *a priori*" ("Le bien d'un individu ou d'un groupe d'individus mérite d'être pris comme un but absolu de notre action; mais nous ne sommes pas autorisés à décider à priori de ce bien"; *PMA,* 198). Each case must be decided on individual grounds, without a general principle of authority. The consequence is tension and, in Beauvoir's terms, inescapable ambiguity.

Beauvoir concludes her ethics by arguing that it is a philosophy of the individual—granting an absolute value to each human being—but is not a solipsistic one, since each freedom must transcend itself toward others. It is thus not escapism but a courageous confrontation of the human condition, and it is not pessimistic but optimistic, positing freedom to act for the good. In her later evaluation (1963) of *Pour une morale de l'ambiguïté,* the author was very severe toward the work, which in her view was permeated by a bourgeois idealism of which she had not yet rid her work. Her judgment is itself suspect, however, distorted by her obsession with social and political inequities and by her increasing dislike of the French middle class. Criticizing the arbitrariness and abstractions of some of the arguments and portraits, she blames herself in particular for having attempted, by means of arguments founded on ontology, to show *why* one should act for others' freedom, instead of having stated baldly that the oppressed must be freed. She overlooks the obvious fact that simply to call for justice for the oppressed is not enough; significant progress must be based on new understandings of the human situation. To that end, philosophers can contribute immeasurably.

The essay is thus not so weak as she believed. It shares with Sartre's writing an intensity and sense of commitment that invite the reader's collaboration. It is a useful summary of, and can serve as an introduction to, atheistic existentialist ethics prior to Sartre's adoption and revision of dialectical materialism in *Critique de la raison dialectique* (1960); it also sheds light on Beauvoir's imaginative writing of the 1940s and later. The question of its originality arises inevitably, and insolubly. Sartre certainly did not write Beauvoir's books for her. Moreover, as she observed, she would have become a writer even had she not met him. She might very well have written much in the same vein, for her philosophical training was similar to his, and her situation, as a rebellious and atheistic daughter of the bourgeoisie, one imbued with idealism and reluctant to acknowledge historical pressures but ultimately having to do so, would have been identical. One must believe, however, that his encyclopedic mind seconded hers, that he contributed points of view as well as vocabulary, that their discussions allowed her to work out a number of her ideas as well as share his, and that her work was the richer for his intellectual presence.

Collected Essays

Two other volumes of this period consist of articles first published in *Les Temps modernes*.[11] The four essays in *L'Existentialisme et la sagesse des nations* (1948; Existentialism and traditional wisdom), all concerned with contemporary issues, draw on the existentialist vocabulary that Beauvoir, with Sartre and others, was then helping to elaborate; they thus furnish a mirror of the period that will doubtless be valuable to future cultural historians. Many of their points are still highly pertinent in the last years of the twentieth century.

The title essay is a defense of existentialist philosophy against its critics, who attack its pessimism, subjectivism, and *misérabilisme*. Surveying their objections, Beauvoir finds them wanting. Pessimism, she argues, is not new: a Christian variety—represented by Pascal in the intellectual tradition and, in practice, by clerical attitudes—has for centuries emphasized human *misère* (depravity) and weaknesses, as has a social type, expressed by La Rochefoucauld, who contended that the universal motive of behavior is self-interest. Age-old wisdom holds that "man is a mechanism whose essential motives are self-interest and lust" ("L'homme est une mécanique dont l'intérêt et la luxure sont les ressorts essentiels").[12] This mechanistic view of action, denying freedom, exists concurrently with a popular humanistic idealism that stresses human goodness and the reality of abstract virtues. Yet in fact people resist both pessimism and idealism, the pessimist acting as if life were good (having friends, children, and so on), the idealist carefully hedging his bets with a dose of skepticism. In practice, then, people adopt an ethics of mediocrity that is barely moral, since instead of representing choice and affirmation it constitutes a denial of possibilities; they expect little and ask chiefly not to get involved. Beauvoir points to the incoherence of these positions, which people manipulate for their own purposes and refuse to synthesize.

In contrast, existentialism demands responsibility in the face of freedom and risks. Rejecting the essentialist (or, as Beauvoir calls it, immanent) view that man is either depraved or innocent and that values are already given, it says that man *is* nothing and is free to go beyond his situation. Even the separation of consciousnesses, emphasized by all pessimistic moralists in the form of the failure of love and friendship, can be surpassed. Nothing is more optimistic, proclaims Beauvoir, than to assert that human beings are masters of their destiny. But this morality is disquieting because it stresses responsibility, whereas a deterministic moral view encourages people to believe they can do nothing to modify the world. If this is so, all is vanity, as Ecclesiastes says, and the only logical position is passive resignation or hedonism. Beauvoir argues, to the contrary, that virtue is neither easy, as the essentialists have it, nor impossible, but possible and difficult. Existentialism, a realistic philosophy, is intended to help people assume their human condition, in which morality must be conquered.

The central concern of "Idéalisme moral et réalisme politique" is the relationship between morality and politics. It argues against both conservative idealism, which, as the author notes, is represented in literature by Antigone and is characteristic of the French bourgeoisie, and realism, characterized by expediency and represented by Creon. Idealistic morality, which emphasizes justice, truth, and so forth, is rejected, again on the grounds that it is impossible to derive from general moral principles—a legacy of Kant—any specific application of them. All actions risk violating universal imperatives, whereas none can be shown unequivocally to carry them out, whence the temptation (again, displayed by Laurence's father) to refrain from action.

The political realist rejects idealism on the grounds that it never achieves its goals; justice does not yet exist, good has no universal definition, and the golden age, which is the extreme form assumed by such idealism, is as distant as ever. The political realist points instead to the reality of his achievements, concrete and visible, which he takes to be desirable in themselves. But as Beauvoir correctly observes, this desirability is a function of an *idea* of how things should be; the realist thus joins the idealist. Believing that the goal exists by itself, in advance, beyond human beings, and that they have simply to *move* toward it, the realist becomes purely a technocrat, ready to sacrifice the meaningless present to the goal, and hence adopts an extreme policy of expediency, to the point where sacrificing a million lives is nothing.

In short, neither the idealist nor the realist has a just view of the relationship between action and the future. That even its adherents sense the sterility of idealistic morality is indicated, argues Beauvoir, by their vague sense of a dialectical relationship between unjust means and a just end. The idealists' opponents, the realists, make this relationship the cornerstone of their ethics by arguing that the end always justifies the means. Beauvoir agrees with neither; rather, she stresses the synthetic relationship between end and means, which form a single process. She writes, "The end is part of the means by which it is actualized" ("La fin est solidaire du moyen par lequel elle s'actualise"; *ESN,* 72). To be pessimistic about what is possible is as false as to be utopistic. While mindless optimism, such as that of French pacifists in the 1930s, is destructive, to believe things possible or impossible may be part of the movement that makes them so. Present attitudes, in short, help to *forge* reality: "Awareness is commitment, adhesion, or refusal" ("La prise de conscience . . . est engagement, adhésion ou refus"; *ESN,* 63). Morality is not a system of preestablished rules; Beauvoir notes that great moralists have not docilely followed a code of behavior but rather created a new world of values. Neither wholly subjective nor wholly objective, morality consists of choosing within a situation a totality of means and ends. It will always involve "scandal," that is, some violation of a principle: one cannot, for instance, free captives without doing violence to their captors and thus denying the latter's freedom, perhaps radically. But this "scandal" helps create a totality of human meaning.

In "Littérature et métaphysique" the author is concerned with defending the metaphysical novel against its critics, who suppose that it is a lifeless, intellectual construction, characterized by obvious theses and precepts that belong only in a treatise. Beauvoir argues that, properly conceived, such a novel is the supreme accomplishment of fiction.

Metaphysics as she defines it is not some detached, fleshless speculation; instead, it is an attitude that consists of "placing oneself in one's totality in confrontation with the totality of the world" ("se poser dans sa totalité en face de la totalité du monde"; *ESN, 99*). Metaphysics is thus experiential, like psychological and social experience. The property of fiction is precisely to provide experience, doing so with the same opacity and ambiguity the reader confronts in his own life but in such a way as to widen perspective and deepen insight.

Such a work is entirely different, Beauvoir asserts, from a novel conceived as an exemplum, for the express purpose of illustrating theses. In that case, the sense of adventure—that is, the moral freedom, the unforeseeable that are the mark of real human action—is lost; the reader even senses that the work derives from a formula or didactic purpose, not from a genuine creative experience. The *roman à thèse* and *pièce à thèse* are inferior not because they deal with meaning—all literature signifies something, if only its own refusal to point beyond itself—but because this meaning is *imposed* by the author by manipulation of characters and situation or simply added on. Instead, it is the reader who should draw conclusions from the story, in the course of living an experiential adventure.

In this connection Beauvoir brings up the topic of the so-called freedom of characters. She deals with the problem more efficiently and clearly than Sartre, who treated it in *Qu'est-ce que la littérature?* No one wishes to claim, she observes, that characters dictate their behavior to the writer. But the authentic novelist creates existential situations so fraught with the freedom and the risks of life that their trajectory brings him to confront experience anew, deepen his own understanding, and make metaphysical and psychological discoveries that carry him beyond the original point of departure; these lend to the characters a density, an independence to which the reader is sensitive.

To those who continue to resist the idea of philosophy in literature, assuming that philosophy cannot lend itself to the concrete experience that is the stuff of drama and fiction, Beauvoir proposes the example of psychology. Although for roughly a century the latter has been recognized as a separate science, no one claims that novels should henceforth avoid psychology, leaving it only to specialists. To put Freud and Bergson into fictionalized form would indeed be absurd; however, they have not exhausted the discoveries to be made, and in any case their scientific explanations cannot take the place of literary experience. To write, by appealing to the imagination, of the human heart and mind in their self-reflection and self-deception, from the depths of experience, can allow an author to be as creative a psychologist as Freud.

That it is possible to create a fiction that represents an authentic imaginary experience and in so doing conveys a genuine metaphysical vision is demonstrated by the works of Dostoevsky, Kafka, and Proust—three writers whose works Beauvoir deemed powerfully totalizing. It is also demonstrated by philosophers such as Plato and Kierkegaard, who have recourse to myths or other inventions; even Hegel used myth. Beauvoir stresses that, the more philosophers are concerned with subjectivity, the more likely they are to tend toward the imaginary and the more confluent their vision will be with that of novelists; those who create great abstract systems concerned only with objective reality, such as Spinoza and Kant, are ill suited to fiction. Since existentialism is a philosophy of subjectivity and concrete experience, it is no wonder that Beauvoir considers the imaginative enterprise to be as crucial for modern philosophers as their other writing.

"Œil pour œil" is one of the author's most lucid essays.[13] Reflecting the moral issues of the *épuration* (punishment of collaborators at the end of World War II), it goes beyond the specific instances to consider in broad terms the issues of vengeance, punishment, and justice. Beauvoir's trenchant prose goes directly to the core of each problem. Here, as in her other writings, true evil consists in denying others' freedom. She observes that the liberal intellectuals for whom she speaks would not denounce a common criminal, because, in their view, thefts, even murders, spring from the injustices of a society that does not afford equal opportunity to all; political crimes, such as those committed by collaborators, are another matter, as are Nazi atrocities.

Personal and social attitudes adopted toward such crimes are generally inadequate. A possible exception is the case of victims of torture and other inhumane treatment who kill their torturers in a direct and immediate act of vengeance, as occurred in a few concentration camps when the camps were liberated. These persons' act was identical to their aim: make the torturer undergo *in his current identity* the reduction of the self to *thing* and, momentarily at least, comprehend in his flesh the objectivity of his being, which he had denied by imposing his project by force. No intermediary is involved, and no abstraction: the sadist lives in his flesh the sadism he has inflicted on others. Even here, however, vengeance is not entirely fulfilled, since one would wish to *force* the sadist *freely* to recognize his own objectivity; such a contradictory recognition cannot be prolonged.

Most other retributions, whether individual or collective, are mediated, and the farther they are from the concrete act, the more they risk miscarrying. During the first days after the liberation of Paris, many were victims of undeserved individual or gang violence. Even the liquidation of genuine collaborators by individual acts of vengeance is philosophically unsatisfying, since there is distance between the concrete acts and the executor, who acts as mediator to avenge others. This action implies judgment more than revenge, and his motives may be suspect. Similarly, random acts of violence inspired by political hatred do not reach those they are intended to punish. What, then, of organized retribution, through the judicial system? The trials of high-placed figures such as Pétain and Laval revealed the inadequacy of justice, which, unlike acts of vengeance and hatred, operates on the symbolic plane. Pétain's commuted death sentence showed that the court felt obliged to distinguish between the traitor, whose death would express the nation's refusal of the evil for which he stood, and an old man who had never understood well the consequences of his actions and who in any case was now *beyond* his act. Moreover, rather than reinforcing the existential meaning of the punishment, striking at the heart of the evil, the elaborate legal proceedings created a ceremonial that added to the distance between the crime and the criminal and, as it were, placed the issue on the abstract plane, removed from the hatred of the evil and from its concrete outcome, punishment.

Similarly, the death sentence of the writer Robert Brasillach, editor of the collaborationist *Je suis partout,* was both satisfying and dissatisfying. Beauvoir, who attended his trial, saw how the accused seemed no longer identifiable with his acts of treason. Bearing himself with dignity, he appeared divorced from the evils represented by his newspaper. Moreover, he had never personally killed or tortured anyone. Yet Beauvoir refused to sign the petition for Brasillach's pardon, on the grounds that there is identity between the self and its acts—especially because, in this case, it was clear that a whole body of attitudes Brasillach had freely adopted in the 1930s had led to his collaborationist stance. The fact remains that only the image of evil was touched by his execution. Yet Beauvoir deems the punishment, like that of Pétain, Laval, and many others, justified in the name of a certain notion of society and justice for which the French struggled during and after the war: "Their crimes reached to our hearts; it is our values, our reasons for being that are affirmed by their punishment" ("Leurs crimes nous avaient atteints au cœur de nous-mêmes; ce sont nos valeurs, nos raisons de vivre qui s'affirment par leur châtiment"; *ESN*, 111).

Punishment is pursued not for realistic motives (to prevent future crimes) but through a need for asserting moral values, through those who have denied them. It is legitimate where there is solidarity between the individual and his actions. As the Allies sensed after the war, wide-scale chastisement of nations and peoples is inappropriate. Beauvoir is aware of the objections that can be made to her positions. An existentialist can argue that no one should be identified totally with a single act, since one is always beyond the act and may regret it; even so, it is the whole person that is penalized. A Christian can observe that judgment and vengeance are both inappropriate, because all human beings are wrongdoers and repentance is always possible. To the latter objection Beauvoir answers that forgiveness belongs to the divine, not the human, plane of values; to the former, that a person must be identified with his acts, since there is nothing else with which to identify him. She concludes that, despite its inevitable share of failure and ambiguity, punishment must be meted out and—contrary to sociologists' claims—with as little abstraction and impersonality as possible: "Punishment must be connected to the crime by concrete relationships" ("Il faut que la punition soit rattachée à la faute par des liens concrets"; *ESN*, 141), without tyranny, as an expression of a concrete will.

Although Beauvoir asserts in the preface to *Privilèges* (1955; republished as *Faut-il brûler Sade?*, partially translated as *Must We Burn Sade?*) that the three essays are connected by the theme of the "privileged," that is, the politically or socially dominant, they have little in common. The first essay, concerned with the Marquis de Sade, has attracted more attention than its companions. While not the first to rehabilitate the "divine Marquis" in this century—Apollinaire was an early defender, and there had been important critical essays by Pierre Klossowski and Maurice Heine, among others—Beauvoir was, in her generation, the best known of those who sought to explain Sade, rather than condemn him. Her thesis is that he is a great moralist, in the sense proposed in "Idéalisme moral et réalisme politique," that is, someone whose mode of existence is the ethical. The paradox involved in making this great immoralist into a moralist does not disturb her; after all, Sartre had called the homosexual convict Jean Genet a "saint."

Seeking a key to Sade's sexuality, Beauvoir concludes that his relationship with his mother is unknown and cannot serve as evidence. A nod is given to Freudian psychology in the identification between avarice and anality; she also identifies intercourse with anger in his case. But it is less the psychology of the individual Sade that interests Beauvoir than its implication, for sexuality is social, always going beyond the self to implicate others. For Beauvoir, Sade's perversions are a direct reflection of his status as an aristocrat in the late eighteenth century, when his caste had lost its function, undermined by bourgeois ideology. He was right, she argues, to reject this society, in which inequity persisted, and its foundations. Disdaining the central thesis of the Enlightenment philosophers that nature is wholesome and that morality consists in following the natural order (as opposed to divine law), Sade, like Hobbes, sees nature as violent and, more crucially, indifferent: man can do nothing to violate it. Contrary to Rousseau, he finds no human relationships inscribed in nature; men are solitary. Seeing no solution to this abandon, he concludes that man's constructs must be in the realm of the imaginary, even if, in true eighteenth-century fashion, they deal with the senses. Individual ideals of goodness and charity, no matter what their origin, are pernicious (hence Sade's appeal to Nietzsche); they are a way of promoting the agent (as when one takes pride in one's generosity) and of giving certification to false relationships; similarly, collective morality is an imposition for which there is no justification.

The solution is to rebel against morality. One way Sade did so was to embrace the republic and its leveling of classes (designed to create new relationships between human beings); however, it, like the previous regime, imprisoned him, recognizing in him a dangerous individualist. Another way was to assume self-gratification as the only value, through domination of other selves. For this purpose, the surest means are crime and cruelty, since unhappiness is always more certain than happiness, pain than pleasure. Whether this pain is exercised on others, as in the perversion that bears Sade's name, or on oneself—for Beauvoir correctly detects a type of masochism in him—it involves an identification between self and other whereby there is an exchange of subjects; one experiences through the other but always in order to dominate.

It is easy to recognize in Beauvoir's analysis the existentialist vantage point. Sade's pursuit of hedonistic sensualism, including writing about it, can be seen as his project—his way of being—assumed in the absence of authentic human relationships—the equivalent of torture in the twentieth century. What he lacks is the ability to conceive of projects that would *join* human beings, thus allowing them to overcome their solitude and simultaneously eliminating the need to subject the other: "The fact is that the only sure bonds among men are those that they create by transcending themselves in a common world by common projects" ("Le fait est que les seuls liens sûrs entre les hommes sont ceux qu'ils créent en se transcendant dans un monde commun par des projets communs").[14]

"La Pensée de droite, aujourd'hui" (Right-wing thinking today) is a lengthy attack on rightist, chiefly bourgeois, ideology. While acknowledging that the latter is not monolithic and indeed invokes plurality, Beauvoir, who is as much a dichotomizer as any right-wing thinker she attacks, reduces it to a single position; anticommunism. This solely negative description implies that there is no real conservative ideology, only reactions to the Bolshevik threat. At the extreme, anticommunism turns for its justification to various totalizing philosophies of history that have in common the denial of freedom and the deification of an abstract history—a right-wing version of Marxist determinism. Such, Beauvoir claims, are the systems of Oswald Spengler, to whom she refers frequently; Karl Jaspers; Arnold Toynbee; the novelist Drieu La Rochelle; and many lesser figures, and such are the systems of fascist totalitarianism. Indeed, according to Beauvoir's logic, all conservatism tends toward fascism. This point is demonstrated, she argues, not only by countless ideological examples and the rise of modern fascism but by the reactions of right-wing thinkers to the defeat of German and Italian fascism in 1945; aware of the bankruptcy of the only political system that is consistent with their positions—that is, aware of their defeat— they lugubriously announce the death of civilization (*their* civilization, that is) and a definitive cataclysm.

All the Western nations on both sides of the Atlantic are, according to Beauvoir, perpetrators of this pessimistic philosophy, which denies that human progress is possible and which ends in *ataraxie,* historical immobility. Yet this philosophy does not imply inaction in the present: conservative thought holds that above the common man, whose life is meaningless, presides a cultural elite (not the same as an intellectual elite, for conservatism is suspicious of the intelligentsia), whose mission is to preserve transcendent values—abstractions inscribed in the universe. These are distinguished by their lack of concreteness; they consist, if one accepts Beauvoir's argument, in a vague harmony between history and some cosmic truth. Concrete values, particularly science and language—which are connected to the human search for control over the universe, on the one hand, and communication with one's fellows, on the other—are, to the Right, particularly anathema.

Beauvoir's critique of the Right is patently crude from the intellectual point of view. In addition to overlooking the contradictions within socialism, holding it up as the sole model for human social progress, she ignores the distinctions to be made in non-Marxist ideology, particularly the liberal strain of American political thought that goes back to Jefferson, and the accomplishments of Jeffersonian democracy in its modern form. She groups thinkers such as Léon Werth—for whom Saint-Exupéry wrote *Lettre à un otage*—and Raymond Aron—a former friend who fell from favor because of his preference for American democracy over Stalinism—with such professed fascists as Drieu La Rochelle and other members of what in English-speaking nations is called the lunatic fringe, and writes as if Spengler's *The Decline of the West* were the foundation of all postwar thinking in the Occident.

Similar hostility to thinkers who do not share her positions reappears in the last essay, "Merleau-Ponty et le pseudo-sartrisme." This piece is a defense of Sartre's thought against the interpretation given it by Merleau-Ponty in *Les Aventures de la dialectique*. In the context of the Korean War, the latter had revised his positions with respect to Marxism and the Communist bloc and had come out in favor of Western democracy as a political ideology and system. Reading Sartre's "Les Communistes et la paix" ("The Communists and Peace") in light of his new positions, Merleau-Ponty thought he discovered there deep contradictions in Sartre's positions and the implied failure of Marxist dialectics. Sartrean thinking, he argued, is characterized by a total subjectivism that renders impossible any genuine social project.

Only those who know Sartre's ontology and political thought alike will be entirely comfortable with Beauvoir's essay; still, she makes numerous points that are comprehensible to all familiar with political theory. She accuses her erstwhile friend of willful distortion of Sartre's essay in an effort to discredit the political philosophy he had just rejected. She cites side by side passages from Sartrean texts, then Merleau-Ponty's statements, as evidence of her claim, leaning on *L'Etre et le néant* for Sartrean ideas of consciousness and freedom, and on his more recent political essays. She distinguishes between (a) Sartre's accurate understanding of history and dialectics, in which the proletariat's aspirations are necessarily identified with the Communist party because the latter is defined as the means toward its ends, and (b) Merleau-Ponty's false and utopistic interpretation of Marxism, according to which dialectics is an exterior historical force descending as if by miracle. It is, she argues against Merleau-Ponty, not Sartre who errs by abstractionism but his adversary. Nor does Sartre believe in the failure of the revolution: his political commitment is positive and concrete, one in which action and consciousness are identical.

Sartre's adversary, on the other hand, disappointed with the failure of Communist revolution to change society totally, irked by its recourse to means that imply limited ends, and particularly annoyed by the reemergence of elites in Communist societies, opts—erroneously, in Beauvoir's view—for change by parliamentary means. She argues that this stance is tantamount to embracing permanent oppression of the proletariat by the bourgeoisie. Merleau-Ponty's vision of a synthesis of the Communist-capitalistic conflict is, for Beauvoir, pure fantasy—a judgment that does not surprise one acquainted with her political views but instead shows how orthodox and unimaginative they were. For her, the privileged are a caste utterly incapable of conceiving any action beyond the defense of their transcendent values and political power, and class warfare thus remains the central tenet of her political philosophy.

Chapter Six

The Self and Others: Memoirs and Documentary Studies

Le Deuxième Sexe

While apparent chronological divisions in an author's development often only approximately match the underlying personal and aesthetic evolution, the publication of *Le Deuxième Sexe* in 1949 was a principal watershed in Beauvoir's public career and in her development as a writer alike. It is not only that her fame, restricted hitherto to the literary and philosophical world in France and to a lesser degree elsewhere, spread widely as she became one of the most quoted, most translated, most admired, and most vilified women writers in the world; she herself was changed by this undertaking, and, while the effects of the change made themselves felt only gradually, she was never henceforth only the writer who was also a woman, but an author and a thinker conscious of the problematizing of herself. After 1949, her fiction began to reflect more broadly feminine concerns, though of course from the beginning women had played central roles in her novels and stories, and there is no radical break between the earlier and later fiction and essays. *Le Deuxième Sexe* was inspired by Beauvoir's interest in her own experience; it would, moreover, lead her back to herself as explicit subject, in her first memoirs, published in 1958. They were followed by others, plus three associated texts, all of which have many concerns in common: the account of her mother's death, as she witnessed it; a sociological study on aging, published when she herself was in her sixties; and a documentary portrait of Sartre's last years.

In a sense, the origins of *Le Deuxième Sexe,* which is a massive monograph of several hundred pages, go back to the author's adolescence, when her coming to terms with herself meant coming to terms with her situation as a woman. Her concern as an adult with thinking her life as much as living it was necessarily connected with her sexual identity. Although that identity had not been a serious impediment to her personally and thus had remained secondary, an increased awareness of its significance developed after 1945. When Sartre pointed out that, despite the common intellectual ground between them, her education and experiences had been distinctly different from his and that this difference should be explored, the study that became *Le Deuxième Sexe* was initiated (*FC,* 109).[1] Begun in 1946, it was finished and published three years later. Beauvoir thought of calling it "L'Autre," a term that would have drawn attention better to the crucial argument of the work: that, to men, woman is always "the other"—the relative, the inessential—and that men acquire self-identity through opposition to this otherness. It was Jacques Bost, to whom the book is dedicated, who proposed the definitive title. The work thus can be said to have two *parrains,* or godfathers.

Some 22,000 copies of the first volume sold in a week; it was favorably reviewed by critics. The second volume, published several months later, caused an uproar; another chapter in the *querelle des femmes,* or argument about women, which dated from the Middle Ages, had been opened. Many male reviewers treated the volume caustically or with hostility. Sometimes the burden of their remarks was that the author was either frigid or a sexual pervert; Mauriac uncharitably made a vulgar, demeaning comment about her (*FC,* 205). In other cases, the reviewers confessed their discomfiture at feeling that their male prerogatives of both situation and sexual definition were threatened by the study's implications. The study was widely declared to be distorted or false, and the spirit in which it was written dangerous.[2] In other quarters, however, the book was praised, and it quickly found audiences in France and elsewhere. It has been noted that since that date, Beauvoir has been, to thousands of readers and thousands more who know her name only, preeminently the author of *Le Deuxième Sexe.* Current feminists have many quarrels with the study but continue to recognize it as pioneering.

Unlike a strictly biological or historical investigation, the work, while generally pretending to be objective, is prescriptive as well as descriptive, since woven into the expository passages concerning women's circumstances, past and present, and the way men have viewed them are judgments on these circumstances and a vast number of arguments adduced in opposition to prevailing views. In short, the study is polemical, a plea for a totally changed view of women. The author put into the work many glimpses of herself and of women she knew, who remain anonymous, of course.

Paradoxically, the work may strike the present-day reader as curiously out of date even for its time; it has certainly become so by now. Some would argue that feminism itself has evolved to the point where Beauvoir's depiction and its underlying assumptions must be rejected. Others could observe that many of the changes in attitude, behavior, and legislation that the work called for, explicitly or implicitly, have been made and have become such a part of Western society that the analyses pertaining to the 1940s are no longer applicable. But Beauvoir's analyses are also marked by the very prejudices, presuppositions, and essentialism that the study undertook to combat. She writes, for instance, "Scandinavian women are healthy, robust, and cold. Passionate women are those who reconcile langor and fire, such as Italian or Spanish women" ("Les Scandinaves sont saines, robustes et froides. Les femmes 'à tempérament' sont celles qui concilient la langueur et le 'feu,' comme les Italiennes ou les Espagnoles"; *DS,* 2:139). Women are said to have physiologically less nervous control than men and to have an affinity with water (*DS,* 2:434, 436). The attitudes of men are assumed to be a homogeneous block, and Beauvoir appears to consider them all guilty for the sins of their forefathers as well as their own. The social changes wrought by World War II are scarcely acknowledged; the wearing of slacks is referred to as a rare oddity.

Moreover, careless use of data leads the author to dubious conclusions and oversimplifications. She often relies on so-called scientific studies by those who specialize in pathological cases and by those (often the same ones) who accept without question the principles of Freudian psychoanalysis. Thus Beauvoir leans on Wilhelm Stekel's *Frigidity in Woman in Relation to Her Love Life* (1929), agreeing with him that all girls are characterized by ridiculous sexual fears (*DS,* 2:142). In other cases, she relies on hearsay and generalizes from one or two examples; this is true notably when she adduces examples of American women. Elsewhere, she is simply wrong, as many female readers—and many male—must have realized. Perhaps the greatest weakness of all is that Beauvoir's study is as culturally conditioned as the images she is combating; many present-day readers would simply refuse to identify themselves with the women portrayed as representative in the course of Beauvoir's analysis, and hence would hardly embrace without caution her generalizations. Such flaws should not lead one to suppose that the entire study is invalid, although they do create in the reader's mind more than a little skepticism. The work makes many valid points, and the evidence amassed is often persuasive.

The study is explicitly grounded in existentialism, emphasizing action, projects, and freedom—the original freedom of all human beings but also its cultural conditioning. The study supposes that women, like men, are what they *do:* "Every subject posits itself concretely through projects as a transcendence" ("Tout sujet se pose concrètement à travers des projets comme une transcendance"; *DS,* 1:31). With respect to psychoanalysis, Beauvoir rejects its dogmatic insistence on universal and irreducible eroticism, preferring to see the erotic as only one element among others composing woman's total situation. Instead of accepting, for instance, the psychoanalytic explanation of why women marry men who resemble their fathers—namely, that they are in love with their father—she argues that since the father has been, from the daughter's earliest age, endowed with the superiority of the male, women seek men who similarly represent this same structure of superiority. As for Marxism, while certain of its principles are taken for granted, the economic monism of Marxism is explicitly rejected as invalid for an accurate picture of women's situation.

Beauvoir's central thesis is based on the distinction between biological fact and what is made of it. While *female* refers to features of anatomy and physiology, the idea of *woman* is a cultural one, derived from and dependent on how men have seen women and how the latter have lived their crucial relationship with the dominant sex. Beauvoir had shown in her novels and philosophical essays that a situation is never just an individual matter; all human beings construct their selves in a social context. Women are, in short, the product of the sum of how they have been seen and how they have defined themselves on the basis of this image. Beauvoir is thus led to survey at length past and present images of women and their resulting situation.

The first part of the work, "Les Faits et les mythes" ("Facts and Myths"), attempts to circumscribe the biological and historical facts defining women and the myths by which these facts have been variously explained, denied, transformed, sanctified, and so forth. The myths are male-dominated but generally accepted by women themselves in a process of interiorization; half victims and half accomplices, as Sartre put it, they have allowed their justification to come at the hands of "the other": "This fall is a moral error if the subject consents to it" ("Cette chute est une faute morale si elle est consentie par le sujet"; *DS,* 1:31). The second part of the study, "L'Expérience vécue" ("lived experience," or, as the English translation has it, "Woman's Life Today"), is a sociological and psychological survey of the experience of girls and women at midcentury. It focuses chiefly on France and the United States, where Beauvoir had become interested in the situation of women during her travels. Indeed, her knowledge of English and the fact that surveys on job opportunities, sexual experience, social attitudes, and so on were then much more common in North America than in Europe led her to draw heavily on American data.

Both the facts—apart from strictly anatomical and physiological ones—and the myths are, Beauvoir argues, the product of what Gerda Lerner, among others, has called patriarchy.[3] Beauvoir assigns to men primary responsibility for women's situation, while observing repeatedly that women have cooperated in perpetuating it; it is human beings, not nature or some higher principle, that are at its origin: "Historical fact cannot be considered as defining an eternal truth" ("Le fait historique ne saurait être considéré comme définissant une vérité éternelle"; *DS,* 2:558). The historical survey begins with the earliest known organized societies (hunters and gatherers, then those who practiced the first agriculture), in which division of labor between the sexes was developed in connection with food production and other tasks; Beauvoir considers that woman's physiology put her at a disadvantage in this distribution of labor. The author then moves to biblical times and classical antiquity, later to Europe in the Middle Ages and up to the Revolution, and finally to modern times. Except for the recent periods, her precise data concerning the circumstances of women are limited, and much of her evaluation relies on general historical and anthropological information and on older texts (biblical and Greek) whose incompleteness and bias are evident. The survey unavoidably suffers, then, from inadequate historical grounding.

The identification and untangling of an enormous corpus of "myths" surrounding women is an early, and valid, instance of what Beauvoir's compatriot Roland Barthes was later to call "mythologies" and "codes," the vast ensemble of idols, clichés, presuppositions, and classifications that are both cultural markers and framers of thought. Beauvoir looks at literary clichés, archetypal images, traditions in painting, religious tradition, the data of psychology, popular wisdom, and so on to identify male dreams and fears as they are embodied in images of women, both positive and negative. She argues that these images—for example, the stock idea of "femininity"—play a role not just in literature and painting but in reality, since, where the images are positive, women are widely expected and pressed to conform to them, and, where the images are negative (as in the myth of feminine impurity), they mark individuals and the entire sex. Beauvoir challenges in particular the traditional religious assumptions that had colored views of women in France. She also draws evidence from the contribution made by literature to the perpetuation of misunderstandings about women. Her commentaries on the portraits of women and their situation by such authors as Stendhal, Paul Claudel, D. H. Lawrence, and Henri de Montherlant—perhaps the most thoroughgoing mysogynist among major French writers of this century—not only are perspicacious studies of the individual authors but also provide examples of how, according to Beauvoir, woman has been turned into angel or devil, a detestable or adorable, an admirable or fearsome creature whose changeless nature emprisons her in an essence.

Philosophically speaking, these myths are false because they make a *subject* into an *object;* they propose an *essential* and *immanent* nature for a human project that, just like the male project, is always in a state of becoming and transcendence. Beauvoir again rejects the idea of ideal *model* and *given nature:* "For us, woman is defined as a human being in search of values in the midst of a world of values" ("Pour nous la femme se définit comme un être humain en quête de valeurs au sein d'un monde de valeurs"; *DS,* 1:94). For men to make an idol of the second sex is only superficially to honor it; the idol is an object, transcended by its worshiper. Beauvoir could have cited as supporting evidence one of the novels her father had enjoyed, Marcel Prévost's *Les Demi-Vierges* (1894); in that book the high honor in which virginity is held has as its corollary the absolute enslavement of girls, not just their bodies but their minds, so that the male psyche as well as the male body can be their sole master.

It may seem paradoxical for Beauvoir to claim that men are viewed as the transcendent sex, women the immanent one, given the privileged position of the latter as childbearers, whose body transcends itself in the creation of a new being. But she argues that superiority has been granted not to the sex that brings forth new life but to the sex that goes beyond the claims of life, to remake the earth by acts, in what is a sort of imperialism. Women's lot has been *reproduction* and essential values, those of the body and the earth, to which the species remains attached; men's has been *production* and those values which deny the earth, affirming the mind and proclaiming human ability to remake the world and to be *more* than one is.

Concentrating on types of feminine experience and behavior, especially in the twentieth century, the second part of *Le Deuxième Sexe* is based on the antideterministic premise set forth in the previous section, that the feminine is a social construct: one is not born but *becomes* a woman; one is what one makes of one's sex. Yet throughout, the practical absence of choice for women is visible. The result is a contradiction that obliges the author to devote many pages to explaining how, originating from a situation of entire freedom, women are nevertheless forced to behave as if they were not free. It is not just a matter of social roles, although they are very important; in the most fundamental aspects of feminine sexuality, the author identifies complexes that seem close to those identified by deterministic Freudian psychology, although she contends that these complexes derive from the history and myths examined earlier, rather than from inherent structures of the sex.[4]

Beauvoir's treatment of the feminine experience first traces the development of the female human being from childhood through adolescence to young womanhood—stages in the acquisition of a sense of self that is obliged to come to terms with sexual impulses and establish a sexual identification. The author takes to task a number of Freud's disciples for their reductive and monistic views, although, as has been observed, she makes generous use of case studies, including pathological ones. The relationships girls establish with the opposite sex, on the basis of the situation into which they are thrust (basically, the very existence of men, but especially the presence and prestige of male family members, friends, and so on), are crucial. In almost all cases, the individual repeats what has historically been true: men are accepted as subjects to the woman's sense of being object, and value is acknowledged as being assigned by them; the woman interiorizes the judgment of the other.

The roles women can adopt, on the basis of their childhood development and of the whole social situation, include those of lesbian, wife, mother, prostitute, and kept woman, each of which Beauvoir analyzes. In each case, woman is always more than her biological function as a female reproductive being. She either objectifies herself in some manner as an erotic object or, less frequently, refuses to be an erotic object; in either case, she thus acknowledges the power of the myths of the feminine, which demand that the purely physical be transformed. The institution of marriage is the prime example, but not the only one, of the institutional transformation of woman in her function as a sexual partner and childbearer.

With respect to the question of women's freedom, marriage poses particular problems. Marriage is so universalized, and its moral and social value so proclaimed, that women accept it as the course to follow, the only one that will give them value in men's eyes, hence their own. Few choose other paths, and those who do are always regarded by others as inferior, even the spinsters who are excluded from the wedded state by men's choice rather than their own; ordinarily, they tacitly accept this judgment. Marriage, in short, is not an option but a fate. Within the conjugal state itself, choices are again restricted, because, obviously, of the privileged status accorded to the husband, the head of the household, to whom until well into the twentieth century wives were expected by law and by custom to be obedient. But such restriction springs also, Beauvoir says, from the very structure of marriage as it has been molded in both past and present societies. Posed as an end in itself, marriage effectively confines the human project of freedom, which the woman may not recognize clearly in herself but which is nonetheless fundamental.

The result is marital unhappiness and often infidelity. The picture of marriage presented in *Le Deuxième Sexe* resembles that of the popular plays of boulevard theater, with their dissatisfied partners who take refuge in illicit affairs, except that Beauvoir's depiction is unrelieved by comic lightheartedness. Much of the evidence for this portrait is textual, drawn from subjective expressions of unhappiness in letters, diaries, and other forms. Beauvoir cites the example of Tolstoy's wife, utterly miserable in her union with the great man; the example, despite its poignancy, has little representative value. Other illustrations come from statistics of infidelities as established by sociologists and from case studies. In any event, Beauvoir speaks about what she does not know firsthand, and her depiction, while not without elements of truth, betrays her own conditioning by literature and doubtless by the marriages she saw in her parents' world. The procreation of children does little, according to this picture, to redeem marriage and the family, both of which Beauvoir would wish to see redefined to the point where they might be a "pact," like her and Sartre's.

The situation of the woman who takes lovers is scarcely better, sometimes worse, than that of the legitimate spouse. Prostitution, tolerated even in Christian societies, is a state of subjection, perhaps adopted by the woman as the most acceptable alternative but reflecting the absence of genuine choice. Prostitution is especially degrading when the woman is dependent on a pimp. Only kept women and high-class courtesans escape from this subjection of their caste; historically, Beauvoir points out, some of the freest women have been courtesans—for example, Ninon de Lenclos, who had a brilliant salon in the seventeenth century.

One aspect of women's situation that particularly draws Beauvoir's attention is aging. The inevitable physical transformations of the body mean entirely different things to men and women. To the latter, the changes are more sudden and more radical. Some deplore chiefly the loss of childbearing ability, with its implied justification; others feel threatened by declining beauty and seductiveness, on which their self-image depends. Men, on the contrary, in the fullness of middle age are usually (as Beauvoir sees them) at the height of their powers as masters of their world—thinkers, executives, entrepreneurs; their body continues to serve them as an instrument for their goals, and social recognition of their accomplishments presents them with a favorable image of themselves.

The classic question of women's character, a question at the center of countless literary works, songs, and popular lore, must be asked anew in the context of Beauvoir's survey of women's roles. The answer is predictable: character is not a predetermined essence but the product of a situation. Like slaves, colonized peoples, and other oppressed castes, women are traditionally considered to be childlike, in need of discipline and management, idle, inane, devious, competent to perform only routine tasks, and prey to their emotions. Beauvoir contends that the matter is simple: restricted to the situation of a child, domestic servant, or sexual object, women behave accordingly; when the oppression is lifted, they show themselves fully capable of going beyond their behavior, assuming their liberty as men do.

The individual reactions to oppression have generally fallen into a number of patterns, including submission, complicity—a widespread posture, with grave consequences—revolt (often powerless and self-defeating), depression, paranoia, schizophrenia or other mental illness, and three types of self-justification that Beauvoir analyzes: narcissism, passion, and mysticism. While men also can be narcissistic and fall passionately in love, evidence suggests that these forms of self-affirmation are much more widely adopted by women, as is mysticism: of the 321 persons whom the Catholic Church recognizes officially as having borne stigmata, only 47 are men (*DS,* 2:516). With the exception of genuine mysticism, these projects at self-justification normally fail. The woman narcissist cannot *really* love herself as another would; she is in bad faith when she attempts to deny the self-awareness (Sartre's nonreflexive consciousness) that sees through such sham. The woman in love—she who makes of love her sole reason for being and stakes all on a beloved object—is almost always disappointed, not because men are cads but by the very structure of passionate devotion, which would have the partner be both subject and object, god and slave. Even the attempts at artistic self-expression that are frequently found among women of the leisure class are poor means of escape: painting and writing require discipline, prolonged work, commitment, and especially creativity; they are not just vessels into which one can pour one's discontent.

The conclusions Beauvoir draws at the end of her study are far from being entirely somber. Throughout, it has been clear that what has made men superior to women has been primarily not their greater strength or freedom from childbearing and child-nurturing duties but their relationship to *work,* a relationship that is not just passive continuation of the species but *praxis,* an active remaking of what the world proposes. This praxis is open to women also—nothing in the structure of the world makes it uniquely male—and when woman is free to engage in a project that goes beyond herself and her passivity, her situation approaches that of men. She is then able to be a partner, rather than a slave, and the slavish characteristics that had marked her in her immanence and dependence disappear. Beauvoir cites numerous cases of women, even shop girls, who have identified themselves with what they have accomplished. To this end, woman must be allowed economic freedom—the chance to work not just as a pastime or to supplement family income but on an equal footing with men. Like some social thinkers both before and after her, Beauvoir contends that such economic equality cannot be achieved in a capitalist state, since inequality among classes produces conditions under which the freedom of a proletarian woman to find satisfaction in work is only virtual; socialism alone will extend such freedom genuinely to all.

In this context, the relations between the sexes can be redefined on a basis of equality in difference. What will be lost, according to conservatives, is either no loss at all or one that is justified by the gain. The author compares women's status to that of pre–Civil War slaves: their labor was the condition of a way of life whose products did include, for the privileged, a life of ease and refinement among beautiful surroundings, but the human price was too high. As for the so-called mystique of woman that will be lost, opponents say, if she is emancipated, it is a mystification, a hoax. Men have held in their arms women whom they loved greatly, but no one has embraced the eternal feminine. Equality with difference does not mean, Beauvoir argues, that the relations between the sexes will no longer allow for sexual attraction, pleasure, and deep love, for each sex will relate to the other through its own sexual structure, which remains distinct.

Le Deuxième Sexe is an imposing work, affording insight into the situation of women historically and at midcentury, and also—although this aspect is secondary—revealing much of the author herself. Martha Noel Evans has argued that, early in Beauvoir's career, fiction represented for her a feminine pursuit, dealing as it does with emotion and the imaginary, and nonfiction a masculine one.[5] This distinction cannot be accepted without qualification, since it ignores the fact that both are based on language, but it may well be that, with her philosophical training and its emphasis on the rational, Beauvoir valued fiction less highly than the products of reasoning. *Le Deuxième Sexe,* like her philosophical essays, displays Beauvoir's abilities as an expository and polemical writer but does so on a topic that is as feminine as possible. As the synthesis of both intelligence and feeling, it is indirectly a kind of self-portrait. Some critics have even argued that the work contains reflections of the author's very difficult relationships with Sartre and Algren during the years of its composition. Perhaps this is why it has appealed to readers of several persuasions who, whether with ease or with difficulty, have found themselves living the same situation, experiencing in a woman's body the aspirations toward freedom and achievement that Beauvoir argues have been the prerogatives of the other sex.

The book has been so influential, especially on American feminists, that its points have become truisms. Some subsequent students of the topic contend that Beauvoir was too timid in her claims and her calls for change. It has been fashionable recently to reproach her with taking as a standard those values, such as action and freedom, which have been embodied by the very sex that has subjugated women; Beauvoir's supposition that "the masculine is the absolute human type," as Appignanesi puts it (3), overlooks the essential difference of the sexes and downgrades what is peculiarly feminine. Mary Evans is one of several critics who see in Beauvoir's writing not a model for a genuine liberation of women but a surrender to male power and male values, attitudes, and patterns of thought (xi).

It is true that the uniquely feminine functions of childbearing and associated nurturing tasks are seen, in *Le Deuxième Sexe*, as an impediment, historically and currently, as women aspire and begin to achieve the right to pursue lives outside the home. Furthermore, the author herself certainly considered such functions to be obstacles to her own self-fulfillment as a writer. And her work can make no special place in the moral sphere for what is characteristically feminine, because she considers these attributes the sign of passivity, relativity, and inferiority. It has been left to French women writers of a later generation, such as Marie Cardinal, Hélène Cixous, and Monique Wittig, to identify and reclaim a domain that is feminine and then attempt to find, as Cardinal put it in the title of her best-known book, "les mots pour le dire" (the words to say it). It can be argued, however, that by their extremism these later writers have separated women from their psyches more than male domination has done: few want to recognize themselves in the physical illness, hysteria, schizophrenia, and lesbianism that either mark these writers or represent for them the rejection of male values and institutions, such as the family, that are said to embody such values.

The Memoirs

To many readers, the volumes in which Beauvoir speaks directly of herself, in the personal mode, are the most appealing. Translated into numerous languages, the four volumes of her memoirs have from the beginning attracted a large audience; in the decades to come they could easily prove to be among the works by which she will be best known. Only the first is categorized generically, through its title, *Mémoires d'une jeune fille rangée* (1958); the others bear no generic indication. Commentators habitually refer to the series as Beauvoir's autobiography; she herself usually called these works her memoirs.[6] Not all critics recognize a difference; James Olney, for instance, construes the term *autobiography* so loosely that it can include many forms of personal expression, such as Montaigne's *Essais* and T. S. Eliot's *Four Quartets*.[7]

It is useful, however, to draw some distinctions. Wide variations in autobiographical writing, from Saint Augustine's *Confessions* to Alain Robbe-Grillet's *Le Miroir qui revient* (*Ghosts in the Mirror*), to take a recent French example, need not obscure the common purpose of true autobiographies: not just to recount a life but to illuminate it.[8] By that is meant identifying and scrutinizing those elements which shape a destiny and thereby plumbing the meaning of the self in its temporal trajectory. An autobiography may thus be legitimately restricted to the early, formative years, as is the case with Gide's *Si le grain ne meurt* (*If It Die*) and Sartre's *Les Mots* (*The Words*). These works concentrate on what existential psychology calls original choice—the free assumption by a subject of a destiny that shapes the future. Or the autobiography may aim at comprehensiveness through the author's maturity. The point is that the linguistic process of verbalizing by small units (words and sentences) and larger units (paragraphs, sections) becomes the means of, and is one with, the writer's project of self-understanding; the self is "inscribed" in the text, thereby attaining a new reality that both reproduces and extends the self. The narrating of experiences is a major element of this *prise de conscience* but is not the only one; other types of discourse, such as sociological and psychological analyses or introspective reflection that can become poetic, even oneiric, can function as self-revelation.

In contrast, the term *memoirs* can usefully be applied to a text, primarily narrative, whose purpose is to recount the subject's experiences and associated events but to do so without subordinating these to the search for, or portrait of, an inner self. In other words, memoirs are principally the record of what happened to and around the self, not the interpretation of the self. Some memoirs are more personal than others; even when they largely treat events of public scope and thus tend toward history, the personality of the writer, if powerful, can make itself felt through the narrative: such is the case with the memoirs of Charles de Gaulle and those of André Malraux, whose title (*Antimémoires*) disclaims any traditional purpose. In fact, the distinction proposed here between autobiography and memoirs indicates tendencies more than firm categories, the parameters remaining flexible.

According to this distinction, Beauvoir's records of the self should be classified as memoirs. As Mary Evans has observed (114), they are documentary rather than interpretative. The first volume comes closer than the others to being a true autobiography. Beauvoir stated that her aim had been to resuscitate the girl lost in the depths of time, to make her exist on paper, thus answering an appeal from the past, made by the person she had been to the person she would become (*FA*, 9). Through a temporal narrative, she proposed to elucidate a freedom becoming cognizant of itself and, paradoxically, to eliminate the effects of time by identifying the unity of the self through its multiplicity, of which Marguerite Yourcenar has said, "Unus ego et multi in me."[9]

Confined to her childhood and youth, including her university studies, Beauvoir's first volume of memoirs explores this period in function
of a certain self seeking its explanation in the past, especially—as in the
corresponding texts by Gide and Sartre—the explanation of her intellectual and artistic vocation. She writes, for instance, speaking of the
differences in temperament and attitude between her parents, "This
imbalance which destined me to challenge explains to a great extent
why I became an intellectual" ("Ce déséquilibre qui me vouait à la
contestation explique en grande partie que je sois devenue une intel-
lectuelle"; *MJF,* 44). The choices that, in terms of Beauvoir's plotting
of her own life, were the most important ones—to take up philosophy,
to choose literature, to fall in love with Sartre—stand out by virtue of
being the end to which the previous narrative was directed; they shape
and give meaning to what precedes them.

This element is less apparent to the novice than to the reader familiar
with the work, for it is long and detailed—the typical Beauvoirian
mode when she is speaking of what is closest to her. The large number
of facts about her family, milieu, and early experiences may seem to be
there simply for fact's sake. But the volume nevertheless carries out a
project of illumination of the self, or *moi,* as the author said; it is, to use
Montaigne's expression, consubstantial with the writer. The book's
concluding sentences, while dealing with an event that was beyond
Beauvoir's will, nonetheless show how she took an event, related it to a
self-project, reassessed her past in terms of this relation, and turned its
light on her future. Speaking of Zaza's death, she writes, "Together we
had struggled against the miry destiny that lay in wait for us, and I
thought for a long time that I had paid for my liberty with her death"
("Ensemble nous avions lutté contre le destin fangeux qui nous guettait
et j'ai pensé longtemps que j'avais payé ma liberté de sa mort"; *MJF,*
359). It is this vision, shaping the past, that makes of *Mémoires d'une
jeune fille rangée* a narrative of the self.

La Force de l'âge, dedicated to Sartre, was published two years later
(1960). Rather than responding to the question of self-identity, it proposes to show what the author did with her freedom and especially how
her artistic vocation was realized; Beauvoir wanted, she said, to "bear
witness to what my life was" ("témoigner de ce que ma vie a été"; *FA,*
11). While personal, the volume is thus closer to the genre of memoirs
than that of autobiography. It furnishes a record of her pursuits from
Zaza's death in 1929, the same year in which she became involved with
Sartre and passed the *agrégation,* to the liberation of Paris in 1944.

Among the activities recorded are her reading and writing, including the first success, with *L'Invitée;* her teaching (mostly marginal); her relationship with Sartre; her friendships, including the complicated trio; her travels; and, during the somber period of the Occupation, her daily life in the context of a national humiliation and the apparent triumph of a political ideology that was inimical to her. (Her important sexual affair with Bost is missing.) Beauvoir's nearly constant activity is paralleled by intellectual pursuits that spill over into her social life and are reflected in sections in the past tense concerning her reading, thinking, and discussions with others, as well as in passages in the present tense devoted explicitly to the expression of ideas—passages that on occasion lend to the work the tone of a philosophical essay.

Readers are often less interested, however, in the ideas or even the woman behind them than in the picture of her times afforded by *La Force de l'âge.* Its 622 pages are rich in glimpses of the 1930s and 1940s. How left-wing but mostly non-Communist professors, writers, and other intellectuals lived and thought in the second decade between the wars can be seen from the accounts of her activities and attitudes, to which the worsening political situation in Europe furnishes a poignant backdrop. Although Beauvoir was not politically active, the implications of Hitler's assumption of power, the Spanish civil war, the Munich crisis, and finally the trauma of war as viewed by a sensitive, intelligent observer are not overlooked. Long excerpts from her diary under the Occupation, before Sartre returned from prison camp, provide a valuable document on the difficulties of daily life in Paris and the distress of the French.

Lest it be thought that the volume does not partake at all of the autobiographical enterprise of interpreting experience, one must note that within the private and public record are reflective passages on the self, frequently as it relates to the human situation and the anguish of being. The work reveals an important transition in the author's relationship to the world, from one of intense preoccupation with the self and her "schizophrenia"—a willful optimism that made her deny the negative force of much of the reality around her, even as she rebelled against it—to a rationalized commitment to the collectivity. It was through this sense of the collectivity that her life assumed, she concluded, its meaning; since she, like Sartre, was persuaded that in midcentury Europe the significance of an individual life could not be determined outside the social and historical context, private figure and public figure were, in existentialist terms, a single project.

It is on this foundation of a dialectics of the self inscribed in an underlying dialectics of history that *La Force des choses,* published in 1963, is constructed. From the outset the book posits the author's sense of solidarity with her time: "I knew now that my fate was tied to that of all; the freedom, oppression, happiness, and grief of people concerned me intimately" ("Je savais à présent que mon sort était lié à celui de tous: la liberté, l'oppression, le bonheur et la peine des hommes me concernaient intimement"; *FC,* 14). Beauvoir proposes an image of herself that can be understood only in the context of the collective drama, a context that includes the reader, with whom the text establishes a relationship of solidarity. As noted earlier, admirers of the first two volumes had urged Beauvoir to continue recounting her life, doubtless because they recognized in her narratives something of both the existential and the historical quality of their own experiences. She had previously remarked that the cases of Samuel Pepys and Rousseau, among others, showed that when writers, no matter how eccentric, speak with sincerity about the self and its experiences, people are drawn to them, although less by their individuality, their oddity, than by the universal truths of the portrait (*FA,* 10). Such general truths include, in the modern context, the impingement of history on individuals—an impingement that contemporary French readers of Beauvoir's memoirs had recently experienced in great anguish and recognized in her texts, reflected through her sensibility and intelligence.

The title echoes by contrast the previous one: to the energies of her life that Beauvoir depicted in *La Force de l'âge* corresponds the pressure of things, or the practico-inert, on human projects. The third volume of memoirs begins with the euphoria of the Liberation, but after scarcely a page it is qualified by a passage on the historical conditioning of personal liberty, or what the author calls historicity (*FC,* 15). The latter is illustrated throughout the work, from the failures (in Beauvoir's eyes) of the post-Liberation governments and the rise of Gaullism, through the cold war and the pressures of the hated American imperialism, to the moral irresponsibility of France in aligning itself with the West and the unconscionable prolonging of colonialism and the horrors of the Indochinese and Algerian wars. Beauvoir especially brings out the divisions wrought in French society by political polarization on domestic and European issues and the conflict in Algeria.

Sometimes directly, sometimes obliquely, there is also the personal, subjective experience of the pressure of circumstance, in the form of aging. Not old, certainly, in 1944—she turned 36 that year—or even in 1962, the last year treated, Beauvoir was nevertheless living the experience of being, as she said, imprisoned by the years (*FC,* 683). If her consciousness of aging became acute around age 50, it did so perhaps less because of subtle changes in her body and her mind than because of her alienation, owing to the Algerian war, from the society around her. The experience separated her from her past, to the degree that despite everything she had identified with France, and thus left her in an existential void with only old age as a prospect. The effects of this alienation are explored further in the following volume; in this one, they are felt, often in the form of rage. Despite the vitality the author demonstrates in so many episodes—especially those concerning her lengthy travels—and in the prose itself, she concludes the volume on a note that many readers took as an expression of despair. "Yes, the moment has come to say: nevermore!" ("Oui, le moment est arrivé de dire: jamais plus!"), she admits, as she gazes toward her future, too short, but too long if all her projects must die before she does. She considers everything she has done—the books she has read and written, the people she has loved—in light of the promises of her youth; admitting that these promises have been kept, she nevertheless concludes that she has been "gypped" ("flouée"; *TCF,* 685–86).

Tout compte fait (*All Said and Done*), published in 1972 and dedicated to Sylvie Le Bon, departs structurally from the previous volumes of memoirs, which, with some analepses and prolepses, were organized chronologically. In contrast, the final volume is organized by massive thematic blocks, each dealing with an aspect of the author's life, from 1963 to roughly the date of publication. While the cover page bears the indication "essai," in the prologue the contents are called "souvenirs" (recollections). Beauvoir's first concern is to respond indirectly to the conclusion of *La Force des choses* by a pointed expression of optimism: "I am satisfied with my destiny and would in no way wish it different" ("Je suis satisfaite de ma destinée et ne la voudrais en rien différente"; *TCF,* 13). This statement is made in the context of an almost-Proustian meditation on the continuity and identity of the self, experienced at the moment of waking. Agreeing with Robbe-Grillet that a life cannot really be recounted as it is lived, since life is, in Sartre's terms, a "detotalized totality" and cannot be surrounded and apprehended like a thing, Beauvoir nevertheless believes that her sense of her own life has been enhanced in writing it; her current aim is to continue this project and "salvage" ("récupérer"; *TCF,* 50) her past, particularly by identifying the conjunction of fate and freedom, or chance and choice, that molded it.

The first elements of the picture are historical and human ones: the class and milieu into which Beauvoir was born, the heredity and character of her parents, the situation of France in the twentieth century. The opening chapter explores the consequences of these circumstances, sketching her evolution and dealing again with her early reluctance to accept her historicity and responsibility: "I did not consent to be defined as a Frenchwoman. . . . I thought I was myself" ("Je n'acceptais [pas] d'être définie comme une Française. . . . [j]e pensais que j'étais moi"; *TCF,* 32). The summary of her gradual insertion into history—a process that can be considered a type of conversion—is followed by a survey of her friendships, passages in which she provides information, not essential but of human interest, on figures who had appeared in earlier volumes (usually under pseudonyms), such as Lise and Camille, and in which she introduces more recent friends, including the writer Violette Leduc. Whether or not Beauvoir was aware of the compositional value of including such contrasts, most of these figures are seen as failures, in contrast to her own success.

"Writing," Beauvoir says, "has remained the great business of my life" ("Ecrire est demeuré la grande affaire de ma vie"; *TCF,* 131). In previous volumes she devoted pages to explaining the genesis and meaning of her works in the context of her biography; here in the second chapter she looks at her production as a whole and presents the core of her literary aesthetics. She also addresses the question of the critical reception of *La Force des choses* and the misunderstandings surrounding that work. Literature is an existential project that overcomes the distance between her consciousness and others': "By language I go beyond my particular case" ("Par le langage je dépasse mon cas particulier"; *TCF,* 136). In the course of considering fiction, she attacks the New Novel, which to her is a fleshless construct.

These considerations are followed by sections devoted to such topics as women's situation and Freud's views, the cinema as an art and her favorite films, the theater, music, painting, Western culture as a whole, and politics, chiefly international. Her concern for the third world is a major current. In *La Force des choses* Beauvoir had devoted many pages—doubtless too many, for some tastes—to the trip she made to Brazil with Sartre in 1960 and other travels. (Her first trip to the United States and her travels in China were omitted because she had given full accounts of them elsewhere.) In this volume she relates many more travels, some short trips, as in Italy, facilitated by her presence in Rome with Sartre nearly every summer. A major episode is their trip to

Japan in 1966. These accounts often have a phenomenological flavor as she shows how the means and angle of perception govern what is perceived; she could have agreed with Gide's dictum that perception begins with change in sensation, whence the necessity of travel. These reportings are followed by an account of her visits to Egypt and Israel in 1967 with Sartre and Lanzmann. Like the pages devoted to domestic politics, these sections are of considerable documentary value for those interested in social questions and the complex politics of the Near East.

Indeed, the main value of *Tout compte fait* may be as a depiction of the 1960s by an intelligent and well-read, if biased, observer whose vantage point was at once Paris and the world. But like all her writings, it also bears the stamp of her personality—her craving for success and for stimulation, her project of self-understanding. Conceding that she—unlike Joyce, Proust, and Virginia Woolf, with whom she implicitly compared herself (Dayan, 77)—has not been a virtuoso of literature, Beauvoir affirms that she has succeeded in her own literary project: to make herself "exist for others by communicating to them, in the most direct manner, the flavor of my own life" ("me faire exister pour les autres en leur communiquant, de la manière la plus directe, le goût de ma propre vie"; *TCF,* 513). Even in this final volume of memoirs, so filled with other people and things that she called it an essay, this flavor of her life, as experienced both directly and in reflection, remains at the heart of her writing.

Beauvoir's self-portraits are not strongly marked by either irony or imagination. Despite self-criticism (especially of her younger self), she adheres to herself nearly throughout and does not experience the deep inner divisions that led to the modern ironies in the writings of Kierkegaard, Baudelaire, and their followers. She continued to espouse her self-project as a whole, and its failures are identified not as her own but as those of the human situation—its inevitable separation of consciousnesses, the limitations posed by the body and by death—and of the twentieth century. Some bitterness seeps in, some disappointments, some failures, and, often in the later volumes, the sense that "Ce n'est donc que ça"—the deceptive aftertaste when long-anticipated experience, even life itself, seems by hindsight to have been a cardboard imitation. But Beauvoir remains faithful, by literary rhetoric if nothing else, to two choices by which she had shaped her adulthood: her literary vocation and her relationship with Sartre. Her memoirs stand in contrast to Sartre's self-contestation, by which (in a very literary manner, to be sure) he demolishes in *Les Mots* the self that became the writer of that very work and countless others. It is significant that one must go outside the memoirs, to information afforded by Sartre's *Lettres au Castor et à quelques autres* and by Beauvoir's recently published letters to him and other statements, to obtain a critical perspective on the relationship between the two writers. Like many autobiographers, even those such as Rousseau and Gide, who announce, with some complacency perhaps, their own shortcomings, Beauvoir carefully constructs her narratives to minimize or simply omit the evidence that would have allowed the reader to arrive at a portrait different from the one produced by the author's ostensible sincerity—in this case, to see what, at this remove, has become obvious: that for all her intellect, her will to independence, her nascent and then full-fledged feminism, Beauvoir lived very much in function of a man, and that in their contract of equality she nevertheless often came up short, to the point of intense mental suffering at times.

As for imagination, its role in giving form to Beauvoir's record of herself seems limited. What she retains of the past as she lived it is conveyed without metaphor or other poetic transformation: she sees herself, if imperfectly, in terms of her birth into a certain milieu, her education, her intellectual choices, her friends, activities, writing, and so forth—but not in either symbolic or allegorical terms. She herself agreed that her memoirs were not a work of art (*FC*, 8). Except for the rather commonplace linear and thematic structure, her experiences would seem to be without pattern, an element that imagination alone can bring out of the randomness of event. Thanks to her directness of language and narrative, the reader enters easily into Beauvoir's memoirs, hence their wide appeal. But they fall short of the spiritual power conveyed by artistic transpositions of personal experience in terms of an organizing vision, whether by Saint Augustine, Montaigne, or Proust.

Other Works

In comparison with the memoirs, none of Beauvoir's other accounts of her experience is focused so centrally on herself. Although *L'Amérique au jour le jour* (1948) is written in the form of a diary, it is not a transcription of notebooks Beauvoir kept during her long trip there in 1947; rather, it is a reconstruction of her notes. Partly personal, directed toward expressing how *she* perceived the United States, the book also aims at imparting general information about the cities she visited (New York, Chicago, Boston, Washington, Los Angeles, New Or-

leans), the ways of life she observed, and the nation as a whole, especially what she identified as the American mentality, which she misread
more often than not. She does not include the account of her love affair
with Algren, on which one must seek information in *La Force des choses*
and *Les Mandarins*. The work has little value as a portrait of the United
States, given the author's biases and ignorance, but it does reveal well
the way in which left-wing French intellectuals looked at their resented
ally.[10] *La Longue Marche: Essai sur la Chine* (1957; *The Long March*) is
entirely impersonal. Given the short time the author spent in the
People's Republic of China, commentators have questioned the accu-
racy of many of the observations and conclusions in this reportage, as in
the book on the United States.[11] But it extended the scope of Beauvoir's
work and, like other political and social commentary, helped enlarge
her audience.

   Une Mort très douce (1964) and *La Vieillesse* (1970) deal in different
ways with some of the same issues; both can conveniently be treated at
this juncture. *La Vieillesse* is an impersonal documentary, connected to
the topic of this chapter only insofar as it deals with the problems of
older women and the age that the author herself had reached. In contrast, *Une Mort très douce,* while containing elements of social commentary, including an indictment of members of the medical profession,
puts the abstraction of death in a personal context: the author's mother
was diagnosed in 1963 as having cancer; her hospitalization, her decline, and finally her death are reported by the writer in what she calls a
récit (narrative), as she and Hélène de Beauvoir observed those events.

   The experience was painful, but ambivalently so. Beauvoir deplored
her mother's sufferings, which were acute enough to suggest that the
title is antiphrastic. She worried also for her sister, who was greatly
distressed by their mother's illness. At the same time, Beauvoir had to
confront her own ambiguous feelings toward the woman whom she had
loved as a young child but from whom she had become estranged, by
virtue of the intellectual emancipation that had made her what she was.
During her adulthood, the relationship between her and Françoise de
Beauvoir had been amical, and perhaps the latter was able to take pride
in her daughter's accomplishments; a photograph of them together
shows two handsome, intelligent women who resemble each other and
seem equally proud (Madsen, 236). But the distance between them
created by Simone's adolescent rebellion and emancipation, particularly
her atheism, and by her subsequent mode of life was not inconsequential, and one can gather how much resentment the writer, even as a

mature woman, felt toward her mother by her repeated criticisms of the maternal-filial relationship.

During her mother's illness, Beauvoir also had occasion to look back not just to her own past but to her mother's, and, with the comprehension afforded by decades of experience, measure how difficult, how unrewarding her mother's life had been, both as a girl, when her own parents almost ignored her, and in her marriage. Her mother's childhood experiences as recounted to Simone serve to illuminate in an awkward fashion her own unsatisfactory relationship with her parents. Finally, Beauvoir was inevitably led to reflect on her own mortality; the narrative is a meditation on the metaphysical scandal of death. The text becomes a mirror, turned both forward and backward, the main narrative line following the chronological progression of the illness, but with some passages going backward to the childhood of Françoise de Beauvoir and then Simone and Hélène, and others moving forward to a death not inscribed in the narration, that of the author herself.

As early as 1958, before the experience of her mother's decline and death, Beauvoir had considered writing a study on what is designated in France as the "last age." She was drawn to the topic increasingly by her own years: "As old age approached, I wanted to know how the condition of old people is defined" ("Aux approches de la vieillesse, j'ai eu envie de savoir comment se définit la condition des vieillards"; *TCF,* 148). It seems, however, to be social consciousness that was chiefly responsible for her decision to undertake an investigation of the question similar to her exhaustive monograph on women. Her hostility to the capitalistic society visible, for instance, in *Les Belles Images* had not decreased after the Algerian war. She observed that, along with colonials and ex-colonials, women (still, to a great degree), the European proletariat (she claimed) and subproletariat, old people were *marginalisés,* grudgingly tolerated at best, usually economically and even physically abused. Like the members of other subclasses, Beauvoir argued, these persons are not considered fully human; they are "the other." To hide this fact, social myths, such as that of the wise grandparent who has few needs, having given up all projects, have been forged hypocritically. The great oversimplification of Beauvoir's assessment, which rejects traditional humanism and overlooks its accomplishments, is patent. She was convinced that the problems of the elderly deserved a thorough exposé, well grounded in science and sociology, that would be a political document. "I wanted to make their voice heard" ("J'ai voulu faire entendre leur voix"), she wrote on the book jacket. [12]

Like her study of women, *La Vieillesse* opens with considerations on the biological reality of the group. The author argues, however, that aging and even death are never purely natural, or physical, phenomena; they are cultural facts, since all human beings exist in a social context—even if it is only that of a primitive tribe—and this context influences understanding of biological processes and even the processes themselves. It is frequently the case, for instance, that a tribe, judging those no longer able to work like healthy adults to be an unacceptable burden, hastens their decline by its harsh treatment of them, to the point of total neglect or ritual murder.

Biology can thus be understood only in a social and historical context, and Beauvoir quickly moves to ethnography and sociology, giving a sample of what is known about aging in primitive cultures and surveying advanced societies. Again she calls liberally on literary sources to furnish information on past societies for which reliable statistical data are unavailable—Greek and Roman culture, Europe in the Middle Ages and the Renaissance, and so on. For more recent periods, she cites a variety of anthropological and sociological data, but even there she uses literary texts as documentary evidence, quoting from Victor Hugo and Samuel Beckett, among others. Her ambitious historical survey is akin to the undertakings of the *Annales* school of historiographers, including Fernand Braudel and Emmanuel LeRoy Ladurie, except that it offers no original data, only an illumination of segments of societies frequently neglected by historians. She then passes to a lengthy study of current gerontological questions. In fact, the latter could easily be understood without the long ethnographic and historical background, which, while of interest, does little to illuminate current attitudes.

What aging means, both subjectively and objectively speaking, concerns the writer in the second part of her study. Diaries, eye-witness accounts, and personal observations furnish a rich selection of testimony on what it is like to age and apprehend oneself as aging. Beauvoir employs existentialist concepts and terminology and additional literary evidence to explore how the old, or even those only on the edge of aging, see themselves in relation to time. She observes the alienation they undergo within themselves. For the aging, there is no subjective sense of being changed; they still identify themselves as they have been, in terms of existential projects. Objectively, however, they are seen as deteriorating, hence in a different relationship to the world than before. Faced with the evidence of this judgment by "the other," they interiorize it, in humiliation.

While this picture is distressing, Beauvoir does not neglect to identify many possible advantages, especially for women, in the "grand age"
that the poet Saint-John Perse saluted in *Chronique* (1960)—advantages
that may include freedom from child-rearing responsibilities, from the
pressures of a profession or job, or from social expectations, that is,
freedom to be oneself. The benefits the elderly may accrue from their
situation depend highly, however, on their economic condition. Studies
Beauvoir cites show that manual laborers have more difficulty in adapt-
ing to retirement than white-collar employees and especially intellectuals, and those dependent for care on the state, through pensions or
geriatric homes, are clearly much less favored than those whose income
allows them to enjoy retirement. For a meaningful old age, without
humiliation, anxiety, or suffering, people need to continue to feel
themselves as project and possibility. Beauvoir portrays the old age of a
number of figures who continued to act in the world, among them
Chateaubriand, Verdi, and Freud.

These examples notwithstanding, she concludes that "old age de-
nounces the failure of all our civilization" ("La vieillesse dénonce l'échec
de toute notre civilisation"; *V,* 569). Adopting a more radical position
than she took in *Le Deuxième Sexe,* Beauvoir does not propose simple
remedial social measures; instead, she announces that humankind itself
and all human relations must be redefined, reconstructed. Capitalism,
which is based on the notion of profit and thus rejects the unprofitable
elderly, must be replaced, as must a fragmented, caste-divided society
and the elitism that reserves culture and meaningful activity for the
few, leaving others, at all ages, to stagnate. Even conditions for the
young must be altered, since it is their way of functioning under the
present system that creates a shameful old age. Because even socialist
societies are far from according to the elderly what they need not merely
to subsist but to live as full human beings, the social revolution must
be worldwide. This position is consistent with those adopted by Sartre
in *Critique de la raison dialectique* (1960), his synthesis of existentialism
and Marxism. It is also consistent with some of Beauvoir's statements
in the 1970s on the question of women's rights, although in time she
came to concede that, pending radical social upheaval, women should
campaign for intermediate measures that would improve their lot.

La Cérémonie des adieux (1981; *Adieux*), can well conclude this chapter, since, as Beauvoir's formal literary farewell to Sartre, it is also a
record of herself in the context of their relationship. The first section
presents a summary of the last decade of his life (1970–80), organized

year by year, as Beauvoir observed it. Recording many of their daily activities, it, like *Une Mort très douce* and *La Vieillesse,* is especially concerned with decrepitude and approaching death. Poignantly, she foresees, in the closing sentence, that his death will separate them and hers not reunite them. This second section consists of "Conversations with Jean-Paul Sartre," a series of talks recorded in 1974 and transcribed by Beauvoir with, she claims, a minimum of rearrangement for the sake of order and cohesion. Her questions, which were not planned beforehand but do fall into thematic groups, seem intended to allow Sartre to restate his case for posterity even as he reveals more about himself, adding to and correcting previous glimpses. While focused on him—his development, his reading and writing, his politics, his other intellectual positions, his tastes—the exchanges include some of Beauvoir's own views and reminiscences of her experiences and reveal indirectly a good deal about her; the entire book has been called "intensely Beauvoirian" (Cohen-Solal, 518). By the close of her career she realized how greatly Sartre had dominated the intellectual arena in France; it is fitting that her last work as a *mémorialiste* should reflect his dominance over the period and, ultimately, over her.

What some readers currently criticize as Beauvoir's failure, despite her insistence on demystifying relationships and telling the truth, to confront openly in any but favorable terms her position vis-à-vis Sartre can be assessed in this connection.[13] The comparison between them is inevitable. None of her novels is so original as *La Nausée,* none of her stories so fine as "Le Mur" ("The Wall"), and her philosophical contributions are generally illustrations of principles he had elaborated first; nor did she ever go so far as he in synthesizing her philosophical and political positions or grounding the latter in Marxism. Had she been of as strong and original a mind as he, she might well have taken the lead in literary innovation, philosophical thought, or political commitment. Beauvoir's wisdom in realizing Sartre's greater grasp and brilliance should be conceded by those who criticize her relationship with him as spousal, noting that she often came up short in the bargain. Despite her independence and great intellectual acumen, she was enough of a woman to accept this situation; whatever degree of insincerity enters into her glossing over of difficulties, she was surely truthful in saying that to live so successfully in harmony with another's mind was to live very richly indeed.

As a whole, Beauvoir's memoirs and associated volumes can be considered the work of a *chroniqueur,* or recorder, of her time as well as a record of herself. She compared herself implicitly with the duc de Saint-Simon, whose *Mémoires* portray in detail the last years of the reign of Louis XIV and the Regency (*FC*, 8); his work was not, she noted, that of an artist, but it has endured by reason of its historical and human truth. She stated more than once that she wanted not to create beautiful objects but to transmit her sense of life, her consciousness. This, most readers would agree, she succeeded in doing, within the context of a historical period and a culture that are sometimes only reflected, sometimes analyzed.

Conclusion

The trajectory of Simone de Beauvoir's career is marked by a unity that incorporates its separate strands and resolves certain underlying contradictions. To her single-mindedness as a writer, illustrated by an abundant output—the product of nearly daily writing except when she was traveling—correspond a number of constants in her convictions, values, and philosophical positions. Among these the primary place belongs to freedom, less the abstract liberty of her atheistic philosophy than freedom as lived and experienced by those—among whom she counted herself—who are fortunate enough to concretize their will to conceive, pursue, and carry out projects, thus developing and indeed creating the authentic self. For Beauvoir this realization of freedom meant being able to think and write as she pleased, to love, travel, and enjoy the products of culture. Because such concrete freedom, which is both the foundation of human reality and its realization, is enjoyed by relatively few, the need for political, economic, social, and moral changes that would extend it to all became imperative in Beauvoir's thinking; a phenomenological philosophy of human freedom and consciousness developed into a social ethics. The changes for which she campaigned would entail radical reorganization of society and transformation of relationships among individuals, resulting in a collective freedom in which class, racial, sexual, age, and cultural barriers would disappear. Projects would serve to unite rather than separate human beings.

Thus, long after her belief in an authoritative God and a single morality crumbled, and despite her rejection of bourgeois humanism and abstract universal ethics, Beauvoir remained in her own manner an idealist and a universalist. Her writing belongs to the Enlightenment and post-Enlightenment intellectual tradition, springing from the middle classes and espousing its aspirations. Her anger was always that of the intellectual who *chooses* to embrace a cause, not that of the oppressed who live the cause in their flesh. Beauvoir's feminism was based on what she considered the legitimate claim of both sexes to the same freedom, realized concretely. Her campaigns in favor of the elderly, workers, and ethnic and social groups in France and elsewhere similarly arose from her belief that constitutional freedoms mean nothing if there is no concrete opportunity for self-development, but this belief itself, however radically expressed, is based on a sense of individual rights that is related to the progressivism of the French intellectual tradition over the past 250 years.

It was phenomenological ontology that allowed Beauvoir to transform her early idealism into an understanding of human reality that synthesized her own aspirations toward experience, especially her commitment to her writing, with belief in freedom for all. According to her understanding, every consciousness, being free, re-creates the world, or rather *is* a world, singular and unique—whence the incredible richness of human reality—and each is irreducible—whence the solitude of the subject, which gives rise to so much anguish in her work. But the subjectivity of consciousness can be overcome not only by common action but also by language and thought, within the context of the human condition, which, as Montaigne wrote, everyone bears within himself. The role of the writer and artist is preeminently to universalize the individual. Earlier in the century, Gide had argued that art could be only general but must pass through the particular. Art addresses itself from one freedom to another; it is by its very nature communication. It is the principal way Beauvoir chose to go beyond the abstractions of Cartesian reason, which is supposed to be a universal but ends in divisive analytical thinking, and Kantian morality, which is limited to the general, with no guidelines for any concrete situation.

Beauvoir's choice does not mean that she held art to be the supreme value, or Occidental culture a universal standard. Thanks to her extensive readings in anthropology, history, and politics and to her travels and political activism, she came to denounce Western cultural imperialism, although she was herself a product of Western thought and literature: "I do not believe in the universal and eternal value of Occidental culture, but I . . . remain attached to it" ("Je ne crois pas à la valeur universelle et éternelle de la culture occidentale, mais je . . . lui reste attachée"; *TCF,* 231–32). In a world where two-thirds of the population are undernourished, culture is fraudulent, she argued, and her political activism and journalism demonstrated the force of her convictions. She also understood the contradiction between the general aims of the intellectual and the inevitable subjectivism from which the intellectual speaks, as well as the incommensurability between human suffering and its sublimation in art. The problem of others, which at the early stage of her career was lived and illustrated in fiction in the mode of personal conflict between rival consciousnesses, took on the dimensions of a wide-scale geopolitical problem to which philosophy was not foreign—it was in the name of reason that she argued—but which had to be addressed by means other than academic and literary ones. She looked to the creation of a new man and a new woman, for whom art would then be as different from today's as the new social order would be.

Yet in her own intellectual and artistic undertakings, Beauvoir could not bring herself to think against herself (as Sartre said) totally, any more than she could renounce her aspirations toward the absolute, to which consciousness aspires in its sovereignty even while knowing that it is ephemeral. The intensity that she brought to her writing—as to living, if one believes her memoirs—reflects this aspiration and places her in the company of other writers, among whom one might name Montaigne, Proust, and Colette, whose pages convey a persuasive sense of the *vécu*, the personal experience of living. But Beauvoir's work offers more than the feel of experience. Taken in its entirety, her production shows that she saw life in the twentieth century with remarkable clarity. Her limitations in understanding—one could cite areas of personal and spiritual experience that are entirely foreign to her—and her intellectual biases—in favor of socialist states and against Western democracy, for instance—kept her from seeing it whole, but such inadequacies are the sign of a humanity that places Beauvoir on an equal footing with her audience. The reader concludes that Beauvoir was able to transmit, in many modes, a wide range of the experiences that she shared with Sartre, as well as many others: "I wanted to make myself exist for others by communicating to them . . . the taste of my own life" ("J'ai voulu me faire exister pour les autres en leur communiquant . . . le goût de ma propre vie"; *TCF*, 513). The number of her readers worldwide indicates her success.

Notes and References

Preface

1. Deirdre Bair, *Simone de Beauvoir: A Biography* (New York: Summit Books, 1990), 618; hereafter cited in text.

Chapter One

1. Beauvoir is frequently quoted even in the popular press—to wit, the Abigail Van Buren column of 27 December 1989 (New Orleans *Times-Picayune*).

2. Editorial, *Signs* 5, No. 2 (Winter 1979): 207.

3. Renée Winegarten, *Simone de Beauvoir: A Critical View* (Oxford: Berg, 1988), 3.

4. *Simone de Beauvoir: Un Film de Josée Dayan et Malka Ribowska* (Paris: Gallimard, 1979), 77; hereafter cited in text as Dayan.

5. Simone de Beauvoir, Yves Berger, Jean-Pierre Faye, et al., *Que peut la littérature?* (Paris: 10/18—Union Générale d'Editions, 1965), 73–92. Others who participated in the debate were Sartre and Jean Ricardou.

6. A vast amount of information about Beauvoir's family and life is given in her memoirs; page numbers will normally not be provided in the text. Other details are available in interviews and films; sources will be noted as appropriate. Additional information is provided in Claude Francis and Fernande Gontier, *Simone de Beauvoir* (Paris: Perrin, 1985), translated by Lisa Nesselson as *Simone de Beauvoir: A Life . . . A Love Story* (New York: St. Martin's Press, 1987), on which I have drawn. Similarly, Bair's biography has an abundance of details about Beauvoir's evolution, activities, relationships, and so on.

7. The publication of these assertions and others, which appear to be accurate, irritated Beauvoir, although she herself spoke of the bankruptcy in *Une Mort très douce* (1964; *A Very Easy Death*) and had earlier furnished her biographers with documents and given lengthy interviews. She subsequently denounced the two authors and repudiated their biography. The biographers tell how, after they had submitted some of their text to her, Beauvoir became incensed on reading about details of her life, only to be told that she herself had revealed them. She often contradicted herself during interviews. Some misremembering about the distant past is understandable, as are changes in subjective evaluations of one's own experiences and others'. But apparently Beauvoir occasionally let slip a fact that she later wished to cover up, and

without a doubt she was concerned with putting up a good appearance. There were also taboo subjects that simply could not be broached. See Francis and Gontier 1987, xii–xv.

8. *Tout compte fait* (Paris: Gallimard, 1972), 37; hereafter cited in text as *TCF.*

9. *Une Mort très douce* (Paris: Gallimard, 1964), 159; hereafter cited in text as *MTD.*

10. The real family name was not revealed by Beauvoir, but it is given in Bair, 76.

11. *Mémoires d'une jeune fille rangée* (Paris: Gallimard, 1958), 142; hereafter cited in text as *MJF.*

12. Robert Garric later published *Albert de Mun* (Paris: Flammarion, 1935).

13. See Deborah MacKeefe, "Zaza Mabille: Mission and Motive in Simone de Beauvoir's *Mémoires,*" *Contemporary Literature* 24, No. 2 (Summer 1984): 204–21.

14. It may have simply been a long term paper; there is no record of a finished thesis deposited anywhere (Bair, 628).

15. See *La Cérémonie des adieux* (Paris: Gallimard, 1981) for Sartre's comparison between men and women.

16. That theme is particularly visible in *Les Séquestrés d'Altona* and is suggested in *Les Mouches.* In *Les Mots* (Paris: Gallimard, 1964), 41–42, Sartre noted the incestuous relationship of a man and woman as one of the poles of his affective imagination, springing probably from his childhood closeness to his young mother, who was treated like a child by her aged parents.

17. Winegarten (1), citing evidence from *TCF,* believes the relationship meant less to Beauvoir than her writing did.

18. See Alex Madsen, *Hearts and Minds: The Common Journey of Simone de Beauvoir and Jean-Paul Sartre* (New York: Morrow, 1977), 206; hereafter cited in text.

19. *La Force de l'âge* (Paris: Gallimard, 1960), 92; hereafter cited in text as *FA.*

20. A list of the institutions at which she appeared is found in Francis and Gontier 1979, 52–53.

21. *La Force des choses* (Paris: Gallimard, 1963), 177; hereafter cited in text as *FC.*

22. *Le Deuxième Sexe,* 2 vols. (Paris: Gallimard, 1949), 2:545; hereafter cited in text as *DS.* On female homosexuality, see Alice Schwarzer, *Simone de Beauvoir aujourd'hui: Six conversations* (Paris: Mercure de France, 1983), translated by Marianne Howarth as *After "The Second Sex": Conversations with Simone de Beauvoir* (New York: Pantheon Books, 1984), 112–14.

23. See *Lettres à Sartre,* ed. Sylvie Le Bon de Beauvoir, vol. 1 (Paris: Gallimard, 1990), 377 and passim. See also Bair, 510.

24. Annie Cohen-Solal, *Sartre: A Life,* trans. Anna Cancogni (New York: Pantheon Books, 1987), 518; hereafter cited in text.

Chapter Two

1. Sartre would insist, however, that situation is a "detotalized totality," a never-completed synthesis. See Catharine Savage Brosman, *Jean-Paul Sartre* (Boston: Twayne, 1983), 113.

2. Sartre's ideal society would include the elimination of scarcity, hence competition; otherness would be absorbed by identity; and the result would be transparency of selves. See Catharine Savage Brosman, "Theories of Collectivities in Sartre and Rousseau," *South Central Review* 2, No. 2 (Spring 1985): 24–41, and "Seeing through the Other: Modes of Vision in Sartre," *South Central Review* 4, No. 4 (Winter 1987): 61–73.

3. See Tilde A. Sankovitch, *French Women Writers and the Book* (Syracuse, N.Y.: Syracuse University Press, 1988), chapter 1; hereafter cited in text.

4. Jean-Paul Sartre, *Situations* (Paris: Gallimard, 1947–76), 2:148.

5. The contemporary French feminist Monique Wittig is one of those who affirm that all language as now known is patriarchal and sexist, and should be undone or at least sabotaged as much as possible. See Monique Wittig and Sande Zeig, *Brouillon pour un dictionnaire des amantes* (Paris: Grasset, 1976), translated by the authors as *Lesbian Peoples: Material for a Dictionary* (New York: Avon, 1979).

6. Quoted in Francis Jeanson, *Sartre dans sa vie* (Paris: Seuil, 1974), 235.

7. Mary Evans takes this point of view in her *Simone de Beauvoir: A Feminist Mandarin* (London and New York: Tavistock, 1985), x; hereafter cited in text.

8. See Charles Du Bos, *François Mauriac et le problème du romancier catholique* (Paris: Corrêa, 1933), 56.

9. For sources, see Elissa D. Gelfand and Virginia Thorndike Hules, *French Feminist Criticism: Women, Language, and Literature* (New York: Garland 1985), and Elaine Showalter, *The New Feminist Criticism* (New York: Pantheon Books, 1985). The irony is that, by their *phallophobie* (hatred of the male), some of these writers and agitators on behalf of femaleness end up, in a kind of Amazonism, resembling the male, through their denunciation of the feminine roles of (a) sexual relationships with men and (b) motherhood, and through their pursuit of other women. Beauvoir shows absolutely no evidence of such hatred of the male. Sexual oppression, as she analyzed it in her writings and opposed it through activism, was to her chiefly a social issue, and she was or would have been opposed to *any* essentialist and dogmatic view of what women must be, even if proferred in the name of women's liberation.

10. Julia Kristeva, "Women's Time," *Signs* 7, No. 1 (Autumn 1981): 13–35.

11. At a Harvard panel discussion, a biographer of Beauvoir was dismayed to see that questions directed to her concerned Beauvoir's life, whereas questions about Sartre addressed to *his* biographer concerned Sartre's *work* (Bair, 18).

12. Beauvoir thought that fiction by women could have such a quality. See Alice Jardine, "Interview with Simone de Beauvoir," *Signs* 5, No. 2 (Winter 1979): 233; hereafter cited in text.

13. See Jardine, 233. The argument that only a woman can properly portray a woman and so forth has been deflated through reductio ad absurdum by Cleanth Brooks, quoted in Calvin S. Brown, "Faulkner: The Unabated Spate," *Sewanee Review* 97, No. 4 (Fall 1989): 559.

14. The phrase is borrowed from Hélène Cixous.

15. See note 5.

16. It has been argued, however, that she does create in her writing her own versions of myths. See Sankovitch, chapter 5.

17. See Hans-Robert Jauss, *Toward an Aesthetic of Reception* (Minneapolis: University of Minnesota Press, 1982).

18. Dorothy Kaufman McCall, "Simone de Beauvoir, *The Second Sex,* and Jean-Paul Sartre," *Signs* 5, No. 2 (Winter 1979): 209–23.

19. Elizabeth Fallaize, *The Novels of Simone de Beauvoir* (London and New York: Routledge, 1988), 7; hereafter cited in the text.

Chapter Three

1. Her father, for instance, appreciated the novels of Marcel Prévost. See Francis and Gontier 1987, 15.

2. In *FA* (231) Beauvoir admits that she had been subject to the same errors as her model and that, in creating Chantal, she was depicting herself.

3. See *L'Invitée* (Paris: Gallimard, 1943), 82: "a novel of which I'm the heroine" ("un roman dont je suis l'héroïne"). This was one of Roquentin's desires in Sartre's *La Nausée* and is fundamental to its interpretation. Given the date of composition of both works, it is plausible that the two authors discussed this desire, which, Beauvoir admitted, was one of her most cherished illusions: "a beautiful story that would become true" ("une belle histoire qui deviendrait vraie"; *MJF,* 168, 316; *FA,* 498).

4. Terry Keefe is an exception; see his *Simone de Beauvoir: A Study of Her Writings* (London: Harrap, 1983), 145; hereafter cited in text.

5. *Quand prime le spirituel* (Paris: Gallimard, 1979), 200; hereafter cited in text as *QPS*.

6. For example, Keefe (157) views it as "too long," although it has considerable merit. Robert D. Cottrell views it as a "major novel"; see his review of Winegarten's book in *French Forum* 14, No. 3 (September 1989): 367.

7. Fallaize notes that the ordinary social world is also very peripheral: the characters seem to "float on the margin of" social ties and forces (28).

8. *L'Invitée* (Paris: Gallimard, 1943), 12; hereafter cited in text as *I*.

9. To read the novel simply as an illustration of Sartre's tenets, however, is a critical error, because he composed his work after the manuscript of *L'Invitée* was submitted. But he had discussed his views at length with Beauvoir. For a Sartrean reading, see Hazel E. Barnes, *The Literature of Possibility* (Lincoln: University of Nebraska Press, 1959), 121–36.

10. For further elaboration on conflict and Sartre's views on others, see Brosman 1987.

11. Pierre's domineering attitude can be compared with Sartre's demanding from Olga "a friendship as absolute, as exclusive as love" ("une amitié aussi absolue, aussi exclusive, qu'un amour"; *FA,* 264).

12. There is a close parallel here between Pierre and Sartre. For a short analysis of Sartre's sexuality as compared with Beauvoir's, see Lisa Appignanesi, *Simone de Beauvoir* (London: Penguin, 1988), 37; hereafter cited in text.

13. Compare *FA,* 325, where Beauvoir says she relied on Sartre to justify her life.

14. Critics' opinions vary concerning whether Françoise experiences true jealousy. Appignanesi, for instance, considers her simply jealous (59), whereas Keefe argues that, since she has not known sexual jealousy before, the sentiment must be different (152–53). Françoise's jealousy—for such indeed it is—springs from the complicated motives explored in the text and is not simply "sexual"—but this novel suggests that jealousy never is, since sexuality is tied up with power and power with the self.

15. This rivalry has been seen as acting out the Electra drama: rivalry of mother and daughter for the father's love. See Fallaize, 30, who calls it "pseudo-oedipal."

16. Keefe has noted the implausibility of Françoise's even imagining that the girl could share the life of two older intellectuals in Paris and the difficulty of understanding how they could be drawn to her (154, 157).

17. The scene of the hand-burning itself has sexual overtones.

18. Fallaize (35) sees this as the power to narrate a story (impose a version of events). Such a reading fits Beauvoir's view of her own life as story (see note 3).

19. Beauvoir later acknowledged the murder to be an implausibility, although she attempted to justify it by foreshadowing (e.g., *I,* 300, 312, 369).

20. I am indebted to Vaheed Ramazani, *The Free Indirect Mode: Flaubert and the Poetics of Irony* (Charlottesville: University Press of Virginia, 1988), for a brilliant study of the phrase "free indirect style" and similar terms, although my usage is slightly different from his.

21. Fallaize suggests (46–47) that the first person serves to present Jean

in his subjectivity, the third person to present "his younger self in terms of object in the world, in terms of a social classification." Beauvoir said (*FA*, 558) that Jean uses the first person when he accepts his past and the third person when he considers, from a distance, how he has appeared to others. This latter description does not, however, entirely conform to the text, as Keefe observed (169).

22. *Le Sang des autres* (Paris: Gallimard, 1945), 13; hereafter cited in text as *SA*.

23. See his *Narrative Discourse: An Essay on Method*, trans. Jane E. Lewin (Ithaca: Cornell University Press, 1980), 40.

24. This episode is based on the death of the child of the Beauvoir's servant Louise; other details are drawn from the family of Jacques Champigneulles (*MJF*, 132; *FA*, 555).

25. Madeleine was modeled in part on Simone Weil, whom Beauvoir had known slightly at the Sorbonne.

26. See, for instance, Carol Ascher, *Simone de Beauvoir: A Life of Freedom* (Boston: Beacon Press, 1981), 60.

27. This existentialist theme had been foreshadowed by such earlier twentieth-century novelists as François Mauriac, in *Thérèse Desqueyroux*, and Gide, in *Les Faux-Monnayeurs*.

28. Beauvoir was mindful of this similarity; she had been struck by Kierkegaard's argument that the authentic man cannot have a clear conscience (*FA*, 556).

29. Counterfinalities are associated with what Sartre called the practico-inert—the action and counteraction of objective factors.

30. This argument was not widespread but was made by some resisters, especially Communists. See H. R. Kedward, *Resistance in Vichy France* (Oxford: Oxford University Press, 1978), 144; Henri Michel, *La Guerre de l'ombre* (Paris: Grasset, 1970), 227–28; John F. Sweets, *Choices in Vichy France: The French Under Nazi Occupation* (New York: Oxford, 1986), 199–230.

31. This basic tenet of the existentialism shared by Beauvoir and Sartre is supported by research in child psychology by Jean Piaget and Jacques Lacan. See Jean Piaget, *The Child's Conception of the World* (London: Routledge & Kegan Paul, 1929), 128–31.

32. The similarity between the concerns of this novel and those in Sartre's *Les Mains sales* is reinforced by this conclusion.

33. Maurice Blanchot, *La Part du feu* (Paris: Gallimard, 1949), 204–5.

34. Maurice Nadeau, *Le Roman français depuis la guerre* (Paris: Gallimard, 1963), 114.

35. Victor Brombert, *The Intellectual Hero* (Chicago: University of Chicago Press, 1960), 232.

36. *Tous les hommes sont mortels* (Paris: Gallimard, 1946), 250; hereafter cited in text as *TLH*.

37. Sartre likewise was interested in the period of the Reformation. See *Le Diable et le Bon Dieu* (Paris: Gallimard, 1951).

38. Serge Julienne-Caffié, *Simone de Beauvoir* (Paris: Gallimard, 1966), 162–63, quoted in Konrad Bieber, *Simone de Beauvoir* (Boston: Twayne, 1979), 164.

39. Among French existentialist or quasi-existentialist dramatists, one should also mention Camus and Gabriel Marcel.

40. *Les Bouches inutiles* (Paris: Gallimard, 1945), 55; hereafter cited in text as *Bln*.

41. For a comparison between the idea of the general good in Rousseau's *Le Contrat social* and some political implications of Sartrean existentialism, see Brosman 1985.

Chapter Four

1. Bair (427) incorrectly credits Bost with the title.

2. Bieber's statement (165) that the intellectuals are "helplessly engaged in a game of politics too complicated for them" may overstate the case as they are not inadequate as *individuals;* it is a question of what singular acts can accomplish when vast historical forces are in motion.

3. See *FC,* 284, 291, for the author's comments on technique.

4. Sartre and Beauvoir maintained this affected convention throughout their public lives.

5. Beauvoir was criticized for not presenting a more positive—more independent and vigorous—heroine; she countered that she portrayed women as she knew them, divided. See *FC,* 286.

6. *Les Mandarins* (Paris: Gallimard, 1954), 255; hereafter cited in text as *M.*

7. Anne represents to some degree what has been called the missing mother—physically present but emotionally absent. See Mickey Pearlman, *Mother Puzzles: Daughters and Mothers in Contemporary American Literature* (Westport, Conn.: Greenwood Press, 1989).

8. Elaine Marks, "Simone de Beauvoir," in *Dictionary of Literary Biography 72: French Novelists 1930–1960,* ed. Catharine Savage Brosman (Detroit: Gale, 1988), 51; hereafter cited in text.

9. Beauvoir attempted to defend the inclusion in this novel of the lengthy liaison, which has been considered marginal, by saying that it gives Anne a personal life, so that she is not merely an observer (*FC,* 286).

10. See Beauvoir's "Œil pour œil" (treated in chapter 5).

11. Jean-Paul Sartre, "We Write for Our Own Time," *Virginia Quarterly Review* 23 (April 1947): 236–43; translated in *Les Temps modernes* 33 (June 1948): 2113–21.

12. Beauvoir gave an interview to the Communist *L'Humanité-Dimanche*

to emphasize that her novel was not to be construed as "reactionary" or hostile to the French Communist party; see Francis and Gontier 1979, 358–62.

13. A recent judgment that the novel has a thin plot and an artificial mechanism can be found in Winegarten, 114.

14. See Fallaize, who calls the novel the most writerly and ambitious (118), and Winegarten, who writes, "It is perhaps her most accomplished work of fiction in the formal sense" (114).

15. In *Thérèse Desqueyroux* (Paris: Grasset, 1927), François Mauriac addresses his heroine in an omniscient fashion; Sartre objected, of course, to such displays of authorial omniscience. See *Situations,* 1:45–46. In *La Modification* (Paris: Editions de Minuit, 1957), Michel Butor uses a narrative *vous* throughout.

16. Beauvoir had already used this technique in *Le Sang des autres.*

17. This detaching of words from their context and meaning was practiced previously by both Proust and Sartre—the latter, for instance, in the Sunday promenade scene in *La Nausée.*

18. Simone de Beauvoir, *Les Belles Images* (Paris: Gallimard, 1966), 57; hereafter cited in text as *BI.*

19. Brigitte, the classmate, is Jewish. This fact may awaken an echo in Laurence of the anguish she felt as a girl on learning of persecutions of Jews during the war. It also reflects Beauvoir's pro-Jewish feelings, strengthened by her ties with Lanzmann.

20. Some readers have connected the father to Sartre, whom they take as a father figure for Beauvoir; see Bieber, 172. It may be more accurate to see a reflection of Beauvoir's *father* and the disappointment she felt when she came to realize his moral and intellectual limitations.

21. Beauvoir's opposition to Freudian psychology, which dated from the 1930s, had been nuanced, but she remained wary of reductive explanations. In Jardine, 228, she said she admired Freud greatly as a thinker but that he knew "absolutely nothing" about women. See also *TCF,* 167.

22. See Brosman 1987, 69–70.

23. Wanda Kosakiewicz and Michelle Vian served as partial models for the heroines. See Bair, 498.

24. See his *The Rhetoric of Fiction* (Chicago: University of Chicago Press, 1961), 158–59.

Chapter Five

1. See my paper, "L'Objet et l'œil: La Visualisation chez Simone de Beauvoir," American Association of Teachers of French, New Orleans, July 1990; see also my "Sartre's Phenomenological Art Criticism," in *Seen Fictions and Visual Essays,* ed. Rima Drell Reck (Baton Rouge: Louisiana State University Press, forthcoming).

2. Jean-Paul Sartre, *L'Etre et le néant* (Paris: Gallimard, 1943), 678.

3. Jean-Paul Sartre, *Cahiers pour une morale* (Paris: Gallimard, 1983).

4. This essay was not, contrary to claims, included in *Pour une morale de l'ambiguïté*. See Francis and Gontier 1979, 127.

5. *Pyrrhus et Cinéas* (Paris: Gallimard, 1944), 16; hereafter cited in text as *PC*.

6. *Pour une morale de l'ambiguïté* (Paris: Gallimard, 1947), 158; hereafter cited in text as *PMA*.

7. There is a resemblance between this position and certain principles in Camus's *Le Mythe de Sisyphe* (Paris: Gallimard, 1942), which may have influenced Beauvoir and to which she alludes, as when she says that the crucial question is not suicide but in what conditions one wants to live (*PMA*, 23).

8. "Monstre incomparable . . . que tout être est pour soi-même et qu'il choie dans son cœur." André Malraux, *La Condition humaine* (1933; Paris: Gallimard, Livre de Poche/Université edition, 1946), 46.

9. The point must be made that freedom is total but power is not: "To be free is not to have the power to do just anything; it is to be able to go beyond the given toward an open future" ("Etre libre, ce n'est pas avoir le pouvoir de faire n'importe quoi; c'est pouvoir dépasser le donné vers un avenir ouvert"; *PMA*, 127).

10. Beauvoir acknowledges (*FC*, 80) the influence of Hegel on the portraits of the adventurer, nihilist, and aesthete. She may also have in mind types of the absurd man in *Le Mythe de Sisyphe*.

11. These essays were first published in *Les Temps modernes*. Data on magazine publication is given in Francis and Gontier 1979.

12. *L'Existentialisme et la sagesse des nations* (Paris: Nagel, 1948), 39; hereafter cited in text as *ESN*.

13. This essay was partially translated by Mary McCarthy as "Eye for Eye," *Politics* 4, No. 4 (July–August 1947): 134–40.

14. *Privilèges* (Paris: Gallimard, 1955), 83.

Chapter Six

1. Sartre had noted, in his *Carnets de la drôle de guerre* (Paris: Gallimard, 1983), that the question of women needed to be reexamined (342).

2. For a full-length refutation of Beauvoir's positions on femininity, see Suzanne Lilar, *Le Malentendu du deuxième sexe* (Paris: Presses Universitaires de France, 1969).

3. Gerda Lerner, *The Creation of Patriarchy* (New York: Oxford University Press, 1986).

4. On Beauvoir and Freud, see Juliet Mitchell, *Psychoanalysis and Feminism* (New York: Pantheon, 1974), 305–18.

5. Martha Noel Evans, "Murdering *L'Invitée*: Gender and Fictional Narrative," *Yale French Studies* 72 (1986): 181–200.

6. Appignanesi calls the series a "massive autobiography" (3). Beauvoir also used the terms *souvenirs* and *autobiographie* (*FA*, 9; *FC*, 7).

7. James Olney, *Metaphors of the Self: The Meaning of Autobiography* (Princeton, N.J.: Princeton University Press, 1972).

8. Philippe Lejeune in *L'Autobiographie en France* (Paris: A. Colin, 1971), 14, similarly says that autobiography should emphasize the history of a personality.

9. Marguerite Yourcenar, *Œuvres romanesques* (Paris: Gallimard, 1982), 699.

10. For a perceptive commentary on Beauvoir's distorted portrait of the United States, see Mary McCarthy, *The Humanist in the Bathtub* (New York: New American Library, 1964), 20–27; reprinted in Elaine Marks, *Critical Essays on Simone de Beauvoir* (Boston: G. K. Hall, 1987), 44–49.

11. Mary Evans, for instance, speaks of "the mixture of somewhat simple interpretation and official propaganda" in both works (111–12).

12. *La Vieillesse* (Paris: Gallimard, 1970); hereafter cited in text as *V*.

13. Judith Okley, *Simone de Beauvoir* (London: Virago, 1986), 127–30; Appagnanesi, 3.

Selected Bibliography

PRIMARY WORKS

A full bibliography, including books, articles, interviews, prefaces, recordings, and other texts, is given in Claude Francis and Fernande Gontier, *Les Ecrits de Simone de Beauvoir* (Paris: Gallimard, 1979). English translations are included. The following listing consists of all full-length French-language publications.

Fiction and Drama

Les Belles Images. Paris: Gallimard, 1966. Translated by Patrick O'Brian as *Les Belles Images*. New York: Putnam's, 1968.
Les Bouches inutiles. Paris: Gallimard, 1945. Translated by Claude Francis and Fernande Gontier as *Who Shall Die?* Florissant, Mo.: River Press, 1983.
La Femme rompue. Paris: Gallimard, 1967. Translated by Patrick O'Brian as *The Woman Destroyed*. New York: Putnam's, 1969.
L'Invitée. Paris: Gallimard, 1943. Translated by Yvonne Moyse and Roger Senhouse as *She Came to Stay*. London: Secker and Warburg/Lindsay Drummond, 1949.
Les Mandarins. Paris: Gallimard, 1954. Translated by Leonard M. Friedman as *The Mandarins*. Cleveland: World, 1956.
Quand prime le spirituel. Paris: Gallimard, 1979. Translated by Patrick O'Brian as *When Things of the Spirit Come First*. New York: Pantheon, 1982.
Le Sang des autres. Paris: Gallimard, 1945. Translated by Yvonne Moyse and Roger Senhouse as *The Blood of Others*. New York: Knopf, 1948.
Tous les hommes sont mortels. Paris: Gallimard, 1946. Translated by Leonard M. Friedman as *All Men Are Mortal*. Cleveland: World, 1956.

Autobiography and Memoirs

La Force de l'âge. Paris: Gallimard, 1960. Translated by Peter Green as *The Prime of Life*. Cleveland: World, 1962.
La Force des choses. Paris: Gallimard, 1963. Translated by Richard Howard as *Force of Circumstance*. New York: Putnam's, 1965.
Mémoires d'une jeune fille rangée. Paris: Gallimard, 1958. Translated by James Kirkup as *Memoirs of a Dutiful Daughter*. Cleveland: World, 1959.

Tout compte fait. Paris: Gallimard, 1972. Translated by Patrick O'Brian as *All Said and Done*. New York: Putnam's, 1974.

Philosophical and Political Essays

L'Existentialisme et la sagesse des nations. Paris: Nagel, 1948.

Pour une morale de l'ambiguïté. Paris: Gallimard, 1947. Translated by Bernard Frechtman as *The Ethics of Ambiguity*. New York: Philosophical Library, 1948.

Privilèges. Paris: Gallimard, 1955. Republished as *Faut-il brûler Sade?* Paris: Gallimard, 1972. Partially translated by Annette Michelson as *Must We Burn Sade?* London: Nevill, 1953; reprinted in *The Marquis de Sade*, edited by Paul Dinnage. New York: Grove Press, 1953.

Pyrrhus et Cinéas. Paris: Gallimard, 1944.

Documentary Studies

L'Amérique au jour le jour. Paris: Morihien, 1948. Translated by Patrick Dudley as *America Day by Day*. New York: Grove Press, 1953.

La Cérémonie des adieux, suivi de Entretiens avec Jean-Paul Sartre. Paris: Gallimard, 1979. Translated by Patrick O'Brian as *Adieux: A Farewell to Sartre*. New York: Pantheon, 1984.

Le Deuxième Sexe. Paris: Gallimard, 1949. Translated by H. M. Parshley as *The Second Sex*. New York: Knopf, 1953.

La Longue Marche: Essai sur la Chine. Paris: Gallimard, 1957. Translated by Austryn Wainhouse as *The Long March*. Cleveland: World, 1958.

Une Mort très douce. Paris: Gallimard, 1964. Translated by Patrick O'Brian as *A Very Easy Death*. New York: Putnam's, 1966.

La Vieillesse. Paris: Gallimard, 1970. Translated by Patrick O'Brian as *Old Age*. London: Weidenfeld and Nicolson, 1970. Republished as *The Coming of Age*. New York: Putnam's, 1974.

Correspondence

Lettres à Sartre. 2 vols. Edited by Sylvie Le Bon de Beauvoir. Paris: Gallimard, 1990.

SECONDARY WORKS

The following listing includes only a few items published before 1975; for others, see the bibliographies by Alden and Brooks and by Bennett and

Hochmann. Similarly, only a small selection is given from the abundant corpus of scholarship, often touching on Beauvoir, that deals with feminist issues in general and women's writing in France; the Gelfand and Hules volume and others listed herein furnish ample bibliographic resources.

Bibliographies

Alden, Douglas W., and Richard A. Brooks, *A Critical Bibliography of French Literature*. Vol. 6, *The Twentieth Century* (3 parts) 3: 1682–90. Syracuse, N.Y.: Syracuse University Press, 1980. An annotated listing of major books on Beauvoir and selected critical articles through approximately 1975. Includes many reviews of her memoirs.

Bennett, Joy, and Gabriella Hochmann. *Simone de Beauvoir: An Annotated Bibliography*. New York: Garland, 1988. A lengthy bibliography of criticism. Index.

Francis, Claude, and Fernande Gontier. *Les Ecrits de Simone de Beauvoir*. Paris: Gallimard, 1979. Lists, chronologically and with commentary, all Beauvoir's publications, in a biographical context. Includes quotations from reviews. Also contains primary texts (unpublished or obscure). Indexes.

Books and Parts of Books

Appignanesi, Lisa. *Simone de Beauvoir*. London: Penguin, 1988. Chiefly a biographical study, from the feminist point of view. Sympathetic.

Ascher, Carol. *Simone de Beauvoir: A Life of Freedom*. Boston: Beacon, 1981. A general study of the life and works, organized chronologically but emphasizing themes such as women's issues, Beauvoir's relations with Sartre, and death. Very personal in tone.

Bair, Deirdre. *Simone de Beauvoir: A Biography*. New York: Summit Books, 1990. A detailed, 718-page study marked by a feminist slant. Based partly on interviews with Beauvoir and her circle over a period of six years; carried out with her approval. Of human interest and useful to specialists. Index.

Barnes, Hazel E. *The Literature of Possibility*. Lincoln: University of Nebraska Press, 1959. Discusses almost all Beauvoir's works to the time of writing; still valid as an existentialist commentary from a major authority.

Berghe, Christian Louis van der. *Dictionnaire des idées: Simone de Beauvoir*. Paris and The Hague: Mouton, 1966. An annotated glossary for scholars. Examines particular uses of vocabulary, with examples and cross references.

Bieber, Konrad. *Simone de Beauvoir*. Boston: Twayne, 1979. Principally a biographical review based on the memoirs, summarized at length. Little close attention given to literary works, and insufficient consideration of philosophical positions. Inadequate.

Cohen-Solal, Annie. *Sartre: A Life*. Translated by Anna Cancogni. New York: Pantheon, 1987. A massive biography of Sartre that deals surprisingly little with Beauvoir, since it was done under the patronage of Arlette El Kaïm. Excessively anecdotal. Index.

Cottrell, Robert D. *Simone de Beauvoir*. New York: Ungar, 1975. A concise, intelligent review of Beauvoir's career and production.

Eaubonne, Françoise d'. *Une Femme nommée Castor: Mon amie Simone de Beauvoir*. Paris: Encre, 1986. An uncritical but perceptive reading of some of Beauvoir's chief themes and works, with a biographical slant.

Evans, Martha Noel. "Simone de Beauvoir: The Murderer." In her *Masks of Tradition: Women and the Politics of Writing in Twentieth-Century France*, 75–101. Ithaca, N.Y.: Cornell University Press, 1987. Treats *L'Invitée* in the context of considerations on *l'écriture féminine* and other French women writers.

Evans, Mary. *Simone de Beauvoir: A Feminist Mandarin*. London: Tavistock, 1985. Deals critically with Beauvoir's social and political positions in the context of her evolution. Very well grounded and documented.

Fallaize, Elizabeth. *The Novels of Simone de Beauvoir*. London: Routledge, 1988. The only full-length study of Beauvoir's fiction; very perceptive and detailed. Concentrates on technique and its relationship to her political radicalization.

Francis, Claude, and Fernande Gontier. *Simone de Beauvoir*. Paris: Perrin, 1985. Translated by Lisa Nesselson as *Simone de Beauvoir: A Life . . . A Love Story*. New York: St. Martin's Press, 1987. A detailed biography based on interviews with the author and her circle, as well as printed material. Overemphasizes the love affair with Sartre. Disavowed by Beauvoir after publication. Index.

Gelfand, Elissa D., and Virginia Thorndike Hules. *French Feminist Criticism: Women, Language, and Literature*. New York: Garland, 1985. Includes a section on *Le Deuxième Sexe*.

Hatcher, Donald. *Understanding "The Second Sex."* New York: Peter Lang, 1984. A summary and commentary for beginners or those unfamiliar with the philosophical background. Unattractive format.

Hewitt, Leah D. *Autobiographical Tightropes*. Lincoln: University of Nebraska Press, 1990. Contains a chapter dealing with Beauvoir's memoirs, particularly their ambiguity as the autobiography of a woman author.

Jeanson, Francis. *Simone de Beauvoir ou l'entreprise de vivre*. Paris: Seuil, 1966. The first biography of Beauvoir, by a friend who knew her well in the 1960s. Studies her achievement very sympathetically.

Keefe, Terry. *Simone de Beauvoir: A Study of Her Writings*. London: Harrap, 1983. A well-balanced, perceptive study that tries to offset excessive attention paid in other volumes to the writer's life at the expense of her works. Deals intelligently with all the major works.

Leighton, Jean. *Simone de Beauvoir on Woman.* Rutherford, N.J.: Fairleigh Dickinson University Press, 1975. Analyzes feminine characters in Beauvoir's novels and her positions on feminism.

Madsen, Alex. *Hearts and Minds: The Common Journey of Simone de Beauvoir and Jean-Paul Sartre.* New York: Morrow, 1977. A popular biography of the two writers. Readable but not entirely reliable.

Marks, Elaine. *Critical Essays on Simone de Beauvoir.* Boston: G. K. Hall, 1987. Twenty-seven selected essays, some by friends, others by philosophers, scholars, and other specialists; all printed in English. An excellent and rich selection.

———. "Simone de Beauvoir." In *Dictionary of Literary Biography 72: French Novelists 1930–1960,* edited by Catharine Savage Brosman, 42–57. A concise and balanced study of Beauvoir's whole career and achievement, especially in fiction. List of her books; references.

———. *Simone de Beauvoir: Encounters with Death.* New Brunswick, N.J.: Rutgers University Press, 1973. A thematic study that relates Beauvoir's obsession with death to her work and the modern temper.

Moi, Toril. *Feminist Theory and Simone de Beauvoir.* Oxford: Blackwell, 1990. By a specialist on feminist literary theory and sexual politics. Sections on Beauvoir consist of an assessment of criticism on Beauvoir, especially the considerable number of hostile reactions, and the essay on "La Femme rompue."

Okley, Judith. *Simone de Beauvoir.* London: Virago, 1986. Concerned almost entirely with Beauvoir and gender issues, seen in the context of the feminism of the 1980s; very personal tone.

Patterson, Yolanda Astarita. *Simone de Beauvoir and the Demystification of Motherhood.* Ann Arbor, Mich.: UMI Research Press, 1989. Examines Beauvoir's views on her own mother and on maternity in general, as illustrated in her imaginative writings as well. Includes interviews with Simone and Hélène de Beauvoir. Good bibliography.

Sankovitch, Tilde. "Simone de Beauvoir: The Giant, the Scapegoat, and the Quester." In her *French Women Writers and the Book.* Syracuse, N.Y.: Syracuse University Press, 1988. Uses myths to explicate the role in Beauvoir's life, as she saw it, of Zaza and Jacques.

Sartre, Jean-Paul. *Lettres au Castor et à quelques autres.* 2 vols. Edited by Simone de Beauvoir. Paris: Gallimard, 1983. Provides information on Beauvoir's activities as well as Sartre's and sheds an interesting light on their relationship. Minimal notation.

Schwarzer, Alice. *After "The Second Sex": Conversations with Simone de Beauvoir.* Translated by Marianne Howarth. New York: Pantheon, 1984. Extensive interviews with Beauvoir and Sartre. Deals chiefly with feminine questions and *Le Deuxième Sexe* but also with her relationship to Sartre.

Simone de Beauvoir: Un film de Josée Dayan et Malka Ribowska. Paris: Gallimard,

1979. Transcription of a film in which Beauvoir, Sartre, Lanzmann, Hélène de Beauvoir, and others converse and are interviewed by the filmmakers.

Simone de Beauvoir et le cours du monde. Edited by Claude Francis and Janine Niepce. Paris: Klincksieck, 1978. Iconography, with quotations from Beauvoir's work to accompany the photographs.

Wenzel, Hélène Vivienne, ed. *Simone de Beauvoir: Witness to a Century. Yale French Studies* 72 (1986).

Whitmarsh, Anne. *Simone de Beauvoir and the Limits of Commitment.* London: Cambridge University Press, 1981. A general study of the work, organized thematically. Well balanced.

Winegarten, Renée. *Simone de Beauvoir: A Critical View.* Oxford: Berg, 1988. A somewhat jaundiced, if justified, view of Beauvoir's achievements and claims; a useful antidote to excessive adulation by other writers.

Index

The Author

Catharine Savage Brosman, who received her Ph.D. from Rice University, is professor of French at Tulane University. Her scholarly publications include *André Gide: L'Evolution de sa pensée religieuse* (1962), *Malraux, Sartre, and Aragon as Political Novelists* (1964), *Roger Martin du Gard* (1968), *Jean-Paul Sartre* (1983), *Jules Roy* (1988), *Art as Testimony: The Work of Jules Roy* (1989), and *An Annotated Bibliography of Criticism on André Gide, 1973–1988* (1990). She has edited three volumes in the *Dictionary of Literary Biography* series on French novelists of the twentieth century; her two volumes on nineteenth-century French novelists in the same series are forthcoming. She was managing editor of the *French Review* from 1977 to 1980. Her poems and essays have appeared in leading quarterlies, and she is the author of three collections of poetry, including *Journeying from Canyon de Chelly* (1990).

The Editor

David O'Connell is professor of foreign languages and chair of the Department of Foreign Languages at Georgia State University. He received his Ph.D. from Princeton University in 1966, where he was a National Woodrow Wilson Fellow, the Bergen Fellow in Romance Languages, and a National Woodrow Wilson Dissertation Fellow. He is the author of *The Teachings of Saint Louis: A Critical Text* (1972), *Les Propos de Saint Louis* (1974), *Louis-Ferdinand Céline* (1976), *The Instructions of Saint Louis: A Critical Text* (1979), and *Michel de Saint Pierre: A Catholic Novelist at the Crossroads* (1990). He is the editor of *Catholic Writers in France since 1945* (1983) and has served as review editor (1977–79) and managing editor (1987–90) of the *French Review*.